# A Guide to the Data Protection Act 1998

# A Guide to the
# Data Protection Act 1998

**Ian Lloyd**
Professor and Director of the Centre for Law, Computers
and Technology, University of Strathclyde, Glasgow

**Butterworths**
London, Edinburgh, Dublin
1998

| | |
|---|---|
| United Kingdom | Butterworths a Division of Reed Elsevier (UK) Ltd, Halsbury House, 35 Chancery Lane, LONDON WC2A 1EL and 4 Hill Street, EDINBURGH EH2 3JZ |
| Australia | Butterworths, a Division of Reed International Books Australia Pty Ltd, CHATSWOOD, New South Wales |
| Canada | Butterworths Canada Ltd, MARKHAM, Ontario |
| Hong Kong | Butterworths Asia (Hong Kong), HONG KONG |
| India | Butterworths India NEW DELHI |
| Ireland | Butterworth (Ireland) Ltd, DUBLIN |
| Malaysia | Malayan Law Journal Sdn Bhd, KUALA LUMPUR |
| New Zealand | Butterworths of New Zealand Ltd, WELLINGTON |
| Singapore | Butterworths Asia, SINGAPORE |
| South Africa | Butterworths Publishers (Pty) Ltd, DURBAN |
| USA | Lexis Law Publishing, CHARLOTTESVILLE, Virginia |

A CIP Catalogue record for this book is available from the British Library.

ISBN 0 406 98100 0

Printed and bound in Great Britain by The Cromwell Press, Trowbridge, Wiltshire

**Visit us at our website: http://www.butterworths.co.uk**

# Preface

Time is a relative commodity. The Data Protection Act 1984 had a life span of 14 years, which in human and legal terms is a relatively short period of time. In computer terms, the world has changed dramatically. A 'Kray' computer (reputed to be the most powerful machine on earth) produced in 1985 would have cost in the region of $8 million: today, a Nintendo Game Station costs less than £200 and has the equivalent processing power (plus a clever graphics capability). The capability of computers is estimated to be doubling every two years with no indication that this exponential rate of growth will reach an end. Today, microprocessors outnumber humans and it is estimated that by the year 2010, 95% of telecommunications traffic will be between machines. This is the 'brave new world' that the Data Protection Act 1998 will seek to regulate.

Given these technological developments, it is, perhaps, a cause for concern that much of the 1998 Act, which was introduced in order to comply with the requirements of a 1995 European Directive, will be familiar to those accustomed to the 1984 Act. The Data Protection Registrar transmogrifies into the Data Protection Commissioner with some additional powers and duties (Parts I, III and VI). The number of data protection principles remains at eight although with some changes in terminology (Sch 1). The 1998 Act moves away from the widely criticised system of universal registration of data users (now to be known as data controllers) to open the way for a more selective system of notification (Part III). Data subjects will benefit from enhanced rights to be informed of (and to object to) the nature and purposes of processing (Part II). The 1998 Act includes new special provisions relating to media activities (ss 3, 44–46) and much more stringent controls over the export of data (transborder data flows) to countries outwith the European Economic Area (Schs 1 and 4).

The 1998 Act is significantly larger than its 1984 precursor, but in spite of this, it is in many respects only a framework statute, with significant detail being introduced by statutory instrument. It is the need to enact a large volume of secondary legislation that has meant that the UK will not be in a position to implement the EC Directive on the due date of 24 October 1998. At the time of writing it is expected that the Act will enter into force at the end of 1998 or early in 1999.

To enable readers to update their knowledge of the subject, the secondary legislation will be included on a web site at the following address—

http://www.butterworths.co.uk/content/products/publications

The necessary password is—

lions

This site will contain the text of the secondary legislation made under the 1998 Act as and when it is enacted.

In addition to requiring Member States to comply with the general data protection Directive, the EU has also adopted a Directive making specific provision for data protection in the telecommunications sector. It may well be that similar sector specific measures will be adopted in the coming years. This Directive will be implemented in the UK by statutory instrument made under the authority of the European Communities Act 1972 and will also be included on the web site.

Finally, although a single name appears as author of this book, the publication would not have been possible without the contribution of others. I am grateful to the editorial staff at Butterworths whose diligence prevented a large number of my errors making their way into the final text. At Strathclyde I would like to pay tribute to the advice and support that I have received over the years from our former (and much missed) head of department, Robert Burgess. I also owe a great deal to Moira Simpson whose help and friendship is valued greatly.

Ian Lloyd
September 1998

# Contents

# Table of Statutes

# Table of Cases

# 1 Background to the legislation

## THE ARRIVAL OF THE COMPUTER

1.1 Although mechanical devices capable of operating in accordance with recorded instructions have been available for several centuries, the electronic or digital computer is a creature of the second half of the twentieth century. Initially the computer was, as its name suggests, seen primarily as a tool for use in making mathematical calculations, with banks and other financial institutions being early commercial users of the technology. During the 1960s the use of computers for text processing became more prevalent, as electronic databases gradually replaced paper based filing systems. Almost all computers operate on the basis of the digital system, which is capable of representing any form of information in digital format. From the 1970s onwards the computer was used increasingly for processing other forms of data, with sounds, pictures and moving images all becoming subjects for automated processing. As the use of image and voice recognition systems has increased, the range of processing activities covered by data protection legislation is continually expanding.

1.2 The advantages which computers might offer to users, and the threats posed to individual rights, were well described in a 1975 White Paper—

'(1)   they facilitate the maintenance of extensive record systems and the retention of data in those systems;

(2)   they can make data easily and quickly accessible from many distant points;

(3)   they make it possible for data to be transferred quickly from one information system to another;

(4)   they make it possible for data to be combined in ways which might not otherwise be practicable;

(5)   because the data are stored, processed and often transmitted in a form which is not directly intelligible, few people may know what is in the records, or what is happening to them.'.[1]

Essentially, the use of computing technology, now more generally referred to as information technology, significantly reduces such problems as recording and retaining large amounts of data, linking between items of data held at different locations and processing data in ways which might not have been practical using manual systems.

---

[1]   'Computers and Privacy' (Cmnd 6353, para 6).

## COMPUTERS AND PRIVACY

1.3 Data have been recorded and stored since writing was invented. The Domesday Book provides an excellent example of a record system, while more mature readers will recall clearly the mountains of manila folders which could be found in doctors' surgeries. The maintenance of extensive filing systems has tended to be seen as, at best, the talisman of bureaucracy and, at worst, an identifier of a totalitarian state. Although the technology described did not include computers, the state of Oceania as depicted in George Orwell's *Nineteen Eighty-Four* is presented as the archetypal instance of a surveillance society. The classical definition of privacy refers to the 'right to be let alone'[1] and the gathering and processing of large amounts of personal data has come to be seen as a practice requiring legislative controls. In Europe this has primarily taken the form of data protection legislation. In the US and other jurisdictions more attention has been paid to the enactment of privacy protection statutes. Although perhaps seeking to achieve the same end result, the two systems tend to adopt different means, a factor which may pose significant problems for the regulation of transborder data flows following the implementation of the European Data Protection Directive.[2]

---

[1]    Judge Cooley (1888). For an extensive collection of definitions of privacy, see Appendix K of the 'Report of the Committee on Privacy' (Cmnd 5012).
[2]    See Ch 7.

---

1.4    While we recoil from the images presented in Orwell's work, and all surveys of public opinion indicate that protection of individual privacy is seen as an important function for the law,[1] consideration of modern data processing practices indicates a significant degree of surveillance. Our movements are recorded by omnipresent CCTV systems, while almost every action involves interaction with some form of computerised recording equipment. Details of our telephone calls are recorded for billing purposes as are the videos viewed in a hotel bedroom, withdrawals made from cash dispensing machines and transactions entered into using a credit or debit card. With almost all of these examples the point may fairly be made that application of technology is seen as desirable by a majority of the population. Television cameras are perceived as reducing crime, itemised telephone bills allow customers to monitor usage of their equipment while systems of 'caller ID' deter the making of hoax or harassing calls. In the case of shopping, millions of consumers have applied to participate in 'loyalty schemes', thereby volunteering to supply store owners with extensive and individualised information about the nature of their spending patterns. It is sometimes difficult to avoid the conclusion that although privacy may be valued, this frequently is at the level of a can of beans.

---

[1]    See Cmnd 5012. Surveys on public attitudes to privacy and awareness of data protection legislation have also been conducted for the Registrar with the results presented in his Annual Reports.

---

1.5    In addition to the fact that growing amounts of data regarding our activities are recorded on computer, one of the most notable aspects of modern data processing has been the increasing linkage between computing and communication technologies. At one extreme, the World Wide Web (WWW) can be seen as a network of hundreds of millions of computers while at the other, even small offices may link up two or three PCs to allow shared access to peripherals, such as printers. Increasingly, data flow between computers and computer systems and, in many respects, the significant issue may no longer relate to what information is held by a particular user but rather to the information which can be accessed by that person. The practice of data matching[1] is extensively used in the public sector where information is shared between departments to facilitate, for example, the detection of those making multiple and fraudulent claims for social benefits. As networks such as the Schengen Information System[2] providing for the exchange of data between European police forces indicate, data transfers increasingly take place at an international level. There seems to be little doubt that the issue of whether, and to what extent, transborder data flows can be controlled in the age of the Internet will prove to be one of the most contentious aspects of data protection regime in the coming years.

---

[1] Social Security Administration (Fraud) Act 1997 puts such practices on a statutory basis. See also the discussion at para 4.74.

[2] The Schengen Agreement signed by seven member states in 1985 and its implementing Convention signed in 1990 provide the basis for the abolition of frontier controls between the signatory states.

## THE MOVE TO DATA PROTECTION LEGISLATION

1.6    The world's first data protection statute was enacted in the German state of Hesse in 1970. This was followed during the 1970s by legislation in a range of countries including Denmark, Germany (at the Federal level), Sweden and France. Early statutes, sometimes referred to as first generation statutes, placed considerable emphasis on the use of systems of licensing or registration to control data users. By 1980, the Council of Europe had adopted the 'Convention for the Protection of Individuals with regard to the Automatic Processing of Personal Data'.[1] The existence of this Convention, which contained the implied threat of data sanctions against states which did not enact data protection legislation, was crucial to the UK's enactment of the Data Protection Act 1984 ('the 1984 Act').

---

[1] Convention 108.

---

1.7    During the 1980s a number of the pioneering countries adopted revised data protection laws. As the number of computers in use increased dramatically, so the notion of licensing individual users became outdated with more attention being paid to substantive provisions seeking to regulate forms of data processing. The process was taken to its most extreme lengths in Germany which pioneered the notion commonly referred to as 'informational self-determination'.[1] Subject to the inevitable caveats and exceptions, this sought to give primacy to the subject's wishes by providing that consent should be a pre-requisite to lawful processing. A further trend has been to require that those processing data demonstrate that reasonable security measures have been taken to guard against wrongful disclosure or destruction. Therefore, the focus of the legislation has switched from seeking to repair damage arising from improper processing to emphasising the need to prevent the damage occurring.

---

[1] The doctrine originated in a decision of the Constitutional Court which struck down statutory provisions for a national census on the ground that the enabling legislation paid inadequate regard to data protection issues. In particular it was held that there was a need to ensure that no more information was collected than was required for the purposes of the legislation, and that the data should not be capable of being processed so as to identify individuals; see 1984 5 HRLJ 94.

INTERNATIONAL MEASURES

1.8   As reference to the work of the Council of Europe indicates, international bodies have been active in the data protection field from the earliest days. Prior to its Convention, the Council adopted recommendations on the topic in 1973. Subsequently a raft of recommendations have been adopted seeking to tailor general principles of data protection to the requirements of specific areas, for example Recommendation (87)15 regulating the use of personal data in the police sector. In addition to the Council of Europe, both the Organisation for Economic Co-operation and Development (OECD) and the United Nations have promoted initiatives in the field in the form of Guidelines.[1] Even from the 1970s the rationale has been that without such efforts, national laws could easily be bypassed by users transferring data outwith the jurisdiction for processing to take place in another state. This is often referred to as a 'data haven' and imposes few, if any, obligations upon data users. With developments in communications technology, this issue is becoming even more important.

---

[1]   These are discussed in para 7.4.

1.9   Initially, the European Union (EU) took the view that the adherence of all member states to the Council of Europe Convention would remove the need for it to act in this field. A recommendation to this effect was addressed to the member states.[1] By the end of the 1980s this view had changed. In spite of the Commission recommendation, a number of states had failed to adopt legislation.[2] Of equal importance was the fact that significant differences existed between the national data protection legislation that had been enacted. While legislation in states such as the UK contained the minimum provisions necessary to ratify the Convention, other states such as Germany and Sweden had adopted much more extensive provisions. The variation in each of the member states' approaches was considered to be a threat to the Single Market. This led to the publication of proposals for a harmonising Directive in 1990.[3]

---

[1]   Commission Recommendation 81/679/EEC, OJ L246, 29.8.81, p 31.
[2]   By 1990, only six of the then member states had ratified the Convention—Denmark, France, Germany, Luxembourg, Spain and the UK.
[3]   COM(90) 314 final, OJ C277, 5.11.90, p 3.

1.10  The Directive proved to be controversial as it passed through the EU's law making process, so much so that five years elapsed between publication of the first proposal and adoption of the final text. Criticism came from both ends of the data protection spectrum. The UK, which had one of the most limited regimes, objected to the measure because it demanded an extension of the scope of their existing legislation. The cost to the UK of enacting legislation that complied with the Directive would be considerable. Criticism was also voiced from Germany, which currently has the most extensive regime, on the basis that the protection afforded to its citizens might be weakened. The basis for this complaint is somewhat convoluted. The Directive establishes basic requirements and does not prevent national laws from imposing higher requirements. The main concern is that the Directive requires member states to allow data to be transferred freely to other member states. From here, the data may be exported to third countries in circumstances where the transfer would be unlawful under the law of the originating state. The Directive has also attracted controversy on a world wide basis, especially within the United States, in relation to its provisions on the control of transborder data flows, as being driven by considerations of economic protectionism and constituting a thinly veiled attack on the US data processing industry.

1.11 These issues will be discussed more fully in subsequent chapters. To conclude, the Directive was finally adopted (the UK abstaining on the final vote in the Council of Ministers) in October 1995[1] with member states being required to implement its provisions by 24 October 1998. This timetable has proved difficult for a number of member states. For both the UK and Germany, the holding of general elections in the implementation period has caused delay in the adoption of implementing measures, albeit by a matter of weeks in the UK. Subsequent to the main Directive, the EU also adopted a Directive[2] making specific provision for data protection in the telecommunications sector. Although this measure was not adopted until December 1997, it contains the same implementation date of 24 October 1998. The provisions of the Directive will be implemented in the UK by regulations made under the authority of the European Communities Act 1972.

---

[1]   Directive 95/46/EC, OJ L281, 24.10.95, p 31; see Appendix 2.
[2]   Directive 97/66/EC, OJ L24, 30.1.98, p 1; see Appendix 2.

DATA PROTECTION ACT 1984

1.12 As indicated above, the 1984 Act marked the UK's first attempt to legislate in this field. Proposals for legislation to protect the interests of individuals had been floated since 1969,[1] but it was not until the arrival of the Council of Europe Convention that legislation was finally brought forward by a somewhat reluctant government. The Convention, which provided for the free flow of data only between signatory states, had prompted concern from commercial interests at the possible loss of data processing business. In commending the Bill to the House of Commons, the then Home Secretary stated that the purpose of the legislation was to 'meet public concern, to bring us into step with Europe and to protect our international, commercial and trading interests'.[2] All this was to be achieved at the minimum possible cost to data users.

---

[1]   In this year the Data Surveillance Bill was introduced by Kenneth Baker MP. Further private Members' initiatives were unsuccessfully proposed in the 1970s. In 1975 the Committee on Data Protection was appointed with a remit to advise the government on the form of data protection legislation. Its report ('The Lindop Report' (Cmnd 7341)) was published in 1978. It remains one of the largest reports in the field of data protection but its key proposals were rejected by the government of the day as being excessively expensive and bureaucratic.
[2]   HC Debs, 11 April 1983, col 562.

1.13 Although the Data Protection Act 1998 ('the 1998 Act') repeals the whole of the 1984 Act, substantial elements of the old regime will continue, subject to some modification. The Data Protection Registrar (the 'Registrar') has estimated that about 80% of the obligations imposed upon those involved in the processing of personal data will remain unchanged.[1] A major, and certainly the most controversial, area of extension concerns the application of the legislation to some forms of manual records. Such extension is required in order to comply with the Directive, but there has been a difference of opinion between the Registrar and the government concerning the impact of this change.[2]

---

[1]    DPR Briefing Paper; see http://www.open.gov.UK/dpr/dprhome.htm
[2]    See paras 2.14–2.16.

## Key features of the 1984 Act

### *The Registrar and registration*

1.14  One of the key elements of almost all data protection legislation has been the establishment of an independent supervisory agency. This constitutes a key point of difference between the European data protection and the US privacy protection models. In the UK the Registrar has played, and subject to a change in title to the Data Protection Commissioner (the 'Commissioner') (s 6 of the 1998 Act) will continue to play, this role. The Registrar's first and continuing task relates to the compilation and maintenance of a register of data users (and computer bureaux) (under s 4(1) of the 1984 Act). Failure on the part of a data user to apply for registration constitutes a criminal offence (s 5 of the 1984 Act).

### *The data protection principles*

1.15  Beyond this role, the Registrar possesses a mixture of duties (limited) and powers (more extensive) relating to the supervision of data users in order to ensure conformity with the substantive requirements of the legislation. Essentially these relate to the obligation to conform to a set of eight data protection principles. The principles make provision for the obtaining, processing, storage and dissemination (including to the data subject in response to a request for access) of personal data and they constitute what is effectively a code of acceptable processing practice. The general formulations of the principles are expanded upon in the body of the legislation and have also been interpreted by another agency established under the 1984 Act known as the Data Protection Tribunal (s 3 of and Sch 2 to the 1984 Act). This Tribunal sits to hear appeals by data users against action by the Registrar alleging a breach of the data protection principles. The Registrar's powers extend to the service of enforcement, de-registration and, in the case of transborder data flows, transfer prohibition notices. While the number of enforcement notices served is in double figures, a single transfer prohibition has been served, and no de-registration notice has been issued during the 1984 Act's life.

### Towards a new regime

1.16  Although aspects of the 1984 legislation, such as the data protection principles, are relatively timeless, the notion of the (near) universal registration of data users is now considered to be out of date. The concept was reasonable at a time when the country's computer population was numbered in the thousands, but is impractical in an era where virtually every office desk hosts some form of computer. Following a consultation exercise, the Registrar submitted proposals for reform of the system in 1990.[1] A further report[2] was published in 1996. No action was taken on these proposals, in part because the looming presence of the Directive served to deter what might prove to be short lived amendments to the data protection regime. There was little doubt, regardless of the requirement to implement the Directive, that reform would be desirable. It may be a cause for some concern that throughout the passage of the 1998 Bill, government ministers were at pains to point out that the measure sought to do the minimum necessary to comply with the Directive. It will be recalled that the initial proposal for a Directive was published in 1990. Although changes were made during its legislative passage, its basic formulations are now eight years old. In the world of information technology, eight years is a long time and there is a real risk that developments such as the Internet and WWW will render elements of the new data protection regime obsolete before they even enter into force.

---

[1]  The proposals were presented in the 'Fifth Report of the Data Protection Registrar' (HMSO 1989).
[2]  The Future of Registration (Office of the Data Protection Registrar). This report was published following criticisms in 1994 by the Public Accounts Committee of the House of Commons concerning the effectiveness of the registration process.

1.17 Initially, the UK government indicated a preference for implementing the Directive's requirements by statutory instrument under the authority of the European Communities Act 1972.[1] This approach would have meant that reform would have been limited to aspects of the law within the scope of EU legislative competence. The consequence would have been the somewhat unsatisfactory situation where most aspects of data processing would have been regulated under the new system while the 1984 regime would have remained applicable for some forms of processing, including that relating to aspects of criminal law. The change of government in May 1997 brought about a change of approach with the decision taken to introduce primary legislation. Following a further consultation exercise,[2] the Data Protection Bill was introduced into the House of Lords in January 1998. Its progress through Parliament was relatively uncontroversial with only one division being required throughout its parliamentary passage.[3] The major feature of the Bill's progress was the very large number, more than 200 in total, of amendments tabled by the government. The Bill received the Royal Assent on 16 July 1998.

---

[1]  'Home Office Consultation Paper on EC Data Protection Directive (95/46/EC)', March 1996; see http://www.open.gov.uk/dpr/dprhome.htm
[2]  Data protection: the government's proposals (Home Office 1997).
[3]  This was in relation to proposals in the Bill to provide ministers with wide-ranging powers to exempt processing activities from the subject access provisions. The House of Lords voted to remove these powers from the Bill. A more closely defined provision was introduced in the House of Commons.

DATA PROTECTION ACT 1998

1.18  As an initial comment it may be noted that the 1998 Act is considerably larger than its predecessor. The 1984 Act has 43 sections and four schedules while the 1998 Act contains 75 sections and 16 schedules. To a greater extent than its 1984 precursor, the 1998 Act provides only a framework, with significant matters remaining to be determined by statutory instruments. Although this approach will allow for easier modification and updating of the legislation than was possible with the 1984 Act, significant issues relating to the identification of those data controllers who may be exempted from the notification requirement are not covered in the Act.

1.19  The 1998 Act will extend significantly the area of application of the legislation, including the regulation of some systems of manual records. In the Explanatory and Financial Memorandum attached to the Bill as introduced in the House of Lords,[1] it is estimated that compliance with the new regime will result in start up costs to private sector data users of £836 million with recurring costs of £630 million. The start up costs for the public and voluntary sectors are estimated at £194 million and £120 million respectively, with recurring costs of £75 million and £37 million. These figures are in addition to the costs incurred in complying with the present data protection regime although no evidence has been published as to the scale of the present costs. The Home Office Regulatory Appraisal and Compliance Cost assessment makes it clear that estimates are based upon a very small sample of users. Only four large and three small manufacturers were surveyed, for example, and although much publicity has been given to headline figures of a £1 billion cost arising from implementation, the assessment document itself highlights the need to approach these estimates with caution. The Registrar has also questioned the accuracy of the financial calculations, suggesting that this may have resulted from misunderstandings as to the nature of the Directive's requirements.[2]

---

[1]   HL Bill 61.
[2]   DPR Briefing Paper; see http://www.open.gov.UK/dpr/dprhome.htm

## THE 1998 ACT IN CONTEXT

1.20  To date it does not appear that data protection has had a significant impact on the public consciousness. To justify costs of £20 for every inhabitant of the UK, it is to be hoped that the new legislation, coupled with other legislative initiatives in the field of human rights and freedom of information, will increase public awareness of the crucial importance of information in modern society and the need to secure an appropriate balance between the interests of data controllers and data subjects.

1.21  Although a right of access to information held by credit reference agencies had been available since 1976 under the provisions of the Consumer Credit Act 1974, the 1984 Act has been seen as a somewhat isolated measure. Criticism has been voiced by the Registrar that inadequate account had been taken of data protection issues in formulating other Acts, such as those concerned with the community charge or poll tax, which involve the obtaining and use of personal data.[1]

---

[1]   See the Fourth Annual Report of the Data Protection Registrar.

---

1.22  The situation in 1998 is significantly different and the 1998 Act should be seen as one of a trilogy of measures operating in the same general field. The Human Rights Act will incorporate the European Convention on Human Rights and Fundamental Freedoms into domestic law. Of particular relevance to data protection are the provisions of Articles 8 and 10 of the Convention. Article 8(1) provides that 'everyone has the right to respect for his private and family life, his home and his correspondence'. Any interference with such rights by a public authority must be sanctioned by law and be—

> 'necessary in a democratic society in the interests of national security, public safety or the economic well being of the country, for the

prevention of disorder or crime, for the protection of health or morals, or for the protection of the rights and freedoms of others.' (Art 8(2)).

In its jurisprudence, the European Court of Human Rights has interpreted Article 8 liberally to include rights of access to personal data. Indeed following the decision of the court in the case of *Gaskin v United Kingdom*,[1] changes to statutory provisions relating to subject access have been necessary.

---

[1]    [1990] 1 FLR 167, 12 EHRR 36; see further para 5.14 et seq.

---

1.23 Perhaps the most controversial aspect of the interface between the Human Rights Bill and the 1998 Act concerns the activities of the media. Article 10 of the Convention guarantees the right to freedom of expression. Once again this may be subject to derogation on conditions similar to those applying to respect for private and family life. Clearly media activities, especially in the field of investigative journalism, may conflict with Article 8. Both the 1998 Act and the Human Rights Bill contain provisions and procedures for seeking to resolve such conflicts. Rather surprisingly, these differ in certain respects with the 1984 Act's provisions receiving a considerably warmer reception from media representatives than those found in the Human Rights Bill.

1.24 A second area where the 1998 Act may have to relate with other measures is connected with governmental proposals for the introduction of freedom of information legislation. A White Paper was published in December 1997[1] and it is expected that a Bill will follow in the Parliamentary session 1998-99. There is a clear overlap between the two concepts. Indeed in other countries which have freedom of information legislation, it has been estimated that 80% of requests relate to the enquirer's own personal data. In respect of this issue, freedom of information legislation may well supplement rights under the 1998 Act by extending these to a wider range of manual records. However, with proposals for significant variations in access rights and exceptions thereto, the prospect arises of what the House of Commons Select Committee on Public Administration described as a 'confusing and messy patchwork of different provisions under which one may obtain access to one's own file'.[2] Even more significantly, however, there will be the potential for conflict between the aims and objectives of the Acts where personal data relates to a party other than the enquirer: whereas freedom of information may give priority to openness and accessibility, data protection seeks to protect individual privacy and confidentiality.

---

[1]    'Your Right to Know' (Cm 3818).
[2]    Third Report, Session 1997–98, para 17.

---

1.25 It is submitted that it would have been desirable for the data protection legislation to have proceeded in parallel with the freedom of information legislation. The Select Committee, whilst welcoming the prospect of freedom of information legislation, have commented critically on the possibility of overlap and conflict between the two systems.[1] It also noted that the Registrar had not been consulted prior to the publication of the White Paper.[2]

---

[1]    House of Commons Select Committee on Public Administration, Third Report, Session 1997–98, para 21.
[2]    Ibid, para 7.

---

IMPLEMENTATION OF THE NEW REGIME

1.26   The UK, in common with the other EU member states, is required to implement the Data Protection Directive by 24 October 1998 (Art 32(1)). As indicated above, this timetable will not be met although it is expected that the 1998 Act will enter into force before the end of 1998. For those commencing automated processing on or after whatever date may be selected for entry into force, the full provisions of the Act will apply. A variety of transitional provisions apply, and the Act will not enter into force in its entirety until 24 October 2007 (Sch 8).

1.27   Consideration of the phased introduction of the legislation is discussed below in relation to the extension of the data protection regime to some categories of manual data (para 1.28) and in relation to the position of existing data users, ie those who have either registered under the 1984 Act or whose processing activities are covered by one of the exemptions offered under the 1998 Act (para 1.29).

**Manual data**

1.28   As initially drafted, the provisions relating to manual data were relatively straightforward. The Directive allows for a 12 year transitional period (Art 32(2)) and initially it was proposed that this should be utilised with provisions regarding manual records entering into force on 24 October 2007. When the Bill was before Parliament however it was determined that the opportunity should be taken to amend the provisions of the Access to Health Records Act 1990 and the Access to Personal Files Act 1987. These changes were necessary to comply with the decision of the European Court of Human Rights in the case of *Gaskin v United Kingdom*.[1] As discussed in more detail below,[2] the amendments will create more extensive rights of access to data generated by third parties. Given that the Court had found against the UK in this case, it was considered inappropriate to delay the effect of amendment. Accordingly data, referred to as 'accessible records', held under the scope of these Acts will be subject to the new access procedures from the date of the 1998 Act's entry into force, but will benefit from the phased implementation of the remaining provisions of the Act (Sch 8, Pt II). The decision was also taken that the access provisions applying under the Consumer Credit Act 1974 in respect of data held by credit reference agencies should be brought within the data protection regime. Provisions relating to this, which broadly continue the existing system, will also enter into force at the same time as the Act (Sch 8, Pt II).

---

[1]   [1990] 1 FLR 167, 12 EHRR 36.
[2]   See para 5.14 et seq.

1.29   Until 24 October 2001 other forms of manual records coming within the scope of the 1998 Act's definitions will be exempt from the legislation (Sch 8, Pt II). Between October 2001 and October 2007 a further transitional period will operate (Sch 8, Pt III). Within this period, manual records will be exempted from the first data protection principle requiring that data be processed fairly and lawfully, save for requirements that the subject be informed of the purposes for which data are collected or acquired. Exemption will also be available from the second, third, fourth and fifth principles and from the provisions of s 14 which confer rights on data subjects to seek the rectification, blocking, destruction or erasure of inaccurate data.

1.30   From 24 October 2007, the full provisions of the 1998 Act will come into force although it is likely that many systems of manual records will be exempted from the notification requirements.

## Existing users

1.31   For those currently registered under the 1984 Act, register entries will remain valid for their scheduled duration. The substantive provisions of the legislation will come into effect from a date to be fixed by order. However, some modifications will apply to existing users (including those exempted under the provisions of the 1984 Act) to allow processing practices to be brought into line with amended and expanded definitions. The Directive sanctions a three year transitional period for existing users (Art 32(2)) and acting on this the 1998 Act provides that until 23 October 2001—

(1)   Data will not be regarded as being processed unless this occurs by reference to the data subject (Sch 8, Pt II, para 5).

(2)   Exemptions offered under the 1984 Act in respect of—
 (a)   payroll and accounting data (Sch 8, Pt II, para 6),
 (b)   unincorporated members' clubs and mailing lists (Sch 8, Pt II, paras 7–11), and
 (c)   back-up data (Sch 8, Pt II, para 12)
will continue to apply.[1]

(3)   The requirement to give notice to data subjects of the purposes for which data are acquired or collected will not apply (Sch 8, Pt II, para 13(1)(a)(i)).[2]

(4)   Provisions relating to the processing of sensitive data will not apply (Sch 8, Pt II, para 13(1)(a)(iii)).[3]

(5)   Provisions requiring that a data subject exercising rights of access be given information regarding the nature of the data held, the purposes for which it is processed and the persons to whom it may be disclosed, the source of the data and the logic employed in systems where decisions are based solely on automated processing will not apply (Sch 8, Pt II, para 13(1)(d)).[4]

(6)   Provisions empowering the data subject to require that decisions not be taken solely on the basis of automated processing will not apply (Sch 8, Pt II, para 13(1)(f)).[5]

(7)   Provisions relating to transborder data flows will not apply (Sch 8, Pt II, para 13(1)(c)).[6]

(8)   Provisions empowering the data subject to block processing for the purposes of direct marketing and to object to other forms of processing will not apply (Sch 8, Pt II, para 13(1)(e)).[7]

(9)   The expanded rights of compensation established under the 1998 Act with the exception of rights to compensation created in respect of processing for the special (media related) purposes will not apply (Sch 8, Pt II, para 13(1)(g)).[8]

> (10)   Existing data users will not be subject to the 1998 Act's provisions
>         relating to the making by the Commissioner of a preliminary
>         assessment prior to permitting processing to commence (Sch 8,
>         Pt V, para 19).[9]

The overall effect of these provisions is to allow existing processing to continue under
the conditions laid down in the 1984 Act until 24 October 2001.

---

[1]  See also para 3.18.
[2]  See also para 3.25.
[3]  See also para 2.22 et seq.
[4]  See also para 5.2 et seq.
[5]  See also para 5.54 et seq.
[6]  See also Ch 7.
[7]  See also para 5.42.
[8]  See also paras 5.47–5.48.
[9]  See also para 3.32 et seq.

# 2 Scope of the Data Protection Act 1998

## THE DATA PROTECTION ENVIRONMENT

2.1    Under the Data Protection Act 1984, the data protection world was inhabited by data users, computer bureaux and data subjects. Operating under the supervision of the Data Protection Registrar and the Tribunal, they all played roles in relation to the processing of personal data. Although the basic structure remains, the Data Protection Act 1998 makes changes to terminology and, more significantly, makes changes related to the substance of key definitions and requirements. In particular, while under the 1984 Act a requirement to register was a pre-requisite for the application of the substantive provisions of the legislation, the 1998 Act provides for the breakage of this link.

2.2    Initially this chapter will identify those parties who are subject to the data protection regime (see paras 2.3–2.7) before examining in detail the key definitions relating to the activities subject to the control and jurisdictional application of the 1998 Act (see paras 2.8 *et seq*). Chapters 3–8 will consider the status and powers of the supervisory agencies responsible for the operation of the system and the substantive requirements of the legislation. The focus of attention will be on the data protection principles. Both the 1984 and 1998 Acts contain eight principles. Although the terminology differs between the two Acts, the basic purpose of the principles remains to enshrine general formulations of acceptable processing practice. In many respects the principles can be regarded as being a modern equivalent of the Ten Commandments. It may be seen either as a mark of technological progress, or of the limitations of machines, that computer based activities require fewer rules than humanity. Finally, consideration will be given to the new controls imposed over transborder data flows and to the special requirements imposed upon those processing personal data in connection with the provision of telecommunication services.

## DATA PROTECTION PARTIES

### Data controllers

2.3    The 1984 Act regulated the activities of data users. In order to be classed as a data user a party had to be able to control the contents and use of personal data (s 1(5)). The term 'data controller' is substituted in the 1998 Act with little apparent change in extent. An individual or undertaking will be classed as a data controller when it—

> '. . . (either alone or jointly or in common with other persons) determines the purposes for which and the manner in which personal data are, or are to be processed' (s 1(1)).

It is possible that a person could be classed as a data controller without owning any form of computer. The example might be given of a business person who maintains all the records relating to the business on paper. If these are passed on to an accountant who transfers the data into electronic form and subjects it to processing, the client will be regarded as a data controller. It is likely that the accountant will also be considered as a controller on the basis that he or she retains control over the particular manner in which work is conducted.[1]

---

[1]  See *Data Protection Registrar v Griffin* [1993] COD 283. In this case an accountant was convicted of processing data without having registered under the 1984 Act. The processing in question related to data supplied by a client. It was held that as the accountant possessed a measure of discretion as to the manner in which the accounts were to be processed, he exercised sufficient control over the data to be classed as a data user.

## Data processor

2.4  As in the example given above, some data controllers may seek to have processing carried out on their behalf by a third party. This was more prevalent in the early days of computing than is the case today, although one significant example is where undertakings make arrangements as part of a disaster recovery plan to obtain access to external processing facilities in the event of some interruption to service. The 1984 Act made provision to regulate the activities of computer bureaux, which a person carries on if he provides a service in respect of data and—

'(a)  as agent for other persons he causes data held by them to be processed . . . or

(b)  he allows other persons the use of equipment in his possession for the processing . . . of data held by them' (s 1(6)).

2.5  Mirroring once again the terminology of the Directive, the 1998 Act substitutes the term 'data processor' for 'computer bureau'. The term data processor is defined to encompass—

'any person (other than an employee of the data controller) who processes the data on behalf of the data controller' (s 1(1)).

The phrase in brackets was included to avoid the possibility that employees engaged in processing in the course of their employment might be regarded as data processors. Given the expanded definition of processing adopted in the 1998 Act,[1] it will be the case that anyone who collects data for the processor—perhaps by conducting market research surveys—will be classed as a processor.

---

[1]  See para 2.36.

2.6  Although a greater range of persons may be classed as data processors, the requirements imposed on them under the 1998 Act are limited. Under the 1984 Act those operating computer bureaux were required to register details of their activities (s 5(1)) and subsequently were required to comply with the eighth data principle relating to the maintenance of adequate security measures (Sch 1, para 8). It was also possible that an aggrieved individual might bring an action for compensation against a computer bureau (s 23). However, under the 1998 Act data processors will not be subject to the notification requirements (s 17),[1] while in respect of the requirement to maintain appropriate security (now found in the seventh principle), the onus is placed upon the data controller for whom processing is conducted. The controller is responsible for selecting a processor who can provide satisfactory guarantees regarding security (Sch 1, Pt II, para 11). A written contract must also be entered into obliging the processor to act only on instructions from the controller in respect of the processing carried out, and also to comply with the requirements of the seventh principle (Sch 1, Pt II, para 12). Furthermore, it is only the data controller who may be liable to compensate data subjects for losses arising from processing (s 13).

---

[1]   This provision provides for notification and refers only to this obligation being imposed upon data controllers.

---

## Data subject

2.7   The terminology of data subject remains unchanged, as does its definition as 'an individual who is the subject of personal data' (s 1(1)).[1] It would take a unique individual to not be classed as a data subject at all. In contrast to the situation with data controllers and processors, where the focus is very much on the obligations imposed under the legislation, for data subjects the purpose of the 1998 Act is to confer rights. The most important right for data subjects is undoubtedly that of obtaining access to data held by controllers and of securing the correction of any errors contained therein.

---

[1]   The equivalent provision in the 1984 Act is s 1(4).

---

## DATA, PERSONAL DATA AND PROCESSING

2.8   These concepts are critical to the application of the legislation. The 1998 Act will apply only where information relating to a living identifiable individual is processed or held with the intention that it should be processed. Although personal data has been estimated as accounting for only around 5% of all recorded data,[1] the 1998 Act will apply in any situation where there is the presence of information about a single individual in a collection of commercial or financial data.

---

[1]   M Briant in P Hansen et al *Freedom of Data Flows and EEC Law,* Kluwer (1988) p 47.

---

## Data

2.9   The 1984 Act defined data as information 'recorded in a form in which it can be processed by equipment operating automatically in response to instructions given for that purpose' (s 1(2)). The 1998 Act adopts a three stage definition referring to information which—

(a)   is being processed by means of equipment operating automatically in response to instructions given for that purpose,

(b)   is recorded with the intention that it should be processed by means of such equipment, or

(c)   is recorded as part of a relevant filing system or with the intention that it should form part of a relevant filing system (s 1(1)).

2.10 It is difficult to identify any form of data which cannot be processed automatically. As a result of developments in image recognition technology, for example, images recorded by closed circuit television cameras can be processed with a view to identifying particular individuals. Such activities will come within the legislation. It is to be emphasised, however, that the fact that information might be processed automatically will not of itself mean that the 1998 Act will apply. An individual might possess many hours of video recordings, but until the intention is formed to subject these to automated processing, the 1998 Act will not apply.

## Extension to manual records

2.11   The first two paragraphs of the 1998 definition of data in s 1(2) effectively restate the provisions of the 1984 Act. The most significant aspect of the new definition is the provision contained in s 1(2)(c) relating to 'relevant filing systems' which has the effect of bringing some manual filing systems within the data protection regime. Under the 1984 Act, such systems were excluded from the legislation. This extension has been the cause of considerable controversy with some estimates putting the cost of compliance in the region of £2 billion. Such figures are likely to prove an exaggeration. The Registrar has commented that there appears to have been an unrealistic assumption made that those keeping manual files will need to check every file for accuracy.[1] While there will certainly be requirements to take reasonable steps to ensure that information is accurate and to correct any errors which arise, no requirement for individual verification applies in respect of computerised records, and there is no apparent reason why the situation should be different with manual files.

---

[1]   DPR Briefing Paper; see http://www.open.gov.UK/dpr/dprhome.htm. This cites research carried out at Aston Business School and the Universities of Tilburg and Leiden which concluded that the 'financial impact of the proposed Directive will be very small for the majority of organisations studied in the public and private sectors in the UK and the Netherlands'.

2.12   The term 'relevant filing system' is defined in the 1998 Act as—

> '. . . any set of information relating to individuals to the extent that, although the information is not processed by means of equipment operating automatically . . . the set is structured, either by reference to individuals or by reference to criteria relating to individuals, in such a way that specific information relating to a particular individual is readily accessible.' (s 1(1)).

2.13   This definition is rather more complex than that found in the Directive which states that the term—

> ' "personal data filing system" ("filing system") shall mean any structured set of personal data which are accessible according to specific criteria, whether centralised, decentralised or dispersed on a functional or geographical basis' (Art 2(c)).

2.14   The key concept is the notion of a structured set of data. Recital (27) of the Directive states that—

> '. . . whereas files or sets of files as well as their cover pages, which are not structured according to specific criteria, shall under no circumstances fall within the scope of this Directive.'.

In discussion on the extent of the provision in Parliament, it was suggested that it would not be sufficient that information about an individual should be located in a single place, for example a manila folder containing an employee's entire work records. In order for the records to be covered, it would additionally be required that the information within the folder should be held in a structured format so that individual items might readily be extracted. Speaking during the Bill's Report stage in the House of Lords, Lord Williams stated that—

> 'Our intentions are clear. We do not wish the definition to apply to miscellaneous collections of paper about individuals, even if the collections are assembled in a file with the individual's name or other unique identifier on the front, if specific data about the individual cannot be readily extracted from that collection.

> An example might be a personnel file with my name on the front. Let us assume that the file contains every piece of paper or other document about me which the personnel section has collected over the course of my career; and those papers are held in the file in date order, with no means of readily identifying specific information about me except by looking at every document. The Government's clear intention is that such files should not be caught.'.[1]

---

[1] HL Report, 16 March 1998, col 467.

2.15 The Registrar, however, has commented that—

> 'It has . . . been put to us that 'particular information' refers to information of a very specific nature. On this analysis information held in a file relating to an immigration application would arguably be covered as all the information in the file will, or should, be directly pertinent to that application. However, it has been argued that information held in a normal personnel file will not be 'particular information' as there will be a range of information concerning such matters as sickness absence, performance, pay, next of kin. We find this distinction unconvincing. The range of information in a personnel file may be wide because there is a wide range of information relevant to an individual's employment. Nevertheless the information is 'particular' in that it is all information held for, and relevant to, employment.'.[1]

---

[1] DPR Briefing Paper; see http://www.open.gov.UK/dpr/dprhome.htm

2.16 The government's interpretation might seem designed to favour those whose records are less organised than others. Even by its own criteria, however, the approach may create considerable problems. An organisation may have, for example, 10,000 employees with personnel records maintained in the format suggested by Lord Williams. A new employee may at some stage have only one or two documents in the file. Such information must be considered readily available. As employment continues, so the file will grow but it will be very difficult to determine at which point the data protection Rubicon is crossed. A wise controller might pay considerable regard to the views of the Registrar who will (in his new guise as Commissioner) be responsible for enforcing the legislation. In reality, other changes to the law may render the issue of limited importance. One matter which may give some cause for comfort to those keeping manual records is that such controllers are exempted from the requirement to notify details of activities for inclusion in the data protection register (s 17(2)).

**Personal data**

2.17  The premise underlying data protection legislation is that the processing of data relating to individuals constitutes a threat to the subject's rights and freedoms, most specifically the right to privacy. If an individual cannot be identified from the manner in which data is collected, processed or used, there can be no significant threat to privacy and no justification for the application of legislative controls. The question may arise, however, as to when an individual may be identified? In the German census case referred to in para 1.7 the court took cognisance of the fact that modern data processing techniques might permit the de-anonymisation of census data.

2.18  The Directive is stated as applying to the processing of—

'. . . any information relating to an identified or identifiable natural person ("data subject"); an identifiable person is one who can be identified directly or indirectly, in particular by reference to an identification number or to one or more factors specific to his physical, psychological, mental, economic, cultural or social identity' (Art 2(a)).

Recital (26) of the Directive states additionally that in order 'to determine whether a person is identifiable, account should be taken of all the means likely reasonably to be used either by the controller or by any other person to identify the said person.'.

2.19  In implementing these provisions, the 1998 Act provides that—

' "personal data" means data which relate to a living individual who can be identified—

(a)    from those data, or

(b)    from those data and other information which is in the possession of, or is likely to come into the possession of, the data controller,

and includes any expression of opinion about the individual and any indication of the intentions of the data controller or any other person in respect of the individual' (s 1(1)).

Initially it may be noted that this definition removes the 1984 Act's distinction between statements of opinion (included in the definition) and of intention (excluded) (s 1(3)). The basis for the distinction was never clarified but it would appear that it was intended primarily to exclude personnel records relating to career planning from the subject access provisions. Special provision is now made for such records (Sch 7)[1] and few will regret the departure of a distinction which even the Registrar described as difficult to understand.[2]

---

[1]    These provisions are discussed at para 5.31.
[2]    Fifth Report of the Data Protection Registrar, 1989.

2.20  In the situation where information is held solely by one data controller, the question as to whether an individual is identifiable may readily be resolved. We live, however, in the age of the computer network. Distributive computing, demonstrated at its most extensive by the Internet, renders the issue of physical possession of data secondary to the question of access. Practices such as data matching allow controllers to trawl across the contents of a wide range of computers. The term 'data matching' has been defined as involving—

'The comparison of data held by different data users (or by the same data user in different contexts). The aim of the comparison is not primarily the creation of a larger file of information about the data subject but the identification of anomalies and inconsistencies within a single set of data or between two or more different sets.'[1]

One area in which data matching techniques have been applied is in seeking to identify individuals making multiple applications for social or housing benefits.[2] Special provision has been made for such applications in the 1998 Act (s 29(4)).[3]

---

[1]  'A Guide to Developing Codes of Practice on Data Matching' (Office of the Data Protection Registrar). As to data matching, see paras 4.74–4.76.
[2]  See the Social Security Administration (Fraud) Act 1997.
[3]  These provisions are discussed at paras 5.20–5.22.

---

2.21  It is not just in the more formal instances of data matching that there might be a number of separate data controllers. In the case of the Internet, the proliferation of search tools such as 'Alta Vista' and 'Dejavu News' allow users to scan thousands of sites to develop profiles of individual's postings to newsgroup discussions. Anyone placing material on the Internet, an act which will constitute processing as defined in the 1998 Act, should be aware that third parties may engage in such forms of processing. A scenario might be postulated whereby *individual A* posts data on a Web site, *individual B* controls an Internet search engine which is used by *individual C* to compile a collection of personal data including elements originating from *individual A's* Web site. It is likely in such situations that there may be a plurality of data controllers with the resolution of relative areas of responsibility being a task of great complexity.

## SENSITIVE DATA

2.22  The extent to which certain forms of data can be classed as being especially sensitive and deserving of special protection has long been a contentious issue. During the passage of the 1984 Act the attempt to identify sensitive data was compared somewhat scornfully by government ministers with the quest for the unicorn. Both were considered mythical creatures. In the case of personal data, the context in which data was held or used was considered far more important than the data itself. A list of names and addresses for example, would not normally be considered sensitive but this view might change if it referred to details of prominent persons and was in the hands of a terrorist organisation. While this view is not without merit, it seeks to transform the exceptional into the norm. Ultimately it was accepted that there are certain categories of information which would generally be regarded as possessing a degree of sensitivity, and in respect of which, substantial numbers of data subjects might wish to be assured that dissemination would be limited and controlled.

2.23  As enacted, the 1984 Act provided the power to make regulations to strengthen the data protection principles in respect of data relating to racial origin, political opinions, religious or other beliefs, physical or mental health, sexual life or criminal convictions (s 2(3)). This power was never exercised. The 1998 Act brings the treatment of sensitive data within the heart of the legislation and subjects its processing to more extensive requirements than is the case with other forms of data.

The definition of what constitutes sensitive data is broader than under the 1984 Act, with s 2 of the new Act referring to—

'(a)    the racial or ethnic origin of the data subject,

(b)    his political opinions,

(c)    his religious beliefs or other beliefs of a similar nature,

(d)    whether he is a member of a trade union, . . .

(e)    his physical or mental health or condition,

(f)    his sexual life,

(g)    the commission or alleged commission by him of any offence, or

(h)    any proceedings for any offence committed or alleged to have been committed by him, the disposal of such proceedings or the sentence of any court in such proceedings.'.

Specific provisions defining the circumstances under which sensitive data might be processed are contained in Sch 3. Opening with  a general prohibition against the processing of such data, a number of exceptional situations are identified which may justify processing (see paras 2.24–2.33).

## Conditions justifying processing of sensitive data

*Explicit consent*

*(a)    The data subject has given his explicit consent to the processing of those data (Sch 3, para 1)*

2.24  The concept of explicit consent is not defined in either the Directive or the 1998 Act. During the Bill's Committee stage it was stated by the Parliamentary Secretary—

'The Government are content for the issue of whether consent has been validly given to be determined by the courts in the normal way. The matter arises in other legal contexts and the courts are well used to handling it. It is better for the courts to decide according to ordinary principles of law than for the Bill to contain specific consent provisions.'[1]

The Directive does define the notion of 'the data subject's consent' as 'any freely given specific and informed indication of' the data subject's wishes regarding processing.[2] It must be assumed that 'explicit consent' imposes a stricter requirement and may, for example, require the obtaining of written consent.

---

[1]    HC SC D, 4 June 1998, col 310.

[2]    Art 2(h).

---

*Employment related processing*

*(b)    The processing is necessary for the purposes of exercising or performing any right or obligation which is conferred or imposed by law on the data controller in connection with employment (Sch 3, para 2(1))*

2.25  It is further provided that the Secretary of State may either exclude the application of this provision in certain cases or impose additional conditions (Sch 3, para 2(2)). It may be noted that in respect of the processing of employment related data, the Directive requires the provision of 'adequate safeguards' (Art 8(2)(b)). Unless it can be assumed that existing employment law provides 'adequate safeguards' for the data subject, UK law will not comply with the Directive unless and until an order is made.

*Vital interests*

(c)   *Processing is necessary to protect the vital interests of the data subject or of another person where consent cannot be given by or on behalf of the data subject or where the controller cannot reasonably be expected to obtain consent (Sch 3, para 3(a))*

2.26   Examples of such situations might be where medical data relating to the subject has to be processed in order to treat the subject who is unconscious in hospital. Again, processing may be justified where the subject is a carrier of an infectious disease and where the information is needed to provide treatment to a third party. It is further provided that processing may take place when this is—

'necessary to protect the vital interests of a third party and the subject unreasonably withholds consent' (Sch 3, para 3(b)).

This situation may well be similar to that discussed above but with the distinction that the subject has been identified by the controller. An example might be where the subject suffers from an infectious disease but refuses to consent to the disclosure of a list of persons who might have come into contact with the subject and who might need to be contacted to receive treatment.

*Processing by specified bodies*

(d)   *The processing is carried out in the course of its legitimate activities by a non-profit making body or association existing for political, philosophical, religious or trade union purposes. In such cases, appropriate safeguards must be provided for the rights and freedoms of data subjects, the data must relate only to members of the association or those in regular contact with it and the processing must not involve disclosure of the data to third parties without the consent of the data subject (Sch 3, para 4)*

2.27   Given the extension of the definition of processing to include the collection of data, this definition may have some unanticipated consequences. It was conceded in Parliament that political canvassing would be covered if the intention were to transfer returns onto a computer system. A similar situation would apply where religious organisations sought to obtain converts through door to door visits. For political data it was indicated that special regulations might be made.[1]

---

[1] HC Debs, 2 July 1998, col 613.

---

*Information in the public domain*

(e)   *The information contained in the personal data has been made public as a result of steps deliberately taken by the data subject (Sch 3, para 5)*

2.28   It is significant to note in this context that it will not suffice that the information has come into the public domain; this must have occurred through the deliberate actions of the subject. There is clearly a relationship between this provision and the statutory provisions discussed below relating to the activities of the media.[1]

---

[1] See Ch 6.

---

*Legal proceedings and the administration of justice*

(f)   *The processing is necessary for the purpose of, or in connection with, legal proceedings (including prospective proceedings), for obtaining legal advice or in order to establish, exercise or defend legal rights (Sch 3, para 6)*

2.29   This provision was criticised in Parliament as being excessively broad. Certainly the provision relating to 'prospective proceedings' appears to be somewhat opaque.

(g)   *The processing is necessary for the administration of justice, for the exercise of statutory or governmental functions (Sch 3, para 7)*

2.30   Once again the Secretary of State may exclude the application of this provision in certain situations or require that additional conditions be satisfied. An obvious example of such a situation would be the maintenance of criminal records. It should be noted that the Directive provides that 'a complete register of criminal convictions may be kept only under the control of official authority' (Art 8(5)).

*Processing for medical purposes*

(h)   *The processing is necessary for medical purposes and is undertaken by a health professional or by a person owing an equivalent duty of confidentiality (Sch 3, para 8(1))*

2.31   The term 'medical purposes' is defined broadly to include 'preventative medicine, medical diagnosis, medical research, the provision of care and treatment and the management of healthcare services' (Sch 8, Pt II, para 8(2)). It should be stressed that in this case, as with all the exceptions described in paras 2.24–2.33, the effect is to free the controller from the requirement to seek explicit consent to processing. The processing must be carried out in accordance with the data protection principles and other requirements of the 1998 Act.

*Ethnic monitoring*

(i)   *The processing relates to data indicating racial or ethnic origin but is carried out in order to monitor compliance with equal opportunities legislation. Appropriate safeguards must also be taken for the rights and freedoms of data subjects (Sch 3, para 9(1))*

2.32   It is provided that the Secretary of State may define more precisely the activities coming within the scope of this provision (Sch 3, para 9(2)). Care will certainly need to be taken to ensure that information supplied for this purpose, for example by an applicant for employment, is used only for monitoring purposes and retained, at least in a form which can identify the subject, for no longer than is necessary.

*Order of the Secretary of State*

(j)   *The processing occurs in circumstances specified by the Secretary of State (Sch 3, para 10)*

2.33   This provision confers a wide ranging power on the Secretary of State to extend the range of exemptions. As indicated above, it has been suggested that the power will be invoked for the benefit of canvassing by political parties. The Directive requires that additional exemptions must be justified by 'reasons of substantial public interest' (Art 8(4)) and must be notified to the Commission (Art 8(6)).

*Processing*

2.34  The final element of the statutory definitions relates to the act of processing. As stated above, a person may hold a substantial amount of personal data but until this is processed, or the intention to process is formed, the 1998 Act will not apply. Under the 1984 Act, processing is defined as encompassing the acts of—

> '. . . amending, augmenting, deleting or re-arranging the data or extracting the information constituting the data and, in the case of personal data, means performing any of these operations by reference to the data subject' (s 1(7)).[1]

---

[1]  Section 1(8) of the 1984 Act provides that the definition of processing is not to encompass 'any operation performed only for the purpose of preparing the text of documents.' Generally referred to as 'the word processing exception' this was intended to remove this basic activity from the scope of the legislation. As computing and word processing technology has advanced, the need for any justification of the exemption has become more limited and it will vanish with the entry into force of the 1998 Act.

---

2.35  Although it is difficult to identify activities connected with the use of a computer which would not constitute processing, the requirement that the activities be conducted by reference to the data subject constituted a significant, albeit ill-defined limitation. For example, a university might hold on computer a list of the names of all the students attending a particular class together with the marks which each student obtained in the exams. If the data is processed so as to compile a list of all students obtaining a mark of 60% or above, it is clear that data has been extracted—but has it been extracted by reference to individuals? This point assumes considerable importance in relation to direct mail where the goal of the processing may be to produce a list of potential customers. The Registrar has expressed the view that this form of activity will constitute processing conducted by reference to every individual whose details are involved.[1] The Directive and the 1998 Act remove the requirement for processing by reference to a particular subject, the Act defining the activity of processing as involving—

> 'obtaining, recording or holding the information or data or carrying out any operation or set of operations on the data, including—
>
> (a)  organisation, adaptation or alteration of the information or data,
>
> (b)  retrieval, consultation or use of the information or data,
>
> (c)  disclosure of the information or data by transmission, dissemination or otherwise making available, or
>
> (d)  alignment, combination, blocking, erasure or destruction of the information or data' (s 1(1)).

---

[1]  'Questions and Answers on the Data Protection Act' (Office of the Data Protection Registrar, p 11).

---

2.36  The new definition is extremely broad. It has to be read in conjunction with the statutory definition of data with its reference to the intention to process either using equipment operating automatically, or as part of a structured filing system. For example, when a market researcher asks individuals to answer a questionnaire, if the responses are noted on paper, processing will have occurred if it is intended that these will be transcribed into electronic format and subjected to computer processing.

2.37  In terms of the activities involved, the new definition should close the apparent loophole created by the decision of the House of Lords in the case of *R v Brown*.[1] In this case a police officer had caused data relating to individuals to be displayed on a terminal attached to the police national computer. Beyond being seen and noted, it was not alleged that any further use had been made of the data. The defendant was charged under the Data Protection Act 1984 with the wrongful use of data contrary to the provisions of s 5 of the Act and was convicted at trial. Overturning the conviction, the House of Lords held by a majority that a distinction had to be drawn between the activities of processing and of use. As was stated by Lord Hoffmann—

> 'In my view, however, the scheme of the Act as a whole does not permit
> the phrase "use [personal] data" to be construed as including its retrieval.
> This is because the Act quite carefully uses a number of different words
> to describe various things which can be done to personal data. These
> include holding, using, disclosing, transferring, obtaining and, for
> present purposes most significantly, "processing" '.[2]

---

[1]  [1996] 1 All ER 545.
[2]  *Ibid* at 560.

---

2.38  Accepting that the defendant's activities constituted processing, the question was posed as to whether it also amounted to using the data? Lord Hoffmann continued—

> 'I do not think that it can. The Act treats processing differently from
> using . . . So it seems to me that 'using' personal data was not intended
> to include the various operations within the computer which fall within
> the definition of "processing". '.[1]

It was concluded that the concept of 'use' had to be interpreted in line with the normal meaning of the word and would require that some action be taken on the data. The consequence is that unfair or even unlawful processing of data will not constitute a criminal offence under the 1984 Act in the absence of evidence that some further use is made of the data.[2] The broader definition adopted under the Directive will bring together the concepts of processing and use.

---

[1]  [1996] 1 All ER 545, at 560.
[2]  There would appear to be little doubt, as indeed was suggested in the House of Lords, that a prosecution on the basis of an attempt to make unauthorised use of data would have been successful.

---

## WHEN IS DATA RECORDED?

2.39  A further problem which may remain under the Directive concerns the definition of the word 'recorded'. For the purposes of the 1998 Act the word 'data' is defined as information recorded in a form in which it can be processed automatically in response to instructions given for that purpose (s 1(2)). The Directive does not provide a separate definition of 'data' but the definition of 'processing' cited above makes reference to the act of recording data. The question as to when information is recorded may be a matter of some difficulty. In the case of *R v Gold*,[1] the House of Lords held that the word 'recorded' required 'the preservation of the thing which is the subject matter of them for an appreciable time with the object of subsequent retrieval or recovery'.[2] As the Registrar has commented, many modern computer systems require that data be held in the system for only a short period of time.[3] The development of the Internet and WWW means that the availability of access to data is becoming an acceptable substitute for its possession. In *R v Gold*, for example, the particular data was retained for less than one second. The issue may assume considerable importance where information is being transferred from one user to another. Direct communications between computers may allow large amounts of data to be transmitted and received in a very short period of time. Once again, the issue might be more accurately considered as one of control rather than the strict application of the legislation.

---

1   [1988] AC 1063.
2   Per Lord Brandon, at p 1073.
3   'What are your views?' Consultation Paper p 38.

## JURISDICTIONAL ISSUES

2.40  The Data Protection Act 1984 applies to all data users who control the contents and use of personal data from within the UK (s 39). In part this approach was necessary in order to comply with the Council of Europe's provisions regarding mutual assistance. In the situation where information is processed in the UK relating to, for example, French or German data subjects, the 1998 Act will apply with the main issue being the identification of the data user. The question as to whether an undertaking can be considered resident in the UK is one which arises in a number of contexts and which may produce different results. As the Registrar has commented, a company could be regarded as resident in the UK for the purpose of the 1998 Act, but not for taxation purposes. In the event that the company is not considered resident, it may be that it will be represented in the UK by a 'servant or agent' who will be classed as a data user for this purpose. It may also be the case that the undertaking which carries out the processing may be regarded as a computer bureau for the purpose of the legislation.

2.41  Similar problems arise when data relating to UK data subjects is processed abroad. In many instances, the data will remain under the legal control of the UK based user who will therefore be subject to the legislation. The view has been taken by the Registrar that jurisdiction will be claimed even where all aspects of the processing are carried out abroad but where it is intended that the data will be used in the UK, regardless of the form in which it is imported. The correctness of this interpretation has not been tested before the courts or before the Data Protection Tribunal.

2.42  In the Directive it is provided that member states are to apply national laws where processing 'is carried out in the context of the activities of an establishment of the controller on the territory of the Member State'. Such a formulation may lead to extra-territorial application of national laws. Article 28(6) provides further that—

> 'Each supervisory authority is competent, whatever the national law applying to the processing in question, to exercise, on the territory of its own Member State, the powers conferred on it[1] . . . Each authority may be requested to exercise its powers by an authority of another Member State.'.

---

1   Ie to investigate suspected violations of the law and to intervene by legal or administrative measures to terminate breaches.

2.43 There is potential for overlapping jurisdiction in the situation where multinational undertakings process personal data in a variety of member states. In its Consultation Paper, the Home Office asserts that—

> 'While some of the provisions relating to geographical extent are clear enough, others are obscure and possibly ambiguous. There is, therefore, the potential for inconsistent approaches being adopted in different Member States. The danger is that this could make it possible for the national law of more than one Member State to apply to a single processing operation, or for no Member State's law so to apply.'[1]

---

[1]    Consultation Paper on the Data Protection Directive, Home Office, 1996, para 2.27.

2.44 The multiple jurisdiction situation would appear to be an inevitable consequence of the free movement of data within the EU. Given that a major purpose of the Directive is to harmonise the laws of the member states, such a result should not be excessively burdensome for data users and indeed corresponds to the UK Registrar's interpretation of the existing situation under domestic law. It is difficult to envisage that a reasonable interpretation of the Directive's terms could produce a situation where no national law applied. In implementing the Directive's provisions the 1998 Act will apply where—

'(a)    the data controller is established in the United Kingdom and the data are processed in the context of that establishment, or

(b)    the data controller is established neither in the United Kingdom nor in any other EEA State but uses equipment in the United Kingdom for processing the data otherwise than for the purposes of transit through the United Kingdom' (s 5(1)).

An example of the latter situation might be where equipment forming part of a computer network, involving an Internet service provider, is located in the UK but managed from the US.

2.45 The question of establishment is defined in the 1998 Act more precisely than under the 1984 Act. The criteria adopted are that the controller is—

(1)    An individual who is ordinarily resident in the UK.

(2)    A body incorporated under UK law.

(3)    A partnership or unincorporated association formed under UK law.

(4)    A person maintaining an office, branch, agency or regular practice in the UK (s 5(3)).

In the case of multinational companies they will be regarded as established in every country in which they operate. The geographical location of any data processing operation will not be relevant. A company established, for example, in France, Germany and the UK will be required to comply with the national laws of each of these states. The effect will be that the Data Protection Commissioner would be obliged to assist in any enquiries made by the German supervisory authority regarding processing relating to German citizens carried out in the UK, and to apply German law in determining the legality of this processing. The 1998 Act provides that an order may be made by the Secretary of State relating to the manner in which these functions might be exercised (s 51(3)).

# 3 The Data Protection Commissioner

## INTRODUCTION

3.1 The establishment of some form of independent supervisory agency has become a hallmark of European data protection regimes, although the approach adopted has varied significantly. In the UK this role has been exercised by the Registrar who has been responsible for the supervision of all aspects of processing. In other states, different agencies have been given responsibility for public and private sector processing whereas in Germany the responsibilities are divided between Federal and State data protection commissioners.

3.2 The appointment of supervisory agencies is not a requirement of the Council of Europe Convention which, in Art 13(2), requires merely that signatories 'designate one or more authorities' to co-operate with other national authorities and assist nationals of other signatory states to exercise access and other rights. The Directive is more prescriptive requiring the establishment of an independent supervisory authority (or authorities) (Art 28). It may additionally be noted that the Treaty of Amsterdam, which made significant changes to the Treaties establishing the EU, provides that independent supervisory agencies are to be established in respect of the Community institutions.[1]

---

[1]    Article 2, inserting a new Art 213b into the Treaty of Rome.

## REQUIREMENTS OF THE DIRECTIVE

3.3 In addition to requiring the establishment of a supervisory agency or agencies, the Directive prescribes the basic powers to be vested in such supervisory agencies. Article 28(3) provides that these agencies are be afforded—

'—    investigative powers, such as powers of access to data forming the subject-matter of processing operations and powers to collect all the information necessary for the performance of its supervisory duties,

—    effective powers of intervention, such as, for example, that of delivering opinions before processing operations are carried out, in accordance with Article 20, and ensuring appropriate publication of such opinions, of ordering the blocking, erasure or destruction of data, of imposing a temporary or definitive ban on processing, of warning or admonishing the controller, or that of referring the matter to national parliaments or other political institutions,

—    the power to engage in legal proceedings where the national provisions adopted pursuant to this Directive have been violated or to bring these violations to the attention of the judicial authorities.'.

It is further provided, by Art 28(4), that—

'Each supervisory authority shall hear claims lodged by any person, or by an association representing that person, concerning the protection of his rights and freedoms in regard to the processing of personal data. The person concerned shall be informed of the outcome of the claim.

Each supervisory authority shall, in particular, hear claims for checks on the lawfulness of data processing lodged by any person when the national provisions adopted pursuant to Article 13 of this Directive apply. The person shall at any rate be informed that a check has taken place.'.

## THE DATA PROTECTION REGISTRAR

3.4    In large measure the powers described above are already conferred on the Data Protection Registrar by the 1984 Act. The Registrar, who was appointed by the Crown under letters patent and who has the status of a corporation sole (Sch 2), is assisted by a Deputy and Assistant Registrars and a staff of around 100, and had been responsible for the operation of the system of registration of data users and for securing their observance of the data protection principles. In his 12th Annual Report, the Registrar indicated concern that the title of Registrar placed undue emphasis on one (rather bureaucratic) aspect of his role and suggested a change to Privacy Protection Commissioner. This request has been accepted in part although the new legislation, in common with the 1984 Act, eschews any mention of the word 'privacy'. From the date of the 1998 Act's entry into force, it is provided that the 'Data Protection Registrar established by the Data Protection Act 1984 shall continue in existence by the name of the Data Protection Commissioner' (Sch 5, para 1(1)).

3.5    Schedule 5 specifies the terms and conditions under which the Commissioner is to be appointed. This is be for a fixed term not exceeding five years. Within this period the Commissioner may be removed from office only following a resolution passed by both Houses of Parliament, a status equivalent to that of High Court judges. One change made from the 1984 Act is the provision that a Commissioner may only serve for two terms, save where special circumstances make a continuation of appointment 'desirable in the public interest' (Sch 5, para 2(5)). Under the 1984 Act, there was no limit on the number of terms that an individual could serve. Concern has been expressed in the past that the government's role in deciding whether to continue an appointment might deter the supervisory agency from investigating public sector data processing. One incident has been reported from Germany when a state data protection commissioner's appointment was not continued shortly after the individual concerned had been involved in a well publicised disagreement concerning governmental data processing practices. Although the matter is not likely to be of significance in the near future, it might be considered unfortunate that the default has effectively been switched from the assumption that the Commissioner might continue in post for more than two terms, to the assumption that this will not be the case.

3.6    Under the 1984 Act the Registrar possessed considerable discretion as to the manner in which he performed his statutory functions. The role might fairly be described as one involving many powers but few duties. In many instances that Act contains provision to the effect that 'the Registrar may'. Even where a provision opens with a prescriptive, 'the Registrar shall' this is almost invariably qualified by the phrase 'where he considers it appropriate'. This has been a source of some criticism as causing the effectiveness of the role to be very dependent upon the diligence of the Registrar. The 1998 Act retains this basic approach while placing the Commissioner under a general duty to—

'. . . promote the following of good practice by data controllers and, in particular, so to perform his functions under this Act as to promote the observance of the requirements of this Act by data controllers.' (s 51(1)).

It is difficult to see how this duty could be enforced in any meaningful way.

3.7    Initially this chapter will focus on the establishment and maintenance of the data protection register and the obligations imposed on data controllers. Attention will then be paid to the investigative  and enforcement powers conferred on the Commissioner before concluding with an account of the remaining powers and duties imposed on the Commissioner.

## THE DATA PROTECTION REGISTER

3.8    In terms of specific tasks, the major obligation imposed by the 1984 Act was to compile and maintain a register of data users and computer bureaux. The data protection register is the result of this activity. This is a publicly available document which can now be accessed over the Internet.[1] It is unclear, however, how valuable the information contained on the register may be to the average data subject. In part this is due to a somewhat idiosyncratic indexing system. A search for entries maintained by the University of Glasgow, for example, found some under this heading but others under that of Glasgow University. Even if the subject identifies the appropriate entry, many of these are substantial documents in their own right. A printout of the University of Strathclyde's entry in respect of its central and academic services (one entry out of six) extends to 40 pages of text. The main purpose for which individuals might wish to consult the register might be to find out who holds information on them. Given the size of the register (in excess of half a million pages of text), unless a subject knows of a particular organisation, it is unlikely that consulting the register will produce much by way of enlightenment.

---

[1]    http://www.open.gov.uk/dpr/register.htm.

## DATA USERS: REGISTRATION UNDER THE 1984 ACT

3.9    A feature of many of the early data protection statutes was the imposition of a system of licensing of data users. Effectively, this required users to demonstrate fitness to be permitted to process personal data. Although terminology in the field is somewhat inconsistent, the procedure might be analogised to the obtaining of a licence for the possession of a gun or the driving of a motor vehicle. With the massive increase in the number of computers, the impossibility of exercising effective control in this manner has been widely recognised. An initial step, which was implemented in the 1984 Act, saw the introduction of a system of registration of data users. Registration as applied in this statute retains qualitative criteria but switches the onus to the supervisory agency to indicate cause why an application should be rejected.

3.10 The danger of such a halfway house—and a criticism of the 1984 Act—is that these regimes impose bureaucratic burdens and costs on data users while providing minimal benefit to the public. During the Parliamentary passage of the 1984 Act, government ministers were at pains to play down the impact that this system would have on data users. 'The process of registration', it was asserted—

> 'will not be onerous. It is important to make that clear. Registration will entail no more than answering half a dozen questions and paying a small fee and acceptance onto the register will in most cases be automatic. Thereafter, the vast majority of users will not be bothered again by the Registrar. We have deliberately kept the requirements of registration to a minimum to ensure that users do not face unreasonable burdens. The registration process will require data users to specify the purposes for which they hold data . . . and bring into the open the processing of personal data, thereby meeting the fear of unknown activities taking place in secret. The establishment of a register to which anyone can go to discover the use being made of automatically processed information is a key feature of the scheme.'.[1]

---

[1]   HC Debs, 11 April 1983, col 39.

---

3.11 As initially introduced, those applying for registration were presented with a 12 page application form accompanied by a 45 page explanatory booklet. In completing the form, users were required to sign, acknowledging that they had 'read and understood' the booklet. In 1994, the Public Accounts Committee of the House of Commons in a report on the working of the 1984 Act expressed concern at the low number of registrations and recommended that action be taken to increase the number of entries. In 1996 the Registrar published a Consultative Paper noting that—

> 'most organisations, whatever the nature of their business and whether in the public or private sector share a common core of functions; they employ staff, they order and despatch goods or services, they carry out advertising or marketing; they carry out general administration using e-mail, word processing and other computer facilities to do so.'.[1]

Accordingly, much has been done to simplify procedures.

---

[1]   'The Future of Registration', Office of the Data Protection Registrar, para 4.2.

---

3.12 A range of standard form core entries has been developed so that users are presented with a set of pre-completed templates appropriate to the nature of their business. This has now been introduced and it is possible for most users to complete all registration formalities by means of a single telephone call. For the future it is proposed that e-mail applications will be accepted and, hopefully, such a possibility will be available under the new system of notification.

3.13 The 1984 Act describes the information that is required to be supplied at registration. By virtue of s 4(3), a data user must supply—

> '(a) the name and address of the data user;
> (b) a description of the personal data to be held by him and of the purpose or purposes for which the data are to be held or used;

(c) a description of the source or sources from which he intends or may wish to obtain the data or the information to be contained in the data;

(d) a description of any person or persons to whom he intends or may wish to disclose the data;

(e) the names or a description of any countries or territories outside the United Kingdom to which he intends or may wish directly or indirectly to transfer the data; and

(f) one or more addresses for the receipt of requests from data subjects for access to the data.'.

## Treatment of applications for registration

3.14 Acceptance of an application for registration under the 1984 Act was not automatic. Applications are to be considered by the Registrar with a decision concerning acceptability normally being notified to the applicant within six months.[1]

---

[1] See s 7(1), and s 7(5) which provides for the Registrar to extend this period if it is considered that a particular application requires more detailed consideration.

3.15 Applications might be rejected on three grounds. First that, in the Registrar's opinion, 'the particulars proposed for registration . . . will not give sufficient information as to the matters to which they relate' (s 7(2)(a)). Secondly, an application may also be refused if the Registrar is satisfied that the applicant is likely to contravene any of the data protection principles (s 7(2)(b)). Thirdly, an application may be rejected if the Registrar—

'. . . considers that the information available to him is insufficient to satisfy him that the applicant is unlikely to contravene any of those principles.' (s 7(2)(c)).

3.16 The onus was on the Registrar to justify the rejection of an application and only a small number of applications are formally refused. The latest figures indicate that 32 applications were refused in the year 1994–95, 31 in 1995–96 and none in the year 1996–97.[1] Applications for registration may continue to be made until the date of entry into force of the 1998 Act. Registrations in force on this date will continue to be valid for their normal currency. Given the normal three year duration of register entries, this will mean that the registration system will remain relevant until 2001.

---

[1] Thirteenth Report of the Data Protection Registrar, p 45.

## DATA USERS: NOTIFICATION UNDER THE 1998 ACT

3.17 More recent statutes, such as the Data Protection Act of 1990 enacted in Germany have moved away from the requirements of universal registration. The Directive follows this model. Although providing initially that—

'Member States shall provide that the controller or his representative, if any, must notify the supervisory authority . . . before carrying out any wholly or partly automatic processing operation . . .' (Art 18(1)).

It goes on to state that simplification or exemption from notification may be provided—

> '. . . for categories of processing operations which are unlikely, taking account of the data to be processed, to affect adversely the rights and freedoms of data subjects . . .'(Art 18(2)).

The provisions of Art 18(2) are subject to conditions being imposed as to the kind of data to be processed, the persons to whom the data are to be disclosed and the length of time the data are to be stored. A range of other possible exceptions are identified in the Directive, some of which are adopted in the 1998 Act.

3.18  The critical point of difference between the 1984 Act and the 1998 Act in respect of exemption is that while under the 1984 Act, exemption removed a data user from all aspects of the legislation, exemption under the 1998 Act is, with two exceptions, merely from the requirement to notify details of processing. All other aspects of the legislation will apply. The Act does not apply where data are processed solely for the purposes of an individual's 'personal, family or household affairs' (s 36), nor where data are processed for the purpose of safeguarding national security (s 28). This restates the position adopted in the 1984 Act although, as discussed below,[1] there are more stringent provisions allowing the Data Protection Tribunal to quash a certificate issued by the Secretary of State certifying that data are processed for national security purposes.

---

[1]   See para 5.13.

## Exemptions from the requirement to notify

3.19  As with the Directive, the 1998 Act imposes a general requirement to notify details of processing. Section 17(1) provides—

> 'Subject to the following provisions of this section, personal data must not be processed unless an entry in respect of the data controller is included in the register maintained by the Commissioner . . .'

3.20  Breach of this provision constitutes an offence. Unlike the situation under the 1984 Act where liability was strict, a defence of 'due diligence' is available to data controllers. This may be justified on account of the wider range of exceptions potentially available to the requirement of notification and the fact that controllers under the mistaken impression that they are so exempt will nonetheless be required to comply with the substantive requirements of the legislation.

3.21  In respect of the exemptions to be made available to data controllers, s 17(3) of the 1998 Act provides that—

> 'If it appears to the Secretary of State that processing of a particular description is unlikely to prejudice the rights and freedoms of data subjects, notification regulations may provide that, in such cases as may be prescribed, subsection (1) is not to apply in relation to processing of that description.'.

3.22  It remains unclear precisely what activities will be exempted from notification. The Registrar has advocated that extensive use should be made of this provision in order to exclude 'potentially hundreds of thousands of data controllers from notification'.[1] In Parliament it was stated that—

> 'It is too early to say what categories of processing will be exempted. However, the White Paper that sets out the Bill's proposals suggested that exemptions might include payroll, personnel and work planning administration; purchase and sales administration; advertising, marketing and public relations; and general administration. We are talking about the routine information that business compiles which it would be sensible to exempt.'.[2]

---

[1]    'Our Answers' Office of the Data Protection Registrar, July 1996, para 7.5.
[2]    HC, SC D, 19 May 1998, col 145.

3.23 In the 1984 Act, the list of categories of exempt processing was defined exhaustively in the statute itself (ss 32, 33). The approach in the 1998 Act purports to bring a greater measure of flexibility to the determination of what activities should be exempt from notification. Again, unlike the situation in the 1984 Act where the Registrar had no formal role to play in the making of any statutory instruments, the 1998 Act provides that the responsibility for drafting the notification regulations is to lie with the Commissioner who is, 'as soon as practicable after the passing' of the 1998 Act, to submit 'proposals as to the provisions to be included in the first notification regulations' (s 25(1)). The Commissioner is charged with the duty of keeping the working of the regulations under review and may submit further proposals to the Secretary of State (s 25(2)). The Secretary of State may also require the Commissioner to consider specific topics and make proposals (s 25(3)). Although the regulatory power remains with the Secretary of State, there is a statutory duty to consider proposals made by the Commissioner and, more generally to consult with him (s 25(4)).

3.24 The 1998 Act's approach opens the possibility for  significant numbers of controllers to be exempted from the procedural requirements, while remaining subject to the substantive requirements of the legislation. One factor which may limit the take up of this provision is that the fees from registration/notification constitute virtually the only source of income for the Registrar/Commissioner. The 1998 Act provides that in fixing the level of fees 'the Secretary of State shall have regard to the desirability of securing that the fees payable to the Commissioner are sufficient to offset' the costs of running the Commissioner and Tribunal's statutory activities.[1] A significant reduction in the level of those requiring to notify will inevitably increase the level of fees for those remaining subject to the requirement. The 1998 Act contains a further provision allowing different levels of fees to be charged to different categories of controller (s 26(1)).

---

[1]    See s 26(2); it was indicated in Parliament that the cumulative deficit on the Registrar's activities since 1986 is some £4.5 million. The 1998 Act further provides that account may be taken of the amount of any outstanding deficit when fixing fees.

## Information to be supplied on notification

3.25 The 1998 Act specifies the information, the 'registrable particulars', which must be supplied to the Commissioner (s 16(1)). This is broadly equivalent  to the information currently required at registration and relates to the identification of the controller and the purposes for which the data are held, used and disclosed. Notice must also be given of the names or a description of, any countries outside the European Economic Area to which the data may be directly or indirectly transferred. Two further novel points are worthy of note. First, where portions of the data held by the controller are exempt from notification, an indication of this fact must be given. Secondly s 18(2)(b) provides that controllers are required to give—

> 'a general description of measures to be taken for the purpose of complying with the seventh data protection principle.'.

This point has proved more controversial.

3.26   The seventh principle relates to the requirement to maintain appropriate data security measures. While the making of such a statement has been a feature of the German legislation for a number of years, opponents have suggested that to publish such information in a public document might give assistance to hackers and others seeking to obtain unauthorised access to the data. Emphasis may, however, reasonably be put on the phrase 'general description' and a statement that security complies with, for example, a relevant British or international information security standard should comply with the obligation.

3.27   While the 1998 Act specifies the categories of information which must be supplied, it is intended to allow flexibility as to the level of detail which may be required. The lack of such flexibility has been identified as a weakness of the 1984 regime. The Commissioner is required to submit proposals to the Secretary of State as to the provisions to be included in the first notification regulations (s 25(1)).[1] The regulations, it is further provided, may allow the Commissioner to determine the form and level of detail required for any of the items referred to above (s 18(3)). The regulations will also impose duties on data controllers to ensure that the terms of their entries remain up to date (s 20).

---
[1]   See para 3.23.

---

3.28   Problems have arisen under the 1984 Act in cases where two or more persons may have responsibility for data. Partnerships, which may have an ambiguous legal status constitute an obvious example, but problems have also arisen in respect of schools where responsibility for data may be shared between the Board of Governors and the headteacher of the school. It is provided that the notification regulations may make specific reference to these issues (s 18(4)).

3.29   As under the 1984 Act, the act of processing data without notification will expose the controller to criminal liability (s 17). The Commissioner is required to compile and maintain a register of notified processors and provide facilities for making entries available for public inspection (s 19(1)). It appears that the present system will be maintained whereby the register can be consulted at the Commissioner's office and may also be accessed over the Internet.

3.30   At present, an entry on the data protection register will be valid for three years unless the data user requests a shorter period of validity. At the end of this period, the user is required to re-apply for registration. This system will change under the 1998 Act. Once made, notification will be valid indefinitely (subject to an obligation to notify changes in any of the registered particulars) subject to payment of an annual fee.[1] It is suggested that arrangements will be made for this fee to be collected by automatic mechanisms such as direct debit.

---
[1]   HC SC D, 19 May 1998, col 152.

## Handling of notifications

3.31 In most cases, data users will be able to commence or continue operations following submission of notification. Although the Registrar indicated a wish to be able to retain some discretion as to the handling of applications, the terminology used would appear to indicate that there will be no power to refuse a notification, save where incomplete details are supplied.

## Preliminary assessments

3.32 Although a data controller may not commence processing operations without notifying the Commissioner (or without being covered by an exemption) certain forms of processing are subject to additional controls. Article 20(1) of the Directive obliges member states to—

'. . . determine the processing operations likely to present specific risks to the rights and freedoms of data subjects and shall check that these processing operations are examined prior to the start thereof.'.

3.33 As implemented in the 1998 Act, regulatory power is conferred on the Secretary of State to determine categories of processing, referred to as 'assessable processing', which appear particularly likely—

'(a) to cause substantial damage or substantial distress to data subjects, or
(b) otherwise significantly to prejudice the rights and freedoms of data subjects.' (s 22(1)).

3.34 It has been indicated that few forms of processing will be covered by such regulations. In Parliament, specific reference was made to activities involving data matching, genetic data and private investigations.[1]

---
[1]   HC SC D, 19 May 1998, col 160.

3.35 Where processing comes within the ambit of such regulations, the data controller may not commence activities until an assessment of its compliance with the data protection principles has been made by the Commissioner. The timetable within which the Commissioner must act is very limited. When receiving notification from any data controller, the Commissioner must consider whether any of the processing activities described involve assessable processing (s 22(2)) and, if so, whether the processing is likely to comply with the requirements of the statute. The Commissioner is required to give notice of his opinion to the data controller within 28 days (s 22(3)), which period might in special circumstances be extended by a further 14 days (s 22(4)). Processing must not be carried on during this period. In the event that the Commissioner's assessment is that the processing would be unacceptable, there would not appear to be any mechanism to prevent the data controller continuing with the plans although it might be expected that an enforcement notice would be served should this occur.

**Optional notification**

3.36 Although it might appear logical for a data controller to seek to benefit from any exemption which might be on offer, the reality may be more complex. Where details of processing are held on the register, the controller is under no further obligation to inform data subjects as to these matters. A controller whose details do not appear is required to supply the information otherwise required at registration within 21 days of receiving a request from any person. Failure to reply timeously will constitute an offence (s 24). Responding to a single request may be as burdensome as making notification to the Commissioner. Given the nature of this obligation, it is perhaps not surprising that the 1998 Act provides that a normally exempt data controller may voluntarily notify details of processing activities (s 18).

## INDEPENDENT DATA PROTECTION SUPERVISORS

3.37 Under the German data protection law, it is common practice for data controllers to appoint 'in-house' data protection supervisors. Provided that such supervisors possess sufficient independence, this will exempt the controller from the requirement to notify the Federal Data Protection Commissioner. The Directive also sanctions the adoption of such an approach (Art 18(2)) and the 1998 Act provides that the Secretary of State may make an order enabling controllers to appoint a data protection supervisor who will monitor in an independent manner the data controller's compliance with the legislation. Any order will also specify the extent to which such action will exempt the controller from the notification requirement (s 23).

3.38 In debate on this provision, the government pointed out that when such an option had been outlined in the consultation exercise preceding the introduction of the legislation, it had received some expressions of interest but little active support. It was indicated that, given the workload involved in implementing the new legislation, the making of any enabling regulations would not be seen as a priority issue.[1]

---

[1]    HC SC D, 19 May 1998, cols 165, 166.

## ENFORCEMENT OF THE 1998 ACT

3.39 Having established a register of those processing personal data, the ongoing task for the supervisory agency is to seek to ensure that data controllers remain within the scope of their entries on the register and that, in general, processing complies with the substantive requirements of the legislation. Failures on the part of data controllers may constitute an offence and will also expose them to a range of sanctions made available to the Commissioner.

**Powers of entry and inspection**

3.40 Section 50 of, and Sch 9 to, the 1998 Act provide that the Commissioner may approach a circuit judge (or in Scotland a sheriff) seeking a warrant to enter and search any premises. The warrant will be granted if the judge is satisfied that a data controller is in breach of one or more of the principles or has committed an offence under the 1998 Act, and that evidence to that effect is to be found at the address specified. Schedule 9, para 1(3) provides that the warrant will empower the Commissioner or his staff to—

> '. . . inspect, examine, operate and test any equipment found there which is used or intended to be used for the processing of personal data and to inspect or seize any documents or other material found there . . .'.

3.41 Procedures for the award of the warrant are similar to those found in the 1984 Act although one significant loophole has been closed. Under the 1984 Act, if the Registrar had sought entry to premises and had been granted admission only for the occupier to refuse to co-operate further with enquiries, it was not subsequently possible in England to obtain a search warrant. Schedule 9, para 2(1)(b)(ii) to the 1998 Act now provides that a warrant may be sought where entry to the premises was granted but the occupier unreasonably refused to comply with a request by the Commissioner or any of the Commissioner's officers or staff to perform any of the acts permitted in executing a search warrant.

## Enforcement notices

3.42 Under the 1984 Act, the Registrar possessed powers to serve enforcement notices (s 10), de-registration notices (s 11), and transfer prohibition notices (s 13). The 1998 Act retains the existing format of enforcement notices (s 40). Under these, the Commissioner may serve notice on data controllers where he is satisfied that a breach of one or more of the data protection principles has occurred. The notice will identify the act or omission complained of and specify the steps that need to be taken to rectify the situation. Failure to comply with an enforcement notice constitutes an offence (s 47). As with all other forms of notice served by the Commissioner, the recipient data controller may appeal to the Data Protection Tribunal (s 48) save that in exceptional circumstances, the lodging of an appeal will suspend the operation of the notice.

3.43 Experience of the working of the 1984 Act indicates that a period of years may elapse between the initial moves to serve an enforcement notice and the completion of appeal proceedings. To date there has been no appeal from a Tribunal decision to the courts, something which would extend the process even further. The 1998 Act provides that the Commissioner may, if he considers that all of its provisions need not be complied with in order to ensure compliance with the principles, vary or cancel an enforcement notice (s 41(1)). The recipient controller may also make a written request to the Commissioner for variation or cancellation on the ground that a change of circumstances means that compliance with its terms is not necessary to secure compliance with the principles (s 41(2)). In order to avoid the possibility of a double appeal, such a request may only be made after the time available for submitting an appeal to the Tribunal has elapsed.

3.44 With the departure from the much criticised system of (near) universal registration, the role for a de-registration notice (which has never been served) disappears. Again, as will be discussed in Ch 7, changes in the rules relating to transborder data flows render redundant the notion of transfer prohibition notices (only one of which has been served).

**Information notices**

3.45   Although the 1984 Act empowered the Registrar to seek and execute search warrants if a breach of the principles was suspected (s 16), that Act conferred no general investigative power and placed data users under no obligation to co-operate with any enquiries made by the Registrar. The 1998 Act stops short of providing a general investigative power but confers a new power on the Commissioner to serve an 'information notice' requiring the supply, within a specified time, of specified information relating to the matter under investigation (s 43(1)). An appeal against service of an information notice will lie to the Data Protection Tribunal and, save in exceptional circumstances, will suspend the operation of the notice (s 43(4), (5)). Failure to comply with an information notice will constitute an offence, as will the reckless or intentional provision of false information in response to an information notice (s 47).

3.46   An information notice may be served either on the Commissioner's own initiative when he considers that information is reasonably required in order to determine 'whether the data controller has complied or is complying with the data protection principles' (s 43(1)), or following a complaint from a data subject. In this latter respect, the 1998 Act provides that any person may contact the Commissioner seeking an assessment whether it is likely that personal data has been or is being processed lawfully (s 42(1)). The Commissioner is obliged to consider the request and determine an appropriate response taking into account, inter alia, whether the data subject could have obtained the information by means of a request for subject access (s 42(3)).

3.47   Although the information notice does constitute a new weapon in the Commissioner's armoury, it may be queried how useful the power will be in practice. The notice may be served when the Commissioner reasonably requires information to determine whether the principles are being observed. This is a slightly weaker criterion than that required for service of an enforcement notice, where the Commissioner has to be satisfied that a breach has occurred. Beyond this, however, the appeal procedures are identical. While it may be expected that many controllers will be happy to respond to an information notice in order to clarify what might be a misunderstanding as to the nature of their processing activities, the possibility for appeals may persuade less scrupulous controllers to prevaricate in their response. Even if the Data Protection Tribunal ultimately upholds the information notice and the Commissioner obtains information indicating that a breach of the principles has occurred, no action can be taken until an enforcement notice, with its own appeal procedures, has been served.

**Assessment of processing**

3.48   Another new power conferred by the 1998 Act enables the Commissioner to assess any processing 'for the following of good practice and . . . inform the data controller of the results of the assessment'. The consent of the data controller involved must be given (s 51(7)). Such action may provide a data controller with assurance that processing will be considered lawful, thereby minimising the possibility of receiving an information or enforcement notice.

## OTHER POWERS AND DUTIES OF THE COMMISSIONER

### Requests for assessment

3.49 Section 42 of the 1998 Act (in accordance with the requirements of Art 28(4) of the Directive) imposes a new duty upon the Commissioner to receive requests from any person directly affected by processing for an assessment as to whether the processing complies with the requirements of the legislation. By virtue of s 42(3), providing that sufficient information is made available to enable the Commissioner to identify the applicant and the processing in question, an assessment must be made in such manner as is deemed appropriate taking into account—

'(a) the extent to which the request appears to him to raise a matter of substance,
(b) any undue delay in making the request, and
(c) whether or not the person making the request is entitled to make an application under section 7 in respect of the personal data in question.'.

The applicant is to be informed of the fact that an assessment has been made and also, taking into account any relevant exceptions which might justify the refusal of a request for access, indicate 'any view formed or action taken as a result of the request' (s 42(4)).

### Dissemination of information

3.50 The remaining powers of the Commissioner under the 1998 Act broadly follow those established by the 1984 Act. The Commissioner is to disseminate information giving guidance about good practice under the 1998 Act (s 51(1)). Section 51(9) defines good practice as—

'. . . such practice in the processing of personal data as appears to the Commissioner to be desirable having regard to the interests of data subjects and others and includes (but is not limited to) compliance with the requirements of this Act'.

3.51 Under the 1984 Act, a wide range of material was published.[1] Members of the Registrar's office were also frequent speakers at conferences. It is likely that these activities will continue. The 1998 Act provides the Commissioner with a new power to levy fees for any matters concerned with the exercise of his powers (s 51(8)). It was indicated in Parliament that income from publications and presentations might account for 10% of the Commissioners income.[2]

---

[1]   Notably, the series of guidelines giving information about the Registrar's interpretation of the legislation.
[2]   HC SC D, 2 June 1998, col 253.

## CODES OF PRACTICE

3.52 Provision relating to codes of practice was inserted into the 1984 Act at a late stage during its Parliamentary passage by a somewhat reluctant government which pointed to the nebulous legal status of these documents. Under the 1984 regime, the Registrar's role is limited to encouraging 'trade associations or other bodies' to prepare and disseminate codes of practice (s 36(4)). The decision of the Data Protection Tribunal in the case of *Data Protection Registrar v Innovations*[1] lends support to this view. Here the Tribunal held that the appellant was in breach of the data protection principle relating to the fair obtaining of data even though its conduct complied with a relevant industry code of practice.

---

[1]   Case DA/92 31/49/1.

---

3.53  In spite of doubts concerning their legal status, a considerable number of codes were adopted under the 1984 Act. The Directive also envisages a substantial role for both national and Community codes, Art 27 providing—

'1.   The Member States and the Commission shall encourage the drawing up of codes of conduct intended to contribute to the proper implementation of the national provisions adopted by the Member States pursuant to this Directive, taking account of the specific features of the various sectors.

2.   Member States shall make provision for trade associations and other bodies representing other categories of controllers which have drawn up draft national codes or which have the intention of amending or extending existing national codes to be able to submit them to the opinion of the national authority.

Member States shall make provision for this authority to ascertain, among other things, whether the drafts submitted to it are in accordance with the national provisions adopted pursuant to this Directive. If it sees fit, the authority shall seek the views of data subjects or their representatives.

3.   Draft Community codes, and amendments or extensions to existing Community codes, may be submitted to the Working Party referred to in Article 29. This Working Party shall determine, among other things, whether the drafts submitted to it are in accordance with the national provisions adopted pursuant to this Directive. If it sees fit, the authority shall seek the views of data subjects or their representatives. The Commission may ensure appropriate publicity for the codes which have been approved by the Working Party.'

The major novelty for the UK is the Directive's provision that supervisory agencies should take a view on the conformity of a draft code with statutory requirements. This is akin to giving an unelected agency law making powers, a practice which traditionally has been resisted in the UK.

3.54  The 1998 Act establishes two roles for the Commissioner in respect of codes of practice. Acting either on his own initiative, or under the direction of the Secretary of State, and after consulting with relevant trade associations and representatives of data subjects, the Commissioner may 'prepare and disseminate . . . codes of practice for guidance as to good practice' (s 51(3)). Any code of practice prepared following directions from the Secretary of State is to be laid before Parliament either in its own right, or as part of another report by the Commissioner to Parliament (s 52(3)).

3.55  As with the procedure under the 1984 Act, the Commissioner is once again under a duty to encourage the adoption and dissemination of codes by relevant trade associations. Section 51(4)(b) provides that the Commissioner shall also—

'where any trade association submits a code of practice to him for his consideration, consider the code and, after such consultation with data subjects or persons representing data subjects as appears to him to be appropriate, notify the trade association whether in his opinion the code promotes the following of good practice.'.

In many respects, this provision formalises the practice under the 1984 Act where many of the codes adopted contain a foreword from the Registrar indicating his views on the appropriateness of the code.

**International co-operation**

3.56 As was the case under the 1984 Act, the Commissioner is the UK agency responsible for liaison with other data protection agencies under the auspices of the Council of Europe Convention. The Commissioner is also responsible for working with the various committees and working parties established at EU level by the Directive (s 54(1)). Such bodies have a particularly important role to play in determining whether third countries provide an adequate level of protection for personal data. The Commissioner is charged with the duty of disseminating information about any such findings (s 51(6)) and seeking to implement these within the UK (s 54(4)).

3.57 The Directive also contains provisions requiring national supervisory agencies to co-operate with each other. In particular, Art 28(6) provides that 'Each authority may be requested to exercise its powers by an authority of another Member State'. The 1998 Act provides that the Secretary of State may make an order relating to such tasks and specifying, in particular, the approach to be taken when a request for assistance relates to processing which is exempt under the UK legislation but is included in the national law of the requesting state (s 54(2)).

PROFESSIONAL SECRECY

3.58 In addition to providing that powers be conferred on supervisory agencies, Art 28(7) of the Directive requires that—

'Member States shall provide that members and staff of the supervisory authority, even after their employment has ended, are to be subject to a duty of professional secrecy with regard to confidential information to which they have access.'.

3.59 The interpretation of this provision as applied in the 1998 Act was the cause of a degree of controversy, and indeed, has been criticised by the Registrar as likely to impede the effective performance of his duties. It is provided that an offence will be committed where information obtained in the course of employment and relating to an 'identified or identifiable individuals or business' is disclosed by past or present Commissioners or members of staff without lawful authority (s 59(1)). The term 'lawful authority' is defined as requiring the consent of the individual, the availability of statutory authority, necessity for the performance of functions under the 1998 Act, compliance with Community obligations, or in the course of legal proceedings.

Finally, and most significantly, it is provided that 'having regard to the rights and freedoms or legitimate interests of any person, the disclosure is necessary in the public interest' (s 59(2)).

3.60  Although it is clearly reasonable that confidential information relating to a data controller should not be disclosed, the effect of this provision might be, for example, to prevent the Commissioner from publicising the fact that data controllers have been served with enforcement notices. It was indicated in Parliament that the government has 'found it difficult to get the provision right' and that the issue might be revisited in the context of freedom of information legislation.[1] The format finally adopted is less restrictive than that originally proposed which would have empowered disclosure only when 'necessary for reasons of substantial public interest', but it remains unclear how extensively it might be interpreted. One possible compromise was suggested in Parliament, that notification regulations may require controllers to include information regarding enforcement notices (or other notices) as part of their entry on the register.[2]

---

[1]    HC Debs, 2 July 1998, cols 603, 604.
[2]    Ibid, at col 602.

## THE DATA PROTECTION TRIBUNAL

3.61  This body, which was established under the 1984 Act to hear appeals by data users against decisions of the Registrar, continues under the 1998 Act (s 6, Sch 5, Pt II). With a legally qualified chair and deputy chairs, the remaining members of the Tribunal are appointed as representing the interests of data subjects and data controllers. Three members will normally sit to hear any appeal brought before the Tribunal. The Tribunal may either uphold the Registrar's finding, order the cancellation of the enforcement notice or vary its terms (s 49).

3.62  Under the 1984 Act, the Tribunal's sole function was to hear appeals brought by data users (or computer bureaux) against decisions by the Registrar which were adverse to their interests. The only change of note introduced in the 1998 Act is that, in very limited cases concerned with the application of the exemption for data processed for national security purposes, a data subject will, for the first time, have the right to bring a case before the Tribunal (s 28).

# 4 The data protection principles

## INTRODUCTION

4.1 While notions of the form of supervision of data users have changed significantly over the years, the substantive requirements of acceptable processing practice have remained more stable. The formulation of general statements of acceptable processing practice has been a feature of data protection legislation from the earliest days. The role of such principles may fairly be analogised to that of the Ten Commandments; both establish general formulations of good conduct but need to be interpreted and expanded in the context of specific activities and circumstances. Both the 1984 and 1998 Acts define eight data protection principles. Given the pivotal role of the principles, it is surprising that in both statutes, these should be relegated to a Schedule rather than, as in the Directive and Council of Europe Convention, being integrated into the body of the text.

## 1984 ACT: THE EIGHT PRINCIPLES

The 1984 principles are set out in Sch 1, paras 1–8, as follows—

'1.    The information to be contained in personal data shall be obtained, and personal data shall be processed, fairly and lawfully.

2.    Personal data shall be held only for one or more specified and lawful purposes.

3.    Personal data held for any purpose or purposes shall not be used or disclosed in any manner incompatible with that purpose or those purposes.

4.    Personal data held for any purpose or purposes shall be adequate, relevant and not excessive in relation to that purpose or those purposes.

5.    Personal data shall be accurate and, where necessary, kept up to date.

6.    Personal data held for any purpose or purposes shall not be kept for longer than is necessary for that purpose or those purposes.

7.    An individual shall be entitled—
   (a)  at reasonable intervals and without undue delay or expense—
      (i)   to be informed by any data user whether he holds personal data of which that individual is the subject; and
      (ii)  to access to any such data held by a data user; and
   (b)  where appropriate, to have such data corrected or erased.

8.    Appropriate security measures shall be taken against unauthorised access to, or alteration, disclosure or destruction of, personal data and against accidental loss or destruction of personal data.'.

1998 ACT: THE EIGHT PRINCIPLES

4.2   For the 1998 Act the decision was taken to leave the total number of principles at eight although there are differences from their 1984 equivalents. The 1998 Act provides (in Sch 1) that—

'1.   Personal data shall be processed fairly and lawfully and, in particular, shall not be processed unless—

   (a)   at least one of the conditions in Schedule 2 is met, and

   (b)   in the case of sensitive personal data, at least one of the conditions in Schedule 3 is also met.

2.   Personal data shall be obtained only for one or more specified and lawful purposes, and shall not be further processed in any manner incompatible with that purpose or those purposes.

3.   Personal data shall be adequate, relevant and not excessive in relation to the purpose or purposes for which they are processed.

4.   Personal data shall be accurate and, where necessary, kept up to date.

5.   Personal data processed for any purpose or purposes shall not be kept for longer than is necessary for that purpose or those purposes.

6.   Personal data shall be processed in accordance with the rights of data subjects under this Act.

7.   Appropriate technical and organisational measures shall be taken against unauthorised or unlawful processing of personal data and against accidental loss or destruction of, or damage to, personal data.

8.   Personal data shall not be transferred to a country or territory outside the European Economic Area unless that country or territory ensures an adequate level of protection for the rights and freedoms of data subjects in relation to the processing of personal data.'.

4.3   Generally, the changes from the 1984 principles reflect the expanded definition given to the activity of processing. The new definition incorporates the activities of obtaining and disclosing data. As a consequence, the need for a specific non-disclosure principle disappears. Paradoxically however, a separate principle remains, requiring that data be obtained for specified and lawful purposes even though this activity also comes under the definition of processing. The most notable addition to the 1984 principles is the inclusion of provisions relating to transborder data flows. This topic, together with that of subject access, will be considered separately.[1] The concept of subject access is now expanded to encompass, for example, the receipt of information concerning the 'logic' employed in a data processing system. In respect of transborder data flows, the 1998 Act moves from a situation where international transfers were allowed unless specifically prohibited, to one where, albeit subject to considerable exceptions, such transfers are restricted unless the availability of adequate protection can be established.

---

[1]   See Chs 7 and 5 respectively.

---

4.4   As with the Ten Commandments, few would disagree with the contents of the principles. It is difficult, for example, to object to a requirement that data be processed fairly. The determination of what is fair may be a more difficult task. Detailed guidance concerning the application of the principles can be taken from a variety of sources. No fewer than four schedules to the 1998 Act (Schs 1–4) expand upon the interpretation of the principles, while provisions in the body of the statute (ss 27–37) make additional provisions, often in the form of providing exceptions from their application. In some instances it may be considered necessary to restrict or exclude the application of one or more of the principles giving priority to other interests, for example, the prevention or detection of crime. As with other statutes, further guidance on issues of interpretation will become available through decisions of the courts and the Data Protection Tribunal; a number of decisions of the Tribunal made under the 1984 Act will remain of considerable relevance. Finally, a significant role is envisaged for sector specific codes of practice although the legal status of these is rather unclear.

4.5    The data protection principles cover all aspects of data processing. This chapter will concentrate on the obligations which the principles impose on data controllers (with the exception of the eighth principle relating to transborder flows). In respect of the remainder of the principles, they are considered in relation to various stages of this activity starting with the manner in which data are acquired which will then be processed and put to use. Use may take a variety of forms and would include disclosure of data to a third party. Finally, this chapter will consider the operation of the seventh data protection principle requiring that users adopt appropriate security measures.

## TOWARDS 'INFORMATIONAL SELF-DETERMINATION'

4.6    The concept referred to as 'informational self-determination', is generally regarded as originating in the German system of data protection. Effectively, it moves from a situation where the data controller can process personal data unless otherwise prevented by law, to one where an individual can claim what is almost a proprietary right to prevent processing unless the controller can show cause why this should be permitted. This approach is generally adopted in the 1998 Act. In order for processing to be considered legitimate, the controller must meet at least one of the conditions specified in Sch 2. The first condition is that the data subject has given consent to the processing. As will be discussed below,[1] consent is only one of six conditions which may justify processing. However, even where the controller is not required to seek consent, the principles will generally require that information be given as to the purposes for which data are sought or obtained.

---

[1]    See paras 4.8–4.15.

---

4.7    Even under the 1984 Act, a number of decisions of the Data Protection Tribunal held that information would be considered as having been unfairly obtained, when it was acquired from a data subject who was not made aware of the purpose for which the data was being collected. These provisions remain and have been expanded by the interpretative provisions attached to Sch 1 to the 1998 Act. In respect of subsequent acts of processing, under the 1984 regime, the sole criterion for lawful processing was that the data user should have registered details of the activity. Schedule 2 to the 1998 Act makes significant changes to this situation, while Sch 3 contains even more restrictive provisions in the event that the controller wishes to process sensitive data. Additionally, as will be discussed in Ch 5, provisions within the 1998 Act confer on individuals the right to object to certain forms of data processing, in particular, the use of personal data for purposes of direct marketing.

PRE-CONDITIONS FOR LAWFUL PROCESSING

4.8   Schedule 2 to the 1998 Act specifies a number of conditions, one of which must be satisfied for the lawful processing of personal data.

## The subject has consented to processing

4.9   The 1998 Act does not define 'consent'. The Directive refers to 'any freely given specific and informed indication of his wishes by which the data subject signifies his agreement to personal data relating to him being processed' (Art 2(h)). As discussed above, where sensitive data is to be processed,[1] the legislation refers to the data subject's 'explicit consent'. It may be taken that the requirements for mere 'consent' will be less stringent than that for explicit consent. Accordingly, the system common with many forms of transaction, whereby a customer is informed of the fact that data supplied may be used for specific purposes and given the opportunity to object, (the 'opt out system') would be compatible with the requirements.

---

[1]   See paras 2.22, 2.23.

## Necessity for concluding or performing a contract with the data subject

4.10   Processing may lawfully take place when this is necessary either for entering into, or performing, a contract with the subject. Some stress should be placed on the word 'necessary', which appears frequently in many instruments such as the European Convention on Human Rights. The jurisprudence of the European Court of Human Rights, which has been approved by the European Court of Justice, has adopted an interpretation requiring that the practice in question be close to essential for the specified purpose. Clearly, information about a data subject's income may be necessary for a lender to determine whether to grant a loan, and information as to address will be vital for a mail order sale, but controllers should take care not to require more information than is strictly necessary for the purpose.

## Necessary for the controller to comply with a legal obligation

4.11   Similar comments (see para 4.10) will apply to this requirement. A controller may, for example, require information to ensure that credit facilities are not extended to those under 18 years of age. It would be reasonable for such a controller to require applicants to provide their date of birth.

## Necessary to protect the vital interests of the data subject

4.12   It is easy to envisage situations where the interests of the data subject may require that data be processed in situations where it is not practicable to obtain consent. The limitation to the subject's 'vital interests' might mean in practice that the data is likely to be of a kind considered sensitive and therefore its processing will be governed by the provisions of Sch 3 discussed above.[1]

---

[1]   See para 2.26.

## Necessary for the administration of justice etc

4.13 Data may be processed lawfully when this is necessary for a range of specified public sector purposes. In addition to the administration of justice, processing may be carried out when necessary for the exercise of statutory functions, for example, compiling registers of data controllers, in the exercise of governmental functions or any other functions of a public nature exercised in the public interest. This might include, for example, the operation of systems of educational scholarships.

## Legitimate interests of the controller

4.14 This final justification for processing is perhaps the most controversial. It requires that the processing be—

> '. . . necessary for the purposes of legitimate interests pursued by the data controller or by the third party or parties to whom the data are disclosed, except where the processing is unwarranted in any particular case by reason of prejudice to the rights and freedoms or legitimate interests of data subject.' (Sch 2, para 6(1)).

Regulations may be made to specify the circumstances in which this provision may or may not be applied.

4.15 On this occasion, the 1998 Act diverges from the wording of the Directive which requires, in Art 7(f), that the processing be necessary for the legitimate purpose of the controller or third parties—

> '. . . except where such interests are overridden by the interests for fundamental rights and freedoms of the data subject . . .'.

In Parliament it was suggested that the Directive's wording would be more favourable to data controllers in the situation where financial and other institutions were sharing personal data in order to prevent or detect fraud. The government resisted an attempt to bring the 1998 Act's wording into line on the basis that the Directive's phraseology was insufficiently precise. It was recognised that a balancing act would be necessary in such situations, and it was indicated that representatives of the CBI had indicated satisfaction with the provision as drafted in the 1998 Act.

## ACQUISITION OF DATA 'FAIRLY AND LAWFULLY'

4.16 The key requirement in both the 1998 Act and the Directive is that information be obtained 'fairly and lawfully'. It may be relatively straightforward to determine whether information has been obtained lawfully, but the criterion of fairness raises more subjective issues. In determining whether data has been obtained fairly, Sch 1, Pt II, para 1(1) to the 1998 Act provides that—

> '. . . regard is to be had to the method by which they are obtained, including in particular whether any person from whom they are obtained is deceived or misled as to the purpose or purposes for which they are to be processed.'.

4.17   The second data protection principle requires that—

> 'Personal data shall be obtained only for one or more specified and lawful purposes and shall not be processed further in any manner incompatible with that purpose or those purposes.' (Sch 1, Pt I, para 2).

In interpreting this principle it is provided that the purposes for which data are to be processed may be specified either by the giving of timely notice to the data subject, or in a notification given to the Commissioner.

4.18   The combined requirements of these two provisions place a significant burden on data controllers. Although the principles as found in the 1998 Act appear broader than their 1984 predecessors, decisions of the Data Protection Tribunal in cases brought under the 1984 Act have interpreted these broadly. The Tribunal decision in the case of *Innovations (Mail Order) Ltd v Data Protection Registrar*[1] is of considerable relevance to the present discussion.

---
[1]   Case DA/92 31/49/1.
---

## The importance of timely notification

4.19   In the *Innovations* case, the appellant operated a mail order business. It solicited custom in a variety of ways including the distribution of catalogues and the placing of advertisements in various types of media including newspapers, radio and television. Customer orders might be placed either in writing or over the telephone. In order to secure the delivery of goods, it was clearly necessary that customers would have to provide details of their names and addresses and it was accepted that there was no need to inform them specifically that the information would be used for this purpose. It was accepted also that customers should have realised that their details would be retained by the appellant and used as the basis for future mailings of its catalogues. However, in addition to using the information to solicit further custom from the individuals concerned, the appellant made the information available to other organisations, a practice known as 'list broking'.

4.20   The appellant's catalogues gave customers notice of this possibility and its order forms offered customers the opportunity to exclude the use of their data for broking purposes. However, some advertisements, especially those appearing on radio or television, made no mention of this. Furthermore, in the event that catalogue orders were placed by telephone, no mention was made of this secondary purpose. An acknowledgement of order would, however, be sent and this would convey the message—

> 'For your information. As a service to our customers we occasionally make our customer lists available to carefully screened companies whose products or services we feel may interest you. If you do not wish to receive such mailings please send an exact copy of your address label to . . .'

The Registrar took the view that notification of the intended use came too late in the contractual process. An enforcement notice was served alleging a breach of the first data protection principle and requiring, inter alia, that where notice was not given in promotional material, the subject's positive consent must be secured prior to the data being used for list broking purposes. Effectively, therefore, the system would become one of 'opting in' rather than 'opting out'.

4.21 A number of arguments were put forward by the applicant to justify their practices. It was suggested that at the time of placing an order, customers would be concerned primarily with obtaining the goods and that a notice along the lines referred to above would have limited impact. Where orders were made by telephone, giving specific notice would increase the length of the call thereby increasing costs for both the supplier and the customer. It was also pointed out that the details would not be used for list broking purposes until 30 days from the date the acknowledgement or order was sent. This, it was suggested, allowed ample time for the customer to 'opt out'. It was further argued that the appellant's practices were in conformity with an industry code of practice and the Council of Europe's Recommendation (85/20) on the protection of personal data used for the purposes of direct marketing.

4.22 Notwithstanding these factors, the Tribunal upheld the Registrar's ruling. Use of the data for list broking purposes, it was held, was not a purpose which would be obvious to the data subjects involved. Fair obtaining required that the subject be told of the non-obvious purpose before the information was obtained. While a later notification might 'be a commendable way of providing a further warning', it could not stand by itself. Where prior notification might not be practicable, the Tribunal ruled 'the obligation to obtain the data subject's positive consent for the non-obvious use of their data falls upon the data user'.

4.23 The question as to what constitute obvious and non-obvious purposes will need to be asked in the context of particular applications. It might be considered that given the amount of junk mail the average person receives, there may be a general awareness amongst the public that customer details would be made available to other organisations. The decision indicates, however, that a restrictive interpretation will be applied and data controllers may safely assume only that the most obvious and direct purposes need not be specifically drawn to the subject's attention.

4.24 The decision of the Tribunal in the *Innovations* case was affirmed by a differently composed Tribunal in the case of *Linguaphone Institute v Data Protection Registrar*.[1] Once again, the conduct complained of lay in the obtaining of information from customers or potential customers enquiring about the appellant's products and services, without disclosing at the time of obtaining the information that it might also be used for list broking purposes. In view of the decision in *Innovations*, there was no doubt that this conduct was unlawful. By the time of the Tribunal hearing, the appellant had modified its advertising to include a notice—

> '(Please) tick here if you do not wish Linguaphone to make your details available to other companies who may wish to mail you offers of goods or services.'.

The Tribunal expressed concern that—

> 'the opt out box appears in minute print at the bottom of the order form. In the Tribunal's view the position, size of print and wording of the opt out box does not amount to a sufficient indication that the company intends or may wish to hold, use or disclose that personal data provided at the time of enquiry for the purpose of trading in personal data. The Tribunal relies upon the Data Protection Registrar to agree a wording which should ensure that a proper explanation is given in all future advertisements.'.

---

[1]    Case DA/94 31/49/1.

4.25 Effectively the Tribunal rulings seek to ensure the data subject's informed consent at the point where data are collected. Although the decision is compatible with the Directive's requirements, it appears to impose even more extensive requirements. Where data are collected from the data subject, it is provided that, save where this is already known, information must be given as to the identity of the controller, the purposes for which the data are intended to be used and any recipients of the data. Where necessary, to ensure that subsequent processing is fair, the subject must also be informed whether providing answers to any questions is voluntary or compulsory and as to the possible consequences of a failure to reply. Notice must also be given of the right of subject access. This information must be supplied at the time the data are first processed. As in the *Innovations* case, delay in giving the information will result in a breach of the principles. Where data are obtained from a third party, notice of the factors given above must be supplied at the time the information is recorded or disclosed to a third party (Sch 1, Pt II, para 2).

## EXCEPTIONS TO THE FAIR OBTAINING REQUIREMENTS

### Parties authorised to supply

4.26 In certain situations, parties may be authorised, or even required, to make information publicly available. Schedule 1, Pt II, para 1(2) to the 1998 Act provides that information is to be regarded as having been obtained fairly if the source is a person who—

> '(a) is authorised by or under any enactment to supply it, or
> (b) is required to supply it by or under any enactment or by any convention or other instrument imposing an international obligation on the United Kingdom.'.

4.27 The provision that information will always be regarded as having been obtained fairly when it is obtained from a person statutorily authorised to supply it assumes considerable significance in the case of electoral registers. These constitute perhaps the most comprehensive listing of names and addresses available to data users. Under the terms of the Representation of the People (Amendment) Regulations 1990 (SI 1990/520), electoral registration officers are obliged to supply copies of the register for their area upon request. Prior to the introduction of these regulations the officers were required to supply copies of the register only where these were readily available. The Data Protection Registrar commented that a number of officers 'had effectively ceased to supply their registers for use for other purposes'.[1] Following representations from the Data Protection Registrar, the Home Office introduced a scheme whereby a list of those purchasing copies of the register is maintained by each officer and made available for public inspection.

---

[1]   Sixth Report of the Data Protection Registrar 1990, p 7.

---

4.28 Although electoral registers may represent the most extensive records of their kind, similar issues arise with other forms of records which are required to be made available to the public. Concern has been expressed on a number of occasions about the use made of lists of company shareholders, particularly in the case of privatised undertakings which might have several hundred thousand shareholders. It may be argued that the purpose of making details of shareholders publicly available is to allow identification of the owners of a limited liability company. Use of this information for the purposes of compiling mailing lists for direct marketing purpose raises different issues, although it is difficult to see how prohibitions might be enforced against the use of publicly available information for such purposes.[1]

---

[1]   In the recent conversion process of the Halifax Building Society, members were encouraged to place their new shareholding in a nominee account administered by the Society so that the shareholder's name and address would not appear on publicly available registers.

## Law enforcement and revenue gathering purposes

4.29   A significant exception to the operation of the first principle applies where data are acquired for the purposes of the prevention or detection of crime, the apprehension or prosecution of offenders or the assessment or collection of any tax or duty. These provisions are carried over from the 1984 Act into the 1998 Act. In such cases, the Commissioner may not take any action against the data user involved in an alleged breach of the principle where this would be likely to prejudice the activity in question (s 29(1)). The rationale behind the exception lies in the recognition that law enforcement agencies might reasonably acquire information in ways which might normally be regarded as unfair, for example, as the result of overhearing or even eavesdropping on a conversation. It might, however, be considered unfortunate that the Commissioner should not be given power to define the concept of fairness, in the light of the particular situation of the user involved, rather than by providing a near complete exception from the requirement to act fairly. It may also be noted that the restriction upon the Commissioner's ability to act exists even where the information has been acquired unlawfully, although in this situation it may be difficult to sustain the argument that observance of the law would prejudice the prevention or detection of crime, the apprehension or prosecution of offenders or the assessment or collection of any tax or duty.

## RELEVANCY AND SCALE OF THE INFORMATION OBTAINED

4.30   The other principle which is pertinent to the acquisition of data is the third principle which requires that data shall be 'adequate, relevant and not excessive'.[1] The Directive uses the same terminology. No further guidance is available in either instrument concerning the application of these requirements. The principle is, however, identically worded to that in the 1984 Act.[2] Breach of this principle was the issue before the Data Protection Tribunal in the course of proceedings brought against a number of Community Charge Registration Officers.[3]

---

[1]   Sch 1, Pt I, para 3 to the 1998 Act.
[2]   The third principle in the 1998 Act was actually the fourth principle in the 1984 Act (see Sch 1, Pt I, para 4 to the 1984 Act).
[3]   The Officers involved represented Runnymede Borough Council, South Northamptonshire District Council, Harrow Borough Council and Rhondda Borough Council.

**The community charge**

4.31  The community charge or 'poll tax' proved to be one of the most controversial forms of taxation introduced in recent times. Although much of the publicity generated concerned its financial aspects, the implementation of the requirement that registers be established of those liable to pay the tax attracted the attention of the Registrar.

4.32  Compilation of the community charge registers was the responsibility of community charge registration officers in each local authority area. Where the intention was that the register should be maintained on computer, an application for registration was necessary under the 1984 Act. In the case of four applications, submitted by the registration officers for, Harrow Borough Council,[1] Runnymede Borough Council,[2] Rhondda Borough Council,[3] and South Northamptonshire District Council[4] registration was refused on the basis that the Registrar was satisfied that the applicants were likely to contravene the 1984 Act's fourth data protection principle by seeking to obtain excessive amounts of data. Appeals against these decisions were brought before the Data Protection Tribunal. The appeal of the officer of Rhondda Borough Council was heard separately, the other appeals being disposed of at a combined hearing.

---

[1]   Case DA/90 24/49/5.
[2]   Case DA/90 24/49/3.
[3]   Case DA/90 24/49/2.
[4]   Case DA/90 24/49/4.

*Rhondda Borough Council*

4.33  Under the terms of the Local Government Finance Act 1988, charging authorities were required to compile and maintain a community charge register (s 6). It was specifically provided that the register should include details of the name and address of every person liable to pay the community charge. The community charge was payable by everyone over the age of 18 years. To this extent, a note of the date of birth of individuals who were about to reach their 18th birthday would be required in order for the registration officers to fulfil their duty of maintaining the register. In many cases, local authorities, including Rhondda Borough Council requested the date of birth of every member of the household, regardless of whether they were over 18 or not. Dates of birth are clearly items of personal data.

4.34  The appellant applied for registration under the 1984 Act. This application was rejected by the Registrar, who expressed the view that the inclusion of information relating to date of birth would, subject to very limited exceptions as described above, be irrelevant to the determination whether individuals were liable for payment of the community charge. The appellant argued that many inhabitants of the Rhondda shared surnames and Christian names. The addition of a record of date of birth would limit the possibility that an individual might escape inclusion in the register because his or her identity was confused with a person of the same name. It was also argued that the inclusion of the information would assist the registration officer in the efficient performance of his or her duties.

4.35  These arguments were rejected by the Tribunal. It heard evidence that nationally fewer than one per cent of households contained persons who shared the same surname and Christian name. Although it accepted that the figure might be higher in the Rhondda, it did not consider that this justified the appellant's actions. The Tribunal concluded—

'We find that the information the appellant wishes to hold on database concerning individuals exceeds substantially the minimum amount of information which is required in order for him to fulfil the purpose for which he has sought registration . . . to fulfil his duty to compile and maintain the Community Charges Register.'.

*Runnymede Borough Council, Harrow Borough Council and South Northamptonshire District Council*

4.36  Similar issues were involved in the second case before the Tribunal. Each of the appellants held, or proposed to hold, on the community charge register details of the type of property occupied by each subject. Again information of this type would be classed as personal data and the Registrar raised an objection on the ground that its inclusion was, or would be likely to, constitute a breach of the fourth data protection principle. In the case of Harrow and Runnymede Borough Councils, action took the form of a refusal to accept the application for registration. In the case of South Northamptonshire District Council, whose application for registration had previously been accepted, an enforcement notice was served.

4.37  In terms of the status of information relating to type of property, the Tribunal held that while there might be justification for holding some information additional to that required under the Local Government Finance Act 1988, the wish to record details of type of property in every case was excessive. The Tribunal endorsed the advice given to data users by the Registrar[1] to the effect that they should seek to identify the minimum amount of personal data which are required in order to enable them to fulfil their purpose. Where additional data might be required in certain cases, these should again be identified and the further information sought or held only in those cases.

---

[1]   Guideline Booklet Number 4; The Data Protection Principles.

## STORAGE OF DATA

4.38  The second data protection principle requires that data be held only for one or more specified and lawful purposes. The question whether data are held for a lawful purpose can be determined only retrospectively. Holding a list of names and addresses might normally be a non-controversial matter, but if the holder is a burglar and the addresses are of houses which are to be burgled, a different viewpoint would be taken. For the majority of users, the requirement that data be held for a specified purpose is of much greater significance. This is to be determined by reference to the controller's entry on the register. If the purpose is not specified therein, there will be a breach of the second principle.

4.39  Both the 1998 Act and the Directive contain provisions relating to the periods of time during which data may be retained. The fourth data protection principle requires that personal data 'shall be accurate and, where necessary, kept up to date', while the fifth data protection principle requires that data 'shall not be kept for longer than is necessary for that purpose or those purposes'. The Directive contains similar provisions relating to the currency of data but adopts a slightly different formulation relating to retention. Article 6(1)(e) provides that information is to be—

> 'kept in a form which permits identification of data subjects for no longer than is necessary for the purpose for which the data were collected or for which they are further processed . . .'.

This formulation appears to allow greater discretion on behalf of the data controller than under the 1998 Act. Given the increasing processing capabilities of computers, it may be difficult to determine what steps will be required to in order to secure the anonymity of particular data subjects.

## PROCESSING OF DATA 'FAIRLY AND LAWFULLY'

4.40 Both the 1998 Act and the Directive require that personal data must be processed 'fairly and lawfully'. In the 1984 Act, the first data protection principle referred separately to the activities of obtaining and processing. The interpretative paragraph applying to the first principle refers only to the act of obtaining data, and the Data Protection Tribunal ruled that a distinction has to be drawn between the two acts, and that different factors may be applied in determining whether conduct is fair. Nonetheless, a series of linked decisions of the Data Protection Tribunal relating to the operation of credit reference agencies is of considerable significance in describing the requirements that processing must be carried out fairly by reference to a particular data subject.

### Processing by reference to the data subject

4.41 Credit reference agencies constitute one of the highest profile sectors of data processors in the private sector. Study of the Registrar's annual reports reveals that a high proportion of complaints from data subjects concern the activities of these organisations.

4.42 The operation of credit reference agencies has been subject to legal controls since the enactment of the Consumer Credit Act 1974. Section 158 of that Act requires credit reference agencies to supply a copy of any information held concerning an individual upon receipt of a written request from that person.[1] Provision is made for the correction of any inaccurate information (s 159), and for details of the change to be transmitted to any third party who had received the inaccurate information within the six month period preceding the amendment.[2]

---

[1]    The subject access provisions of the Consumer Credit Act 1974 have now been incorporated into the access provisions of the 1998 Act. The effect of this is discussed at para 5.7.
[2]    Consumer Credit (Conduct of Business) (Credit References) Regulations 1977, SI 1977/330, reg 5.

4.43 The compatibility of certain aspects of the operations of credit reference agencies with the data protection principles was at issue in a number of cases brought before the Tribunal. Several hundred undertakings have been granted licences under the Consumer Credit Act 1974. Four agencies dominate the UK market; CCN, Credit and Data Marketing Services, Equifax and Infolink, each of which was the recipient of an enforcement notice served by the Registrar.

## The nature of credit reference agency operations

4.44 Although the details of their operations vary, each of the credit reference agencies referred to above holds a core of data culled from public sources. Infolink, for example, are reported as holding—

(1) Electoral registration information in the form of the collected electoral rolls for the UK.

(2) The Scottish Valuation Roll.

(3) County court judgments from courts in England and Wales, Northern Ireland and the Channel Islands.

(4) Scottish court decrees.

(5) Bankruptcy information obtained from court records and other public sources such as the London, Belfast and Edinburgh Gazette.

(6) Bills of sale.

(7) Postal address information taken from a listing of all addresses and postcodes produced and made available by the Post Office.

In addition to this publicly available information, each agency holds information supplied by its subscribers reporting instances of bad debt and maintains records of searches made. An indication of the scale of the agencies' operations can be taken from the report of the Tribunal in the appeal by Credit and Data Marketing Services[1] which indicated that the agency conducted in excess of 5 million searches per year, while Infolink conducted some 30 million searches.

---

[1]  Case DA/90 25/49/10.

*Uses of data*

4.45 The information held by the credit reference agencies and extracted in connection with a particular application for credit might be used in a variety of ways. The established method of operation would be for the agency to supply the information generated to its client, the potential creditor, leaving the determination whether to extend credit facilities entirely to the recipient. All of the credit reference agencies involved in the Tribunal actions operated on this basis. In a number of cases, the agencies also offered more extensive facilities. Instead of supplying a client with raw data, the client's own acceptance criteria might be applied. These might operate at a fairly simple level so as, for example, to reject all applicants who were not home owners. If searches revealed this fact, a recommendation that the application be rejected would be transmitted to the client.

*Method of obtaining data*

4.46 The critical point concerning the agencies' operations, and the aspect to which exception was taken by the Registrar, is that in all cases searches were conducted by reference to an address rather than to a name. Although at first sight the practice might seem illogical, it was based upon a number of factors. Names constitute a rather inefficient means of identification. A glance at any telephone directory will show that most surnames appear more than once. Even full names are unlikely to be unique and most recipients of 'junk mail' will be aware of the many and various permutations of names and initials that may appear on envelopes. By contrast, an address tends to be represented in a reasonably static format and, especially with the

55

use of postcodes, the possibility of duplication is limited. However, the consequence of processing by reference to an address would inevitably be that a search resulting from an application for credit by one individual, would retrieve information about previous residents at the address given and as to members of family or others who shared the address with the applicant.

*Extraction of data: uses: unfair processing*

4.47 The extraction of third party data in making decisions about an individual applicant was considered by the Registrar to constitute unfair processing of personal data and, as such, contravened the first data protection principle. After discussions with the credit industry failed to provide an acceptable solution, enforcement notices were served on the four major agencies in August 1990. The terms of these notices were virtually identical, requiring the recipients to ensure that—

> 'from the 31st day of July 1991 personal data relating to the financial
> status of individuals ceases to be processed by reference to the current or
> previous address or addresses of the subject of the search whereby there
> is extracted in addition to information about the subject of the search
> any information about any other individual who has been recorded as
> residing at any time at the same or similar current or previous address as
> the subject of the search.'.

4.48 A considerable number of issues were raised in separate Tribunal proceedings hearing appeals by each agency. The first question considered in the *CCN* appeal concerned the nature of the processing carried out by CCN. As defined in the 1984 Act this involves—

> '. . . amending, augmenting, deleting or re-arranging the data or
> extracting the information constituting the data and, in the case of
> personal data, means performing any of these operations by reference to
> the data subject.' (s 1(7)).

This definition encompasses a considerable range of operations. In the case of credit reference agencies it was the act of extraction that was critical to the decisions. Relating the definition to the first data protection principle, the question to be answered by the Tribunal was whether the extraction of data by the credit reference agencies was to be considered unfair.

4.49 An initial argument put forward on behalf of CCN sought to draw a distinction between the extraction and the use of the personal data. The extraction of information, typically by causing the information to be displayed on a monitor was, it was argued, a value-free operation and not susceptible to judgment by reference to any criteria of fairness. What the Registrar was objecting to, it was argued, was the use to which the information was subsequently put, for example, the refusal of an application for credit. Nowhere in the first data protection principle is there any reference to the use to which personal data might be put, mention being made only of the acts of obtaining and processing data.

4.50 This line of argument was rejected by the Tribunal. Such an approach, it was held, would rob the first data protection principle of almost all meaning. Reference was made to the long title of the 1984 Act which described it as an 'Act to regulate the use of automatically processed information relating to individuals and the provision of services in respect of such information'. This made it clear that it sought to control not the technology but its human controllers. Although the data supplied by CCN's computers would be used subsequent to the actual processing, the computers could operate only in accordance with their programs. These specified the criteria by which information was to be extracted. The extraction was not, therefore, 'value-free' and the activity had to be judged by reference to the statutory criteria of fairness.

4.51 The key element of *Equifax's*[1] appeal concerned the requirement that processing be conducted by reference to the data subject. Equifax, it was argued, in common with the other agencies, extracted information by reference to an address rather than to a name. This argument was rejected by the Tribunal. Account, it was held, had to be taken of the intended purpose of the processing. If this was to obtain information concerning a living, identifiable individual, the 1984 Act would apply. It was noted that one of Equifax's registered purposes is to provide 'information relating to the financial status of individuals'. The company was well aware that its customers sought the information in connection with their transactions with individuals and that the results of its processing would affect these persons.

---

[1]  Case DA/90, 25/49/7.

4.52 Applying these criteria, the Tribunal considered evidence submitted on behalf of the appellant arguing that to deprive them of third party information would render their operations less effective. The consequence would be either an increase in bad debts or the denial of credit to persons who might otherwise have been accepted. It might even be that certain creditors would cease to operate in the consumer field.

4.53 The Tribunal accepted that the operation of credit reference agencies provided benefits. It noted that the 1984 Act provided no definition of the word 'fairly' but held that the prime purpose of the legislation was to protect the rights of the individual. While the interests of the credit industry should not be ignored, primacy must be given to the interests of the individual applicant. On this basis it was considered—

> 'unfair for a credit reference agency, requested by its customers to supply information by reference to a named individual, so to program the extraction of information as to search for information about all persons associated with a given address or addresses notwithstanding that they may have no links with the individual the subject of the inquiry or may have no financial relationship with that individual.'.

4.54 In the *Infolink*[1] case it was also argued that much of the information held in, and extracted from, Infolink's computers, for example judgments from county courts, was public information. It was in the public interest that such data should be readily available. While not disputing this argument, the Tribunal pointed out that they were concerned with a much narrower issue, namely whether the extraction of this information in connection with a search relating to an unconnected individual could be considered fair. The answer to this must be in the negative.

---

[1]  Case DA/90, 25/49/9.

## The form of the enforcement notice

4.55 In all of the credit reference agency decisions the Tribunal accepted that a breach of the first data protection principle had occurred which was sufficient to justify the Registrar serving an enforcement notice. In all the cases, however, the Tribunal considered that the terms of the notice were excessively broad. The value of reliable credit reference and credit scoring systems was accepted, the Tribunal commenting that it was—

> 'very conscious of the benefits of reliable credit reference and credit scoring systems in preventing over-commitment by debtors, a measure very much for their benefit and that of the community, and in ensuring a well-managed credit system for the benefit of potentially sound debtors and of the credit and supply industries.'.[1]

---

[1]    Case DA/90, 25/49/9.

---

4.56 Although the unrestricted use of third party information was considered objectionable, the Tribunal did accept that information relating to members of the applicant's immediate family or to persons with whom the applicant shared property might be relevant to a decision concerning the grant of credit. To this extent, the terms of the Registrar's enforcement notice would be varied to permit the extraction of third party information in a restricted set of circumstances.

*Where the third party is recorded as residing at any address concurrently with the applicant and where the third party shares the same surname and any recorded forenames or initials as the applicant*

4.57 An example of this situation is a parent and child sharing the same name and living at the same address. In such a case it might be difficult, if not impossible, for the credit reference agency to be able to avoid extracting information about the non-applicant. Extraction of third party data will not be considered unfair in this situation except where the agency possesses information from which they should reasonably be aware that there are two parties involved. This might be the case when parents, perhaps acting in response to previous incidents, have informed the agency that they were not willing to accept responsibility for the actions of their child, or vice versa.

*Where the third party is recorded as residing at any address concurrently with the applicant and where the third party has a name 'sufficiently similar' to that of the applicant to make it reasonable for the agency to believe that the parties are one and the same*

4.58 The application of this exception is subject to the same proviso as that described in para 4.57 regarding the existence of information contradicting the presumption of commonality. The application of this exception must be less certain than the previous one. It would seem reasonable for it to apply in the case of minor variations in initials and perhaps even in the spelling of surnames.

*Where the third party shares the same or a sufficiently similar surname as the applicant and it is reasonable for the agency to believe that they have 'been living as a member of the same family as the subject in a single household'*

4.59  This exception will allow extraction of information relating to members of the applicant's family. It would appear that this would apply even where the third party is residing at a different address. Extraction will not be permitted where the agency possesses information which makes it reasonable for it to believe that there is no financial connection between the applicant and the third party.

*Where the third party does not share the same surname as the applicant but, from information possessed by the agency prior to extraction, it is reasonable to believe the third party and the applicant are one and the same person*

4.60  This exception will apply in the situation where the applicant is suspected of using a variety of names, perhaps in order to obtain credit by means of fraud. It is subject to the same proviso as operates in the previous exception although the scope for its application must be limited.

*Where the third party does not share the same surname as the applicant but, from information possessed by the agency prior to extraction, it is reasonable to believe has been living as a member of the same family in a single household*

4.61  This exception will operate in the situation where unmarried persons share the same address, but will not apply where the agency possesses information from which they should reasonably conclude that there is no financial connection between the third party and the applicant.

4.62  The scope of these exceptions is potentially broad. An agency will not be able to extract information about third parties previously resident at the same address as that pertaining to an applicant. In cases where there appears to be some link the agency will be able to extract third party data in the absence of specific information. The onus will lie with data subjects to supply any information disclaiming links with other persons and it may be questioned how effectively this might be accomplished in anticipation of the extraction of data. Most likely, information may be supplied only in response to the unfavourable use of the information extracted.


## ACCURACY AND TOPICALITY OF DATA

4.63  The fourth data protection principle requires that 'personal data shall be accurate and, where necessary, kept up to date'. Information is regarded as being inaccurate when it is 'incorrect or misleading as to any matter of fact' (s 70(2)). In the event that personal data are inaccurate, a data subject may be entitled to seek rectification and in certain cases compensation for any resultant damage or distress (ss 13, 14).

4.64  The question as to whether information is accurate will not always be susceptible of a straightforward answer. A statement may be in the format: 'Fred Smith informs us that Joe Bloggs has defaulted on three loan agreements.' If it is assumed that Joe Bloggs is in reality a person of the utmost financial probity, can it be said that the statement is false? Schedule 1, Pt II, para 7 provides interpretation for the fourth principle—

> 'The fourth principle is not to be regarded as being contravened by reason of any inaccuracy in personal data which accurately record information obtained by the data controller from the data subject or a third party in a case where—
>
> (a)    having regard to the purpose or purposes for which the data were obtained and further processed, the data controller has taken reasonable steps to ensure the accuracy of the data, and
>
> (b)    if the data subject has notified the data controller of the data subject's view that the data are inaccurate, the data indicate that fact.'.[1]

---

[1]    These provisions are substantially similar to those applying to the data subject's claim to compensation for, or rectification of, inaccurate data. See paras 5.45–5.48.

4.65    These requirements are cumulative and mark an extension from similar provisions in the 1984 Act which required only that the data user mark data which had been challenged by a subject with an appropriate indication. The 1998 Act's requirement should not only oblige a controller to accept data only from sources which they have reason to believe are reliable, but also to take such steps as are practicable to verify information prior to subjecting it to processing.

4.66    The second element of this principle requires that the necessary updating of data shall be carried out. The 1998 Act does not expand on this requirement, but it would appear that the question whether updating is required will be dependent upon the nature of the information and the purpose for which it will be used. If the information is merely a record of a transaction between the data user and the data subject, no updating would be either necessary or justified. Where the information is being used as the basis for continuing decisions and actions, regular updating may be essential. Thus, where information is to be used for assessing an employee's suitability for promotion, an indication of periods of absence would need to be supplemented by any explanations which might subsequently have been provided.

## DURATION OF RECORD KEEPING

4.67    Linked to the issue of the topicality of data, are the provisions of the fifth principle which require that information should be retained for no longer than is necessary for the attainment of the purpose for which it is held. The Directive contains an equivalent provision.[1] Neither the 1998 Act nor the Directive expands on this provision. In many cases data users will be under an obligation to maintain data for a specified period of time, for example, solicitor/client data. In more general terms, there would appear to be justification for retaining data until the expiry of any limitation period for possible legal action. Save in the situation where data are maintained as a matter of historical record (Sch 8, Pt IV), the fifth data protection principle would appear to require that users operate some form of policy for monitoring their data holdings and for removing items which are no longer of value or relevance to their activities.

---

[1]    Article 6(1)(e).

USE OF DATA

**1984 Act**

4.68  The 1984 Act made specific provision as to the extent to which data might be used or disclosed. The third data protection principle, frequently referred to as the 'non-disclosure principle' stated—

> 'Personal data held for any purpose or purposes shall not be used or disclosed in any manner incompatible with that purpose or those purposes'.

The determination whether use by a data user was lawful would be made by reference to the relevant entry on the register. Likewise, the range of potential dissemination of data would be specified therein.

**1998 Act**

Specific reference to use and disclosure of data is not found in the 1998 principles but the equivalent provision is now contained in the second principle. Sch 1, Pt I, para 2 to the 1998 Act provides—

> 'Personal data shall be obtained only for one or more specified and lawful purposes, and shall not be further processed in any manner incompatible with that purpose or those purposes'.

4.69  In interpreting this principle it is again provided that the terms of an entry on the register will determine whether use is lawful. In the case of data controllers who are exempted from the notification requirement, use will be limited to the purposes for which exemption was granted. In determining the legality of any disclosure of the data it is provided that—

> 'In determining whether any disclosure of personal data is compatible with the purpose or purposes for which the data were obtained, regard is to be had to the purpose or purposes for which the personal data are intended to be processed by any person to whom they are disclosed.' (Sch 1, Pt II, para 5).

This is very much in line with the 1984 Act and requires that the disclosure must be made in circumstances compatible with the purpose for which the data were originally obtained and processed. As with the 1984 Act, the 1998 Act provides for a significant number of exceptions enabling disclosures to be made in situations which might not have been envisaged, and are not connected with the original purpose of the processing.

EXCEPTIONS TO THE NON-DISCLOSURE PRINCIPLE

4.70  Reference has been made to the fact that the act of disclosing data is subsumed within the expanded definition of processing. Comments which have been made above concerning this definition will apply also to the disclosure of data.[1] Thus the subject may consent, or the disclosure may be necessary to protect the vital interests of the data subject or of a third party. These provisions replace a range of specific exemptions provided in the 1984 Act. In a more limited number of cases, the 1998 Act does retain specific provisions, and it also confers regulatory power on the Secretary of State to—

> '. . . by order exempt from the non-disclosure provisions any disclosures of personal data made in circumstances specified in the order, if he considers the exemption is necessary for the safeguarding of the interests of the data subject or the rights and freedoms of any other individual.' (s 38(2)).

It would be preferable that this power be used to clarify the range of permitted disclosures, rather than placing undue reliance upon the somewhat nebulous formulation of the principles.

---

[1]   See para 4.40 et seq.

## Crime and taxation

4.71   Few data users will anticipate a need to make disclosures to law enforcement agencies at the time of completing their register entry. Circumstances might arise, however, in which they, and possibly also the data subject, may want information disclosed. An example might concern the situation where details of a person's attendance at work might be relevant in a criminal investigation. To avoid the situation where a user could not legally assist criminal investigations, s 29(3) of the 1998 Act provides that the non-disclosure principle will not apply where information is disclosed in circumstances where the user has the reasonable belief that it is for purposes connected with—

(a)   the prevention or detection of crime,

(b)   the apprehension or prosecution of offenders, or

(c)   the collection or assessment of any tax or duty;

subject to the condition that a failure to so disclose would prejudice the attainment of the purpose in question.

The need for some exception in this area is not seriously questioned. Nonetheless, Sir Norman Lindop who chaired the Committee on Data Protection, criticised this provision in the 1984 Act as 'perpetrating a fraud on the public'.[1] The basis for this opinion is that a cardinal feature of the legislation is its promise to the public that the purposes for which their data may be used will be a matter of public record yet, in these significant areas, the Act sanctions contrary and secretive disclosures.

---

[1]   The Times, 26 March 1984.

4.72   The criticisms which may be made of this exception are germane to many aspects of the legislation. The need for some provision is unarguable, but rather than attempting to analyse the extent of the requirements and make limited provision, the 1998 Act provides a blanket exception. There is no requirement that the disclosure be in connection with a serious offence and there are no provisions regarding the procedure to be followed. Although both parties may face internal disciplinary measures, there is nothing in the 1998 Act to prevent a request for disclosure being made by the most junior police officer and acceded to by the most junior member of the data user's staff. No records need be kept of the disclosure and no form of notification given to the Commissioner.

## Legal requirements or advice

4.73 Where disclosure is required by any other statute, by the order of a court, or where it is made for the purpose of obtaining legal advice or in the course of legal proceedings the non-disclosure principle will not apply (s 35).

## DATA MATCHING

4.74 The practice referred to as data matching has received considerable publicity. Operating principally in the public sector, it can be seen as the equivalent of some of the direct marketing techniques described above[1] but with the essential difference that it involves searches across a range of databases controlled by different government departments. In the past, strict controls have limited, or in many cases prevented, the exchange of data held by different departments. However, the Social Security (Administration) Fraud Act 1997, ss 1–3 provide a statutory basis for the exchange of information between the Department of Social Security and other departments, including the Inland Revenue, for the purpose of detecting fraud. Information may also be exchanged with local authorities responsible for the administration of various housing and council tax benefits with the view to identifying inconsistencies. With the development of computer networks, it is a comparatively simple matter for such exchanges to take place automatically so that although there may not be a single computer database, the effect may be chillingly similar.

---

[1]   See para 4.41 et seq.

4.75 Although the application of data matching is a new phenomenon in the UK, the technique has been applied in a number of other countries including Australia, New Zealand and the US. In New Zealand the practice has been attacked by the Privacy Commissioner who has challenged both the ethics of placing innocent individuals under surveillance as well as the benefits obtained by government. Many calculations, it was suggested, were 'based on frankly heroic assumptions'.[1] Further support for this scepticism comes from the US where a General Accounting Office report on the practice—

> 'found many problems with implementation of (statutory provisions regulating data matching) including poor quality or non-existent analyses. In 41 per cent of cases, no attempt was made to estimate costs or benefits or both. In 59 per cent of cases where costs and benefits were estimated, the GAO found that not all reasonable costs and benefits were considered . . .'.[2]

Indications of the scale which data matching activities can assume come from Australia where a programme similar to that introduced by the 1997 Act anticipates between 375–750 trillion attempted file matches each year. Vast to human eyes, these figures are eminently manageable using computer technology. The Australian figures illustrate a further consequence of the activity. Almost no one can escape being the subject of data matching. Every database contains errors and the inevitable consequence is that suspicion of wrongdoing may fall upon innocent individuals.

---

1    Dominion (Wellington), 5 December 1996.
2    Simon Davies, *Big Brother* (Pan 1996), p 86.

---

4.76  Data matching can, of course be put to positive as well as negative uses. In Parliament during the passage of the 1997 Act the suggestion was made that data matching techniques could be used to identify individuals who were entitled to benefit but had not submitted a claim. In terms of data protection, the exemptions from the non-disclosure principles are sufficiently broad to justify most of the disclosures of data which would occur in the context of data matching. Following the expression of concern by the Registrar with regard to the privacy implications of the new provisions, the government agreed to enter into discussions with a view to compiling a code of practice and offered an undertaking that data matching would not commence until this work had been completed.[1]

---

1    Thirteenth Report of the Data Protection Registrar, p 36.

---

## DATA SECURITY

4.77  Under the terms of the seventh data protection principle, data users and the operators of computer bureaux are obliged to ensure that—

> 'Appropriate technical and organisational measures shall be taken against unauthorised or unlawful processing of personal data and against accidental loss or destruction of, or damage to, personal data.'.

Additionally, controllers will be responsible for ensuring that any data processors used by them comply with the requirements of the principle.

4.78  The comparable requirement in the Directive is that, taking account of the state of the art and making an assessment of costs and risks involved—

> '. . . the controller must implement appropriate technical and organisational measures to protect personal data against accidental or unlawful destruction or accidental loss, alteration, unauthorised disclosure or access, in particular where the processing involves the transmission of data over a network . . .' (Art 17(1)).

4.79  The Registrar has identified a considerable number of matters which are relevant to data security including—

  (1)    the physical security of premises,

  (2)    the security measures incorporated into computer systems, for example password requirements,

  (3)    the level of training and supervision of employees, and

  (4)    the manner in which data and equipment are disposed of.

A number of instances have been reported where the purchasers of second hand computers have discovered that data belonging to the original owner remained in the machine's memory. Such lapses might constitute a breach of the principle, as might any deficiency in respect of the disposal of print-outs of computer-generated data.[1] In 1992, the EC adopted a 'Decision in the field of the security of information systems'.[2] This is concerned principally with establishing the basis for Community action and, in Art 2, para 2.IV, calls inter alia for the 'development of specifications, standardisation, evaluation and certification in respect of the security of information systems'. Such measures might be of significant value in the field of data protection, although the diversity of processing activities might defeat any simple form of classification.

---

[1]   Guideline No 4.
[2]   Council Decision 92/242/EEC in the field of security in information systems; OJ L123, 8.5.92, p 19.

---

4.80 In November 1997, the Registrar published a consultation paper on information security in the context of the need to comply with the relevant provisions of the Directive. This suggested that data controllers would be required to undertake a risk-based approach in determining the relevant standard of security. Specific reference was made to BS7799 which contains both a code of practice and a specification for information security management. In Parliament, however, the government rejected an amendment which would have recast the interpretative provisions attached to the principle to make specific reference to 'the risks represented by the processing'[1] on the basis that as a—

> '. . . general principle of law . . . it is usually necessary to prove a degree of damage. The words "damage" and "harm" can be taken together. There are not many actions before the courts that are based simply on the prospect of there being a problem.'.[2]

It might be considered, however, that such an approach is a case of closing the stable door after the horse has bolted.

---

[1]   HC SC D, 4 June 1998, col 304.
[2]   Ibid, col 305.

---

## Unlawful obtaining of data

4.81 The seventh principle makes it clear that the data controller is responsible for maintaining data security. A successful attempt whether by means of computer hacking or other techniques, to obtain access to the data may lead to the controller incurring the Commissioner's wrath, perhaps in the form of service of an enforcement notice, and possible claims for compensation brought by aggrieved data subjects. During the 1980s and 1990s considerable publicity attached to the activities of private investigators and investigative journalists who, through various forms of subterfuge or bribery, were able to secure access to personal information held by a data user. Stella Rimington, the former head of MI5, for example, has been quoted as saying—

> 'When I was first appointed DG, the Sunday Times employed a private investigator to find out everything it could about me. Without much difficulty through getting access to . . . (various databases) . . . it found

where I lived, where I banked, how much I had in my account, where I regularly bought my food and on what days, my telephone number (even though I was ex-Directory and who I regularly telephoned.'.[1]

---

[1]   Herald, 17 October 1996.

---

4.82 In the situation where the investigator obtained direct access to data held on a computer, it would be likely that an offence would be committed under the Computer Misuse Act 1990. In many instances, however, the information would be obtained either through bribing an employee of the data user or by misleading the user as to identity and entitlement to access the data. In these situations the investigator would normally commit no offence. To remedy this situation, the Criminal Justice and Public Order Act 1994 amended the 1984 Act to provide that—

'A person who procures the disclosure to him of personal data the disclosure of which to him is in contravention of subsection (2) or (3) above, knowing or having reason to believe that the disclosure constitutes such a contravention, shall be guilty of an offence.'.[1]

Offences would also be committed by a person selling or offering for sale any information obtained in breach of the above provision.

---

[1]   Data Protection Act 1984, s 5(6), as added by the Criminal Justice and Public Order Act 1994, s 161(1).

---

4.83 The first prosecutions under the new provision were brought in 1996. In one case a private investigator secured details about the keeper of a motor vehicle from the Driver and Vehicle Licensing Agency by means of a deception.[1] In the second the employee of a credit reference agency used computer search facilities made available to him in the course of employment to conduct a credit search for non-work related purposes. This conduct resulted in a successful prosecution on the basis of procuring the disclosure of data.

---

[1]   Thirteenth Annual Report of the Data Protection Registrar, p 16; the Registrar's Fourteenth Report discloses 12 prosecutions for obtaining or selling data, p 52.

---

4.84 As formulated in the 1994 Act, the basis for the offence was the intent to cause the user to disclose data outside of the terms of an entry on the register. With the change to selective notification, this approach could not be continued. Section 55 of the 1998 Act seeks to effect the same result providing that an offence will be committed by a person who 'knowingly or recklessly, without the consent of the data controller', seeks to obtain or disclose personal data or procure its disclosure to a third party. An exception is provided where the data is obtained in connection with the prevention or detection of crime or in pursuance of a court order. A further offence is committed by a person who sells or offers to sell data obtained in contravention of this provision.

# 5 Subject access and individual rights and remedies

## FROM SUBJECT ACCESS TO SUBJECT INFORMATION

5.1 The right to obtain a copy of information held, and concomitant rights to correct errors and obtain compensation, constituted the most high profile aspect of the data subject's rights as established under the 1984 Act. However, as discussed at para 5.49, the limited evidence that has been collected about the operation of the 1984 Act indicates that this right has been used to the disadvantage, rather than for the benefit, of the data subject.

5.2 Under the 1984 Act, data subjects were entitled to enquire of a data user whether any personal data concerning them was held and, if so, they were entitled to be supplied with a copy of that information (s 21(1)). The 1998 Act significantly extends the range of information which must be supplied to such an extent that the term 'subject information' is used in place of the term 'subject access'. If personal data are being processed, the data subject must be given a description of the nature of the data held, the purposes for which it is to be processed and the persons, or categories of person, to whom it may be disclosed (s 7(1)). Under the 1984 Act, the assumption was that this information could be obtained by the data subject by consulting the data protection register, but this was unlikely to happen. With the possibility that many data controllers might be removed from the requirement to notify under the 1998 Act, the likelihood that a data subject may obtain information in this way is even more remote. Finally, the 1998 Act provides that an enquiring subject must also be supplied with 'any information available to the data controller about the source of those data' (s 7(1)(c)(ii)). Such information may prove useful in providing a form of audit trail, allowing the subject to track down the source of any erroneous data.

5.3 In addition, where decisions affecting the subject are likely to be taken solely on the basis of automated processing,[1] a subject requesting access is also to be supplied with information regarding the 'logic involved in that decision-taking' (s 7(1)(d)). The extent of the information to be supplied under this heading was the subject of considerable debate in the House of Lords where concerns were expressed that the controller might be required to supply information which constituted valuable intellectual property.[2] It is provided that the obligation is not to extend to any information which 'constitutes a trade secret' (s 8(5)), but as was pointed out in the debates[3] this concept is an ill-defined one.

---

[1] See paras 5.54–5.59.
[2] HL Debs, 23 February 1998, cols 43–45.
[3] Ibid.

## ACCESS PROCEDURES

5.4 The basic features of the system are similar to the 1984 régime. A data controller is required to respond only to requests which are made in writing,[1] which contain sufficient information to allow for identification of the data subject and which enclose any fee required by the controller.

---

[1] Section 64 of the 1998 Act provides in respect of the access procedures (and a variety of other procedures under the 1998 Act) that the requirement for writing is to be satisfied where a notice is transmitted by electronic means, received in legible form and is capable of being used for subsequent reference. An e-mail message would seem to satisfy these requirements although it may be difficult for such a message to supply payment of the access fee.

---

5.5   The existing obligation that a written copy of data be supplied has been replaced by the requirement that the copy be supplied in 'intelligible form' (s 7(1)(c)). With developments in processing technology, it is possible that data may take the form of audio or video clips and although the provision of written copies may be expected to remain the norm, expansion of the definition is clearly desirable. It is further provided that although the copy of the information is normally to be provided in permanent form, this requirement may be waived with the consent of the subject, or in a case where the supply of such a copy would be either impossible or involve a disproportionate effort (s 8(2)).

## Cost of access

5.6   Under the 1984 Act, the maximum fee payable for access was £10. This has remained unchanged since the inception of the access provisions in 1986. No indication has been given that the fee will be amended. Under the 1984 Act, a data user who maintained multiple entries on the Register could require an additional fee for each entry in respect of which the subject wished to obtain access. With the move to notification, the possibility for multiple entries should disappear. Again, whereas under the 1984 Act, only registered data users were subject to the access provision the 1998 Act will apply to all data controllers.

5.7   The concept of subject access was pioneered in the Consumer Credit Act 1974 which provided that individuals should be entitled to obtain a copy of information held by a credit reference agency (s 158). The 1974 Act's procedures were unaffected by the 1984 Act. Given that the majority of the complaints received by the DPR over the years have related to the credit sector, the retention of two separate regimes might be considered illogical. The 1998 Act now deals with the issue of access to data held by credit reference agencies which had previously been regulated by the Consumer Credit Act 1974. Provision is made for different fee levels to be fixed by the Secretary of State and it is intended that requests, which would previously have been brought under the 1974 Act's provisions, will remain subject to the lower fees (currently £1) payable under that régime (s 9). One issue concerning the change was the subject of discussion in Parliament. Under the 1974 Act, a modified access procedure applies where the subject is a business person (s 160). Effectively, this limits the amount of information supplied so that, for example, the applicant would not receive information about adverse credit reports which had been provided by bankers or suppliers. Where the business constitutes a sole trader or partnership, the general access provisions of the 1998 Act will replace the specialised provisions. Concern was expressed that the consequence might be that third parties would be reluctant to supply such information in the knowledge that it could be obtained, with the result being that small businesses might find it more difficult to obtain credit. While giving an undertaking to keep this issue under review, the government indicated that it was not convinced that the concerns were justified and a proposal to amend the Bill to retain the current procedures was rejected.[1]

---

[1] HC Debs, 2 July, 1998, cols 578, 579.

## Access timetable

5.8   Valid requests for access must be satisfied within 40 days (s 7(8), (10)). It is intended that where information is held by a credit reference agency, the current shorter time limit of seven days is to apply. The information supplied must generally be that held at the date of receipt of the access request. Account may be taken, however, of any amendments or deletions made subsequently where these would have been made 'regardless of the receipt of the request'(s 8(6)).

5.9   Having satisfied an access request it is provided that a controller is not obliged to comply with a subsequent identical or similar request until a reasonable interval has elapsed (s 8(3)). In making this determination, account is to be taken of the nature of the data, the purpose of the processing and the frequency with which amendments are made.

## EXEMPTIONS FROM THE SUBJECT INFORMATION PROVISIONS

5.10   In certain situations, the individual's interest in obtaining access to personal data has to be restricted either in the subject's own interests or as a result of giving priority to other competing claims. Access to medical data provides an example of the first situation, while restrictions on access to data held for the purpose of crime prevention or detection illustrate how the subject's desire to know what information is held might reasonably be subjugated to the requirements of the data user.

5.11   An aspect of the new system which prompted critical comment from the DPR, is that in many instances where the controller is exempted from the requirement to provide access, there is also exemption from the first data protection principle, which requires that data be processed fairly and lawfully. Under the 1984 Act, this latter exemption was defined separately from the provisions relating to subject access. In comments on the Bill, it was argued that—

> 'In many cases it is extremely difficult to understand the justification for this. In particular the miscellaneous exemptions in Schedule 7, Paragraph 2, Armed Forces; Paragraph 3, Judicial Appointments and Honours; Paragraph 4, Crown Employment and Crown or Ministerial Appointments; Paragraph 5, Management Forecasts; Paragraph 6, Negotiations; Paragraph 9, Information about Human Embryos; Paragraph 10, Legal Professional Privilege; are all exempt from the subject information provisions. This is a major extension of the existing exemptions.

> The same applies to Health and Social Work Orders in clause 29, Regulatory Activities in clause 30 and Information Available to the Public by or Under Any Enactment in clause 33. The Registrar

questions whether the exemption from the fair obtaining requirements is necessary in all of these cases. For example there would be no requirement under the new legislation to inform donors, in relation to in vitro fertilisation, how their information was to be processed. In many cases it represents a substantial extension of exemptions from control.'.[1]

[1] Comments of the Data Protection Registrar on the Data Protection Bill; 5 May 1998.

5.12 In respect of the various provisions to be discussed below, a variety of approaches exist. Where data are held for national security purposes, total exemption is offered from the legislation. In the case of data held for historical, research or statistical purposes, the exemption relates only to subject access and the related supply of information relating to source, processing purpose and intended disclosures as defined in s 7. In other cases, however, the exemption is stated as applying also in respect of the requirements of the first data protection principle relating to the fair and lawful processing of personal data. Although in many cases, the application of the exemption is limited to instances where it is necessary to avoid prejudicing the purpose for which the information is being processed, its linkage with subject access does mean that provisions which purport to protect data subjects may, in reality, work to their disadvantage.

## National security

5.13 Under the 1984 Act, information held for the purpose of national security was exempted from the legislation (s 27). Given the increasing involvement of national security agencies such as MI5 in crime related functions, for example operations against suspected drug dealers, the division between national security and criminal functions is frequently blurred. This has led the Registrar to express concern that exemptions have been claimed on an organisational rather than a task related basis.[1] Although no changes were required to the 1984 Act in this regard, as national security issues fall outside of the ambit of Community law making competence, the 1998 Act does contain significant new provisions. As under the 1984 Act, a certificate may be issued by a Minister of the Crown indicating that personal data are held for the purpose of national security (s 28(2)). Under the 1984 Act, such a certificate was not open to challenge. However, it is now provided that it may be challenged before the Data Protection Tribunal by any person 'directly affected'. This may include a data subject who, for the first and only time, is given a right to initiate proceedings before the Tribunal. Applying 'the principles applied by the court on an application for judicial review' the Tribunal may quash the certificate if it considers that the Minister did not have 'reasonable grounds' for issuing it (s 28(5)).

[1] See, for example, Sunday Times, 1 February 1998.

## Third party data

5.14 While the grant of access to personal data is a key element of data protection law, many records may contain information relating to third parties. While, as a general proposition, it is clear that a data subject should have no right of access to data relating to a third party, in many cases the data will be closely linked. An example concerns the situation where the third party has compiled a report on the data subject.

5.15 Under the 1984 Act a data user was under no obligation to supply information relating to a third party, including the fact that the third party had been the source of information relating to the data subject. No obligation was imposed on the data user to enquire whether the third party would be willing for the information to be transmitted to the subject (s 21(4)).

5.16 A significant change to the extent of access rights has been introduced following the decision of the European Court of Human Rights in the case of *Gaskin v United Kingdom*.[1] In *Gaskin*, the applicant had spent much of his childhood in local authority care. In adulthood he claimed that he had been the subject of ill-treatment and instituted legal proceedings against the local authority. As part of these proceedings he sought discovery of all documents held by the authority relating to his case. Many of the documents had been compiled by third parties such as doctors and the authority contacted the third parties seeking their approval to disclosure. A number of parties refused to consent to this and the authority took the view that this was determinative of the issue. The European Court of Human Rights disagreed and held that while the applicant did not have an unqualified right of access to data, the failure to provide an independent review constituted a breach of his rights under Art 8 of the European Convention on Human Rights requiring respect for his private and family life.

---

[1] (1990) 12 EHRR 36.

5.17 In seeking to ensure conformity with the decision in *Gaskin*, the 1998 Act provides that a data controller will not be required to supply information relating to a third party unless that party has consented or—

> 'it is reasonable in all the circumstances to comply with the request without the consent of the other individual.' (s 7(4)(b)).

In determining the question of reasonableness, account is to be taken of a number of factors including any duty of confidentiality owed to the third party, the nature of the steps taken to secure consent, whether death or other incapacity might make it impossible for the third party to give consent and whether consent was expressly refused (s 7(6)). An appeal may be made to the courts against any refusal to supply information (s 7(9)).

5.18 A further issue concerns the question as to when a third party is to be considered identifiable. A controller is obliged to supply as much information as is possible without disclosing the third party's identity. In particular, it is stated that this might involve the omission of names or other identifying particulars. Section 8(7) provides that account is to be taken of—

> '. . . any information which in the reasonable belief of the data controller, is likely to be in, or to come into, the possession of the data subject making the request.'.

5.19 This requirement may cause some difficulties for data controllers. In a case such as *Gaskin*, for example, it may be a very difficult task for controllers to assess whether the enquiring data subject would have, after the passage of many years, any recollection of the identity of particular doctors or social workers who had been responsible for submitting reports.

## Data held for the purposes of prevention or detection of crime and revenue gathering purposes

5.20 The 1984 Act excluded data held for the purpose of the prevention or detection of crime, the apprehension or prosecution of offenders, or the collection or assessment of any tax or duty from the subject access provisions, where this would be prejudicial to the attainment of the purpose in question (s 28(1)). The determination as to whether access would be prejudicial needs to be made in the context of an individual request for access. As originally submitted to Parliament, the 1998 Act supplemented this list with provision that the Secretary of State might exempt personal data of a specified description from the subject information provisions, where the exemption was required for any of the above purposes. In such cases, there would be no requirement that the granting of access to a particular subject would prejudice the attainment of the purpose. It was explained on behalf of the government that the provision was intended primarily to benefit the Inland Revenue. An example might be that—

> '. . . the Inland Revenue's recently introduced self-assessment system uses a range of indicators to identify individual tax returns which justify further inquiries. Subsection (4) will allow an exemption to be made for withholding this critical risk assessment information from data subjects. If it was not withheld, tax experts, if not the individuals concerned, could soon start to compare cases and deduce the revenue's criteria for further inquiry.'.[1]

---

[1] HL Debs, 16 March 1998, col 505.

5.21 However, this clause could potentially have been applied to a wide range of public sector processing activities. Following a lengthy debate, the House of Lords voted to remove this provision from the Bill and a more closely defined provision was introduced at the committee stage in the Commons. This provides that subject access will not be permitted where personal data is processed by a relevant authority as part of a system of risk assessment relating to the assessment or collection of any tax or duty, the prevention or detection of crime or the apprehension or prosecution of offenders if 'the offence concerned involves any unlawful claim for payment out of, or any unlawful application of, public funds', and where exemption is required in the interests of the operation of the system (s 29(4)). A 'relevant authority' is defined in s 29(5) as a government department, a local authority, or any other authority administering housing benefit or council tax benefit.

5.22 This provision will be applicable to systems of data matching,[1] a practice which has in itself been the cause of some controversy. It is to be noted that the exemption relates only to the subject access provision and not to the requirements of the first data protection principle that data be obtained and processed fairly and lawfully.

---

[1] As to data matching, see paras 4.74–4.76.

## Health and social work data

5.23 The 1984 Act established the general principle that access should be provided to medical and social work data. The Access to Personal Files Act 1987 and the Access to Health Records Act 1990 extended these rights to manual files with procedures which are now gathered under the umbrella of the 1998 Act. Access might be denied where, in the opinion of a qualified person, this would be likely to cause serious harm to the data subject's physical or mental health (and in the case of social work data, emotional condition). The 1998 Act confers power on the Secretary of State to make regulations exempting or modifying the subject information provisions in respect of health data (s 30(1)). A similar power is created with respect to social work data but subject to the caveat that the power can be exercised only where the application of the provisions would prejudice the carrying out of social work (s 30(3)). From comments made during the 1998 Bill's committee stage,[1] it would appear likely that the provisions adopted will be similar to those applying under the current legislation although, especially for some categories of social work records, the changes to the provisions relating to third party data may have a significant impact.

---

[1] HC Debs, 21 May 1998, col 199.

## Regulatory activity

5.24 A broad range of statutory agencies engaged in regulatory tasks are provided with exemptions from the subject information provisions to the extent that compliance would prejudice the attainment of their purpose (s 31). A number of agencies are specifically identified in the 1998 Act, such as the Parliamentary, Health Service, Local Government, Northern Ireland Assembly and Northern Ireland Complaints Ombudsmen. Exemption is also offered to the Director General of Fair Trading in respect of the discharge of functions in the fields of consumer protection and competition policy. In addition to named agencies, exemption is also offered to those performing 'relevant functions' which are designed to protect against specified risks. The term 'relevant functions' is defined to encompass functions conferred by statute, functions performed by the Crown, Ministers or government departments or 'any other function which is of a public nature and is exercised in the public interest' (s 31(3)). The activities involved relate to protection against loss due to 'dishonesty, malpractice or other seriously improper conduct' within the financial services, corporate and professional sectors or through the conduct of discharged or undischarged bankrupts. Also exempted are functions concerned with the supervision of charities and the protection of health and safety both for workers and for third parties who might be affected by particular activities.

## Research, history and statistics

5.25 The exemption for data of this description continues the approach adopted in the 1984 Act. Where data are 'not processed to support measures or decisions with regard to particular individuals' and where the processing is not likely to cause substantial damage or distress to any data subject, exemption is offered from the subject access provisions, subject to the further condition that the results of processing are not made available in a form permitting identification of data subjects (s 33).

**Information required to be made available to the public**

5.26 In many instances personal data will be contained in some documents which are made available to the public. An example would be the electoral roll, copies of which may be supplied in electronic format. In the situation where the information made available is the only information held concerning the data subject, there would be little value for the subject in exercising a right of access. Such an exemption previously applied under the 1984 Act and continues under the 1998 Act but, again with the additional benefit to the data controller, that there will be exemption from the first data protection principle (s 34).

**Miscellaneous exemptions**

5.27 Schedule 7 to the 1998 Act contains a substantial list of additional exceptions, which may be supplemented by regulations made by the Secretary of State (s 38(1)). The extent of the individual exemptions varies, ranging from the application of modified access procedures, exemption from access, to exemption from the fair processing requirement.

*Confidential references*

5.28 In many cases under the 1984 Act, confidential references would have been excluded from scrutiny under provisions referring to the processing of data purely in order to create the text of a document (the word processing exemption) (s 1(8)). This exemption is not retained in the 1998 Act and the expanded definition of processing in the 1998 Act will bring such documents within its scope. It is provided that the subject access provisions will not apply to references given in confidence in connection with the data subject's education, employment or appointment to any office as well as to the provision of any services by the data subject (Sch 7, para 1).

*Armed forces*

5.29 The subject information provisions will not apply where their application would be likely to prejudice the 'combat effectiveness of any of the armed forces' (Sch 7, para 2). This is a new provision and it is difficult to identify situations in which it is likely to apply.

*Judicial appointments, Crown appointments and Honours*

5.30 Under the 1984 Act, information held about judicial appointments was exempted from the subject access provisions (s 31). Schedule 7, para 3 to the 1998 Act extends the scope of that exemption to data processed in connection with the 'conferring by the Crown of any honour'. Such data are exempt from the subject information provisions regardless of any issue of prejudice. Schedule 7, para 4 gives the Secretary of State the power to exempt from the subject information provisions data processed for the purpose of assessing a person's suitability for any employment by the Crown, or any office to which appointments are made by Her Majesty, a Minister or a Northern Ireland department.

*Management forecasts*

5.31 Personal data processed for management forecast (undefined) purpose benefit from an exemption to the subject information provisions where compliance would prejudice the attainment of the purpose (Sch 7, para 5). Under the 1984 Act, a data user was not required to give access to information indicating intentions held towards the data subject. Such information might frequently be held in records maintained for career planning purposes and this area may benefit from this provision.

*Corporate finance*

5.32 Extensive provisions are made for exemptions under this heading. The exemption will apply to data processed by 'relevant persons' concerned with the underwriting of share issues or the provision of advice on capital structure, industrial strategy and acquisitions and mergers, and will apply when the application of the subject information provisions could affect the price of any shares or other instruments. Where this criterion is not satisfied, it is further provided that exemption may be granted 'for the purpose of safeguarding an important economic or financial interest of the United Kingdom'. The Secretary of State may specify in more detail the circumstances and situations in which this latter exemption is to apply (Sch 7, para 6).

*Negotiations*

5.33 Data processed in relation to negotiations between the controller and subject which record the intentions of the controller are exempt from the subject information provisions where compliance with these would be likely to prejudice those negotiations (Sch 7, para 7).

*Examination marks and examination scripts*

5.34 The 1984 Act made special provision allowing examination authorities to delay responding to requests for access beyond the normal 40 day period (s 35). This was considered necessary for large-scale examinations such as the GCSE, where a period of months might elapse between examination and publication of the results. This approach continues in the 1998 Act (Sch 7, para 8). One point which should be noted is that where an examination authority relies upon the extended time limits upon receipt of an access request, its response must provide information as to the data held at the time of receipt of the request, at the time the request is complied with and any further data which was held at any intervening stage. An enquiring subject will, therefore, receive details of any changes made to exam marks during the various stages of the assessment process.

5.35 A novel exemption from the subject access provision relates to the materials produced by students during the examination process (Sch 7, para 9). Under the 1984 Act, it is unlikely that these would have been covered by the legislation. With the extension to some forms of manual records and the deletion of the text processing exemption the 1998 Act may well govern such materials.

*Information about human embryos*

5.36  Under s 35A of the 1984 Act, access to information indicating that a data subject had been born following IVF treatment could be obtained only following receipt of counselling as specified in the Human Fertilisation and Embryology Act 1990 (s 31). It was originally proposed that such data should be included in the Sch 7 list of exemptions from the subject information provisions. This approach was criticised by the Registrar[1] as providing an excessively broad exemption and the provision was removed at the Report Stage.[2] It may be expected however, that the 1984 provisions will be reinstated by an Order made under the authority of s 38(1) of the 1998 Act empowering the Secretary of State to modify the subject information provisions where this is considered to be necessary in order to safeguard the interests of the data subject.

---

[1] Comments of the Data Protection Registrar on the Data Protection Bill, 5 May 1998.
[2] HC Debs, 2 July 1998, col 614.

*Legal professional privilege*

5.37  Data are exempt from the subject information provisions where they consist of information in respect of which a claim to legal professional privilege (or client/lawyer confidentiality in Scotland) could be maintained in legal proceedings (Sch 7, para 10). This provision replaces an equivalent exemption under the 1984 Act (s 31(2)) but once again with an extension from the subject access to the subject information provisions.

*Self-incrimination*

5.38  By virtue of Sch 7, para 11 to the 1998 Act, data controllers need not supply information in response to a request for access when the provision of the information would indicate that an offence might have been committed, thereby exposing them to the risk of criminal prosecution (other than an offence under the Act itself). Any information supplied pursuant to a request for access is not admissible in any proceedings relating to an offence under the 1998 Act.

# RIGHTS TO OBJECT TO PROCESSING

## Direct marketing

5.39  It is a little known fact that those persons who purchase black ash furniture are 20 times more likely to respond to a fashion promotion than those whose tastes are less exotic. Such nuggets of information may constitute interesting trivia to most people, but to those engaged in the retail industry they can represent the path to fortune. Direct marketing is one of the fastest-growing sectors of the economy. Although it tends to be referred to under the epithet 'junk mail', each item delivered represents a not inconsiderable investment on the part of the sender. In many instances retailers will possess information linking an individual to a purchase and may use this in order to attempt to stimulate further sales. The purchaser of a motor vehicle, for example, is likely to receive a communication from the seller around the anniversary of the purchase in the hope that the purchaser might be considering buying a new model. The increasing use of store-based credit cards coupled with the utilisation of laser scanning cash points, provides retailers with detailed information about their customers and their purchases. There are few technical barriers in the way of processing data enabling one to 'talk to every customer in his or her own life style terms'.[1] It has even been suggested that 'intelligent shopping trolleys' might guide customers towards promotions which analysis of their previous purchases suggests might prove alluring.[2] Assuming that the data users involved have registered the fact that they intend to process personal data for sales and marketing purposes, the only legal barrier to such techniques might come from a determination that such processing is unfair.

---

[1] Roger Hymas, GE Capital executive director; quoted in Financial Times, 4 April 1991.
[2] Ibid.

---

5.40  The use of personal data for purposes of direct marketing has been the cause of some recent controversy. Reference has previously been made to the *Innovations*[1] case and the data protection implications of list broking. Additionally however, organisations are seeking to exploit their customer databases by entering into agreements to provide mailings on behalf of other companies. This may take a variety of forms. Analysis of, for example, purchases made with a credit card may indicate that an individual frequently stays in hotels. The credit card company may then enter into an agreement with a hotel chain to include a promotional leaflet with its statement of account. In this example, no personal data will be transferred between the companies. In a Guidance Note relating to Direct Marketing issued in October 1995, the DPR has indicated that in certain circumstances use of financial data for such purposes might constitute a breach of confidence (paras 81–88).

---

[1] See paras 4.18 et seq.

---

*Right to object to data being used for the purpose of direct marketing*

5.41  Treatment of data obtained and used for the purposes of direct marketing constituted one of the most controversial aspects of the Directive. As originally drafted, the legislation would have imposed strict obligations on data controllers to inform subjects whenever data was to be used for such a purpose. The proposals were weakened in subsequent drafts and, as enacted, the Directive offers member states a choice of control regimes. It may be provided that data subjects be given the right to object to a controller's intention to process or to disclose data for the purposes of direct marketing. No fees are to be charged in this event. As an alternative, the Directive provides that controllers might be required to give specific notice to data subjects before data are used by or on behalf of third parties for direct marketing purposes (Art 14(b)).

5.42  The 1998 Act provides that where data are used for the purpose of direct marketing, a data subject may serve notice on the controller at any time objecting to this form of processing and requiring its cessation. In the event that the controller fails to act on the notice, an application may be made to the court which may make such order as it thinks fit to secure compliance with the subject's wishes (s 11).

**Other forms of processing**

5.43  In the case of direct marketing data, the subject's wishes are absolute. In the case of other forms of processing, the subject may serve notice requiring the cessation of processing on the basis that this is likely to cause substantial and unwarranted damage or distress (s 10(1)). This right will not apply where the subject has previously consented to the processing, where the processing is necessary to conclude or perform a contract with the data subject, where it is necessary to comply with any legal obligation on the data controller, or where the processing is necessary to protect the vital interests of the data subject. Furthermore, the Secretary of State may specify other situations in which the right to object is to be withdrawn (s 10(2)).

5.44  Upon receipt of such a notice, the controller must respond in writing within 21 days indicating either that the subject's request will be granted or giving reasons why, or to what extent, it will be refused (s 10(3)). A negative response may be appealed and the court may make such order, for ensuring compliance, as it thinks fit (s 10(4)).

DATA SUBJECT REMEDIES

**Rectification of inaccurate data**

5.45  Data will be considered inaccurate if they are false or misleading as to any matter of fact. In such an event, the data subject may ask the court to order the controller to 'rectify, block, erase or destroy'[1] the data in question (s 14(1)). These remedies may also be invoked when the data controller has acted in such a fashion as would give the subject an entitlement to claim compensation under the 1998 Act. Additionally, the controller may be ordered to amend any statement of opinion which appears to be based on the inaccurate data. Where data constitutes an accurate transcription of information received from a third party, the court may make one of the above orders, alternatively, it may permit the data to be retained with a proviso that it be supplemented by a further statement of the true facts as determined by the court (s 14(2)).

---

[1]  The distinction between erasure and destruction of the data may relate to the nature of the storage medium involved. Manual files my well be destroyed through burning or shredding. With computer records, the concept of erasure is more relevant given that data may only be completely destroyed following the complete re-formatting of the storage device.

---

5.46  The above remedies are almost identical to those operating under the 1984 Act. However, the 1998 Act introduces one potentially significant extension. Where the court determines that data are inaccurate and requires that it be rectified, blocked, erased or destroyed, it may, where this is considered reasonably practicable, order that the controller notify details of the changes to any third party to whom the data had previously been disclosed (s 14(3)). Such a remedy may provide a valuable audit trail allowing the detrimental consequences of inaccurate data to be minimised.

**Compensation**

5.47  Under the 1984 Act, data subjects were entitled to claim compensation for damage and distress resulting from inaccuracy in data or from their unauthorised destruction or disclosure. These rights were seldom utilised;[1] in particular, the fact that it was necessary to demonstrate both damage and distress proved to be a substantial hurdle.

---

[1] The Fourteenth Report of the Data Protection Registrar cites one case where a credit reference agency wrongly registered adverse data against the complainant. The mistake continued for some considerable time and the report indicates that, following the Registrar's intervention, 'a substantial ex gratia payment was made'; page 88.

5.48 The 1998 Act adopts a more extensive approach. An individual who suffers damage by reason of any breach of the Act will be entitled to compensation from the data controller concerned. Where damage in the form of quantifiable financial loss can be demonstrated, further compensation may be claimed for any related distress (s 13). Where data are processed for media related purposes (the 'special purposes') an aggrieved data subject may seek compensation for distress alone (s 13(2)).[1] In all cases, the controller will have a defence if it can be shown that reasonable care was taken to avoid the breach.

---

[1] See also Ch 6.

## ENFORCED SUBJECT ACCESS

5.49 Some one hundred thousand access requests are received each year by police forces and the DSS. Such a statistic might seem to suggest that subject access is a valuable right for the individual. In reality, however, it is estimated that the majority of requests are made at the behest of third parties. In a neat reversal of history, it is suggested that the Australian immigration authorities are major initiators of access requests wishing to satisfy themselves that potential immigrants do not have criminal records. To achieve this, applicants are required to exercise their rights of access under the data protection legislation and pass the results on to the authorities. Although employers and others are entitled to require information about criminal convictions (and a false reply might be grounds for dismissal) the data obtained pursuant to an access request will include details of convictions which are regarded as 'spent' under the provisions of the Rehabilitation of Offenders Act 1974.

5.50 The situation where access rights imprison rather than empower the data subject has long been the subject of criticism, not least by the DPR. Devising an appropriate method of control has proved more difficult. The major difficulty facing any attempt to control the practice is the imbalance of power typically existing in such situations. If the subject is seeking employment, for example, a request that the information be supplied may carry as much weight as a demand. The initial drafts of the Directive provided that data subjects should be entitled—

> 'to refuse any demand by a third party that he should exercise his right of access in order to communicate the data in question to that third party.'.

In the final text, the Directive contained the somewhat enigmatic provision that data subjects should be guaranteed the right to exercise access 'without constraint' (Art 12(a)). Other language versions of the Directive make it clearer that the provision is intended to apply to enforced access, the German text for example, requiring that access be provided 'frei und ungehindert'.

5.51  Although the government indicated its intention to act against enforced subject access from the earliest stages of the 1998 Bill's Parliamentary passage, finding an appropriate form of prohibition proved a difficult task. A variety of possibilities were considered. Subject access might, for example, be provided only in person rather than in writing. This would, of course, have made a dramatic change to the whole system of subject access and would have caused great inconvenience if, for example, a data subject was located in Glasgow and the data controller in London. An alternative suggestion canvassed was that all access requests should be filtered through the Commissioner. Again, practical constraints might make this solution unworkable. Ultimately, however, it was determined that the only feasible approach was to make the practice criminal. The prohibitions apply only in respect of certain forms of records (criminal records, prison records and DSS records) and in respect of a limited range of situations. A person must not require the provision of information obtained following a request for access (a relevant record) in connection with the recruitment or continued employment of the data subject, or with any contract under which the subject is to provide services. Similarly, when the person is concerned with the provision of goods, facilities or services to members of the public, it is prohibited to require the production of any relevant records as a condition for the provision of such goods, facilities or services (s 56). Section 57 further provides that any contractual terms will be void in so far as they purport to require the production of any medical information obtained pursuant to an access request. Although it is provided that the categories of data specified in s 56 may be extended by statutory instrument (s 56(8)), it may be queried whether the provisions comply fully with the Directive's requirements.

5.52  In this, as in other areas, the provisions of the 1998 Act will not operate in isolation. Under the provisions of the Police Act 1997 new arrangements have been made for providing access to criminal records. Three categories of access are created. A basic certificate may be sought be any applicant and will reveal details of any convictions which are not spent under the Rehabilitation of Offenders Act 1974. A more extensive 'criminal record certificate', adding details of spent convictions, will be issued upon the joint application of the individual and an organisation which is exempted from the provisions of the 1974 Act. This will include professional organisations such as the Law Society in respect of their role in determining whether individuals might be considered suitable for admission to the profession. The most extensive certificate, the 'enhanced criminal record certificate' will include police intelligence data and details of acquittals, but will be reserved for situations where an individual is seeking to work with children or vulnerable adults (or other sensitive positions such as those related to gambling or judicial appointments).

5.53  Given the large numbers of requests for access relating to criminal records, there will clearly be a close relationship between the access provisions of the Police Act 1997 and the information provisions of the 1998 Act. It was stated in Parliament[1] that the 1998 Act's provisions will not be implemented before those of the Police Act 1997. Again, while a public interest defence will be available to parties charged with an offence under the 1998 Act, this will not be available in respect of data relating to the prevention or detection of crime.

---

[1] HC Debs, 2 June 1998, col 276.

## AUTOMATED DECISION MAKING

5.54  There have been reports sending out bills for the sum of £0.00p, followed by reminders and final demands for payment. Many of these reports may be apocryphal, but many individuals have encountered difficulty in persuading some human to intervene in data processing operations when computers are acting with remorseless logic but basing actions on original data containing errors. As the maxim has it, 'garbage in, garbage out'.

5.55  Adopting provisions originally found in the French legislation, the Directive seeks to address the problem by providing that decisions adverse to an individual are not to be made purely on the basis of automated data processing (Art 15). As implemented in the 1998 Act, it is provided that a data subject may give notice in writing to a data controller requiring that—

> '. . . no decision . . . which significantly affects that individual is based solely on the processing by automatic means of personal data in respect of which that individual is the data subject for the purpose of evaluating matters relating to him such as, for example, his performance at work, his creditworthiness, his reliability or his conduct' (s 12(1)).

5.56  Such a prohibition clearly cannot be absolute. The act of obtaining money from a cash dispensing machine, for example, would be prohibited in the situation where the bank's computer system makes a check on the state of the customer's account before allowing the withdrawal to proceed. It would be a uniquely altruistic bank that would accept a restriction to its rights in this situation. The 1998 Act provides that as exemptions to the general rule, automated decisions may be made in the course of entering into, or performing, a contract with the data subject, or under statutory authority where the decision is either favourable or where 'steps have been taken to safeguard the legitimate interests of the data subject (for example by allowing him to make representations)' (s 12(4)). Additional exemptions may be made by order of the Secretary of State (s 12(5)).

5.57  In the case of the cash dispensing example, there would be no problem where the customer's request for money was accepted. In the event that the request was rejected owing to a shortage of funds in the customer's account, it might be argued that the presence of contractual terms specifying in advance the nature and extent of the customer's rights would constitute sufficient steps. Additionally, the right to seek an overdraft facility would appear to satisfy the requirement of allowing the subject to make representations.

5.58  In the event that a data controller is found to have breached the prohibition against automated decision making, the data subject may seek a court order demanding that the controller either reconsider the decision or take a new decision other than on the basis of the automatic process (s 12(8)). It is also possible that such conduct may be considered to constitute a breach of the first data protection principle (fair processing) and might form the subject of an enforcement notice (s 40(1)).

5.59  In cases where no notice is served on a data controller and where decisions are made solely on the basis of automated processing, it is provided that the controller must, as soon as reasonably practicable, give notice to the subject of the fact that the decision was made on such a basis (s 12(2)(a)). The subject may, within 21 days, serve notice requiring the controller 'to reconsider the decision or to take a new decision otherwise than on that basis' (s 12(2)(b)).

# 6 Data protection and the media

## INTRODUCTION

6.1    The application of data protection provisions in respect of media activities raises a number of complex issues. Investigative journalism may involve the use of tactics and techniques which might normally be stigmatised as unfair (if not unlawful). Again, where the text of published articles is maintained in electronic format, the attempt by a featured data subject to invoke rights to have errors of fact rectified, together with changing any related opinion, brings to mind the operation of George Orwell's Ministry of Truth in *Nineteen Eighty-Four*.

6.2    The 1984 Act made no special provision for the media. To a large extent, this approach was justified by the limited use of computer equipment for journalistic purposes, the existence of the text processing exemption and the limited nature of the definition of processing. Time and technology have moved on. A 1992 study produced for the Council of Europe[1] identified a wide range of practices in member states regarding the treatment of media activities within data protection legislation. Some countries, such as the Netherlands and Sweden, provided a total exemption from data protection laws, others provided partial exemption; in the case of Germany, for example, the legislation requires only that media users comply with requirements relating to data security. Other regimes, including that of the UK, provided no form of special treatment. The study identified a potential conflict between the provisions of the European Convention on Human Rights relating to freedom of expression and the right to seek out and impart information, and those concerned with the right to privacy. Providing solutions is a difficult task and the Council of Europe contented itself with a recommendation that the potential conflict should be borne in mind in framing legislation.

---

[1] Data Protection and the Media; A study prepared by the Committee of Experts on Data Protection.

6.3    Such an approach is sanctioned by the Directive which provides in its Preamble that—

> 'Whereas the processing of personal data for purposes of journalism or for purposes of literary [or] artistic expression, in particular in the audiovisual field, should qualify for exemption from the requirements of certain provisions of this Directive in so far as this is necessary to reconcile the fundamental rights of individuals with freedom of information and notably the right to receive and impart information, as guaranteed in particular in Article 10 of the European Convention for the Protection of Human Rights and Fundamental Freedoms . . .' (recital (37)).

The Preamble continues to suggest that national laws should provide for alternative measures, such as the submission of reports to the supervisory agency, to ensure that data subject's rights are not abused. Article 9 states that—

> 'Member States shall provide for exemptions or derogations from the provisions of this Chapter, Chapter IV and Chapter VI for the processing of personal data carried out solely for journalistic purposes or

the purpose of artistic or literary expression only if they are necessary to reconcile the right to privacy with the rules governing freedom of expression.'.

This formula empowers, rather than requires, member states to act. However, the decision was taken to include special provisions for these activities, described as 'the special purposes' in the 1998 Act.

## THE SPECIAL PURPOSES: SCOPE OF THE PROVISIONS

6.4   Section 3 of the 1998 Act defines the concept of 'the special purposes'. These relate to the processing of personal data—

'(a)   for the purposes of journalism,

(b)   artistic purposes, and

(c)   literary purposes.'.

6.5   It was stressed in Parliament[1] that no qualitative criteria would be applied to determine whether a work could be classed as artistic, journalistic or literary. Although much of the debate in Parliament focused on the activities of the media, this definition recognises that literary and artistic works also raise issues of freedom of expression. The prime purpose of the 1998 Act's exemption provisions is to place limits on the ability of data subjects to invoke statutory rights to impede the publication of a work. Similar restrictions are placed upon the powers of the Commissioner and there are modified provisions for the service of information and enforcement notices. Once the work is in the public domain the provisions of the general law will apply, including the law of defamation. However, as indicated in Ch 5, the 1998 Act does provide new rights of compensation for distress caused as a result of processing carried out in connection with one of the special purposes.[2]

---

[1] HC Debs, 21 May 1998.
[2] See paras 5.47, 5.48.

### Activities covered

6.6   The 1998 Act applies a three stage test to determine whether processing for the special purposes should benefit from exemption. Section 32(1) provides that personal data must be subject to processing—

'(a)   . . . with a view to the publication by any person of any journalistic, literary or artistic material,

(b)   the data controller reasonably believes that, having regard in particular to the special importance of the public interest in freedom of expression, publication would be in the public interest, and

(c)   the data controller reasonably believes that, in all the circumstances, compliance with that provision is incompatible with the special purposes.'.

6.7   In determining whether the belief that publication is in the public interest is reasonable, it is specifically provided that account is to be taken of any relevant code of practice. Such codes are to be designated by the Secretary of State (s 32(3)). Examples given in the House of Lords included codes prepared by statutory bodies such as the Independent Television Commission, the Broadcasting Standards Commission and non-statutory bodies such as the Press Complaints Commission.[1] It was suggested that—

> 'We have deliberately placed upon the face of the Bill, I believe for the first time in an Act of Parliament in this country, that the public interest is not the narrow question of whether this is a public interest story in itself but that it relates to the wider public interest, which is an infinitely subtle and more complicated concept.'.[2]

---

[1] HL Debs, 25 February 1998, col CWH 97.
[2] HL Debs, 2 February 1998, col 442.

## THE SPECIAL PURPOSES: SCOPE OF THE EXEMPTION

6.8   Section 32(2) of the 1998 Act defines a range of provisions which will not apply where processing is carried out for the special purposes. With the exception of the seventh principle relating to data security, the data protection principles will not operate, neither will the subject access provisions nor those enabling a data subject to object to data being processed. Also excluded are the provisions of s 12 relating to subject rights in respect of automated decision making, and the general provisions of s 14 relating to the subject's rights to compensation. However, these latter provisions are substituted by special and more extensive rights.

6.9   These exceptions are wide-ranging. One consequence will be that even the unlawful obtaining of personal data will not expose the controller to action under the 1998 Act, although other criminal sanctions, such as a charge of theft, may be imposed in respect of the offending conduct. It should be stressed that these exceptions apply only to the period of time prior to the publication of material. A data subject will not be able to exercise access rights to discover material which a newspaper has obtained about, for example, financial dealings and which will form the core of a report on the subject's activities. But once the story has been published the subject access provisions will apply subject only to the normal exemptions.

### Procedural aspects

6.10   The question as to whether processing is covered by one of the special purposes exemptions is likely to arise in the course of legal proceedings. It is provided that proceedings must be stayed when the data controller claims, or it appears to the court, that the data are being processed for a special purpose and—

> 'with a view to publication by any person of any journalistic, literary or artistic material which, at the time twenty four hours immediately before the relevant time, had not previously been published by the data controller' (s 32(4)).

The relevant time will be the moment at which the controller makes the claim for protection or the court determines that the processing is for a special purpose.

ر

6.11 It will be noted that there is no requirement that the controller's claim that processing is covered by the special purpose should have any merit. As discussed in the next paragraph, procedures for the lifting of such a stay are complex, and the DPR has criticised the situation whereby an unscrupulous party could delay proceedings for a period of months, if not years, with little justification.[1]

---

[1] DPR Briefing Paper; see http://www.open.gov.UK/dpr/dprhome.htm

6.12 Once a court has determined that procedures should be stayed the focus of attention switches to the Commissioner. The Commissioner will be required to make a written determination as to whether the processing is being conducted only in connection with one of the special purposes or with a view to the publication of material not previously published by the data controller (s 45). In obtaining evidence necessary to reach such a view, the Commissioner may need to exercise powers conferred by the legislation to serve a special information notice. However, service of such notice may itself be the subject of an appeal to the Data Protection Tribunal. If the Commissioner determines that the processing is not exempt, this finding may itself be appealed to the Tribunal. It will only be when all the appeal procedures have been exhausted that the determination will come into effect, and the court will be in a position to lift the stay. Although reference was made to the possibility of a 'fast track' procedure[1] for resolving appeals to the Tribunal, the DPR has been markedly less optimistic than the government as to the possibility that disputes can be resolved speedily.[2]

---

[1] HC Debs, 21 May 1998, col 228.
[2] DPR Briefing Paper; see http://www.open.gov.UK/dpr/dprhome.htm

## Special information notices

6.13 A modified form of information notice applies where data are being processed for a special purpose. Section 44 provides that the Commissioner may serve a 'special information notice' in two situations. First, in response to a request from a data subject for an assessment as to whether data are being processed in accordance with the principles (ie, under s 42). Secondly, where there are reasonable grounds for suspecting that a data controller has wrongfully claimed the benefit of the special purpose to, for example, refuse a request for access. The notice will require the controller to supply the Commissioner with specified information to enable the Commissioner to determine whether the processing is being conducted for a special purpose, or with a view to publication of new information. The notice must indicate the ground upon which the Commissioner is making the request and give notice of the controller's rights of appeal. The notice will not come into effect until the expiry of the period allowed for the lodging of appeals. Under the 1984 Act, this period is 28 days.[1] The period under the 1998 Act will be fixed by order (Sch 6, para 7). In cases of urgency it is provided that the notice may require that information be supplied within seven days (s 44(6)).

---

[1] Data Protection Tribunal Rules 1985, SI 1985/1568, r 4.

6.14 Having received the information required, the Commissioner will make the determination whether processing is being conducted only for the special purposes. If the determination is that the processing is not being conducted for these purposes, the Commissioner may serve the normal form of information notice seeking information that allows a determination to be made as to whether processing is lawful (s 46(3)).

### Enforcement notices

6.15 Whether following service of a special information notice or otherwise, a determination by the Commissioner that processing is unlawful may be followed by service of an enforcement notice. Once again, different procedures apply in relation to the special purposes. An enforcement notice may only be served with the leave of the court (s 46(1)). Leave will only be granted if the court is satisfied that 'the Commissioner has reason to suspect a contravention of the data protection principles which is of substantial public importance' and that 'except where the case is one of urgency' notice has been given to the controller of the Commissioner's intention to apply for leave (s 46(2)).

## INDIVIDUAL RIGHTS AND REMEDIES

6.16 As discussed above,[1] the 1998 Act gives extended rights to data subjects to institute proceedings before the courts seeking compensation for damage and distress resulting from a breach of any of the Act's requirements (s 13(1)). In the case of processing for the special purposes, damages may be awarded for distress without the need for any related damage. The data subject may also bring an action, in the normal manner, seeking rectification, blocking or erasure of inaccurate data (s 14). The question as to whether, and to what extent, such remedies are provided is at the discretion of the court. It may be assumed that account will be taken of the requirements of the special purposes so that, for example, the court will not order the alteration of the contents of a database containing the contents of stories which have been published in a newspaper. Even where a story contains errors, a notice of correction appended to the file would appear to be a more appropriate course of action.

---

[1] See paras 5.45, 5.46.

### Granting of assistance by the Commissioner

6.17 Section 53 confers a new power on the Commissioner to provide assistance following an application from a party to proceedings relating to the special purposes (s 53(1)). This will include all the forms of proceedings described in para 6.16, with the assistance taking the form of a contribution towards the costs of legal advice and representation and indemnification against any award of costs to the other party (Sch 10). The criterion for the award of such assistance is that the Commissioner is of the opinion that 'the case involves a matter of substantial public importance' (s 53(2)). The Commissioner's decision whether or not to grant support must be transmitted to the applicant as soon as is practicable. If the Commissioner decides not to grant assistance, reasoned notification to this effect must be given (s 53(3), (4)).

# 7 Transborder data flows

## INTRODUCTION

7.1 During the nineteenth century the development of telegraph networks provided a medium for the speedy transfer of data both nationally and internationally. The possibility that messages might be sent into, or out of, the jurisdiction without the possibility of control caused concern to many governments. As a result it was required that a physical break in the telegraph network be made at the national border and that messages be—

> 'sent to the terminal at the border, decoded and walked across to the next country where the message was again encoded and sent on to the terminal at the next border and so on.'.[1]

The International Telegraph Union (now the International Telecommunications Union) (ITU) was established in 1865 primarily to promote governmental confidence in the integrity of the system, and to avoid such artificial barriers to the use of communications technology.

---

[1] Pelton *Global Talk* (Harvester Press 1981) p 233.

7.2 In keeping with history's tendency to repeat itself, concerns at the implications of transborder data flows have evolved in parallel with the development of national data protection statutes. Typically, the fear is expressed that an absence of control may result in evasion of national controls. As has been stated—

> 'protective provisions will be undermined if there are no restrictions on the removal of data to other jurisdictions for processing or storage. Just as money tends to gravitate towards tax havens, so sensitive personal data will be transferred to countries with the most lax, or no data protection standards. There is thus a possibility that some jurisdictions will become 'data havens' or 'data sanctuaries' for the processing or 'data vaults' for the storage of sensitive information.'.[1]

---

[1] Millard *Legal Protection of Computer Programs and Data* (1985) p 211.

7.3 Controls over transborder data flows have been a feature of almost all national data protection statutes, with restrictions being justified on the basis of safeguarding the position of individuals. However, while there may be concern about the implications of transfers, transborder data flows are essential for commercial activities. Many thousands of messages must be transmitted prior to an aircraft flying from London to New York (for example, passenger details). In this context, the issue of transborder data flows is not merely an esoteric topic: if the data cannot flow, the aeroplanes cannot fly.

INTERNATIONAL INITIATIVES

7.4    As concern about the impact of national controls over telegraphic and voice traffic led to the establishment of the ITU, so international initiatives have sought to establish what are effectively free trade zones in respect of personal data. In 1980 the OECD adopted 'Guidelines on the Protection of Privacy and Transborder Flows of Personal Data'. These guidelines, which have no legal effect, were supplemented by a Declaration on Transborder Data Flows adopted in 1995. This declared its signatories' intention to 'avoid the creation of unjustified barriers to the international exchange of data and information' (para 1). The UN has also adopted 'Guidelines Concerning Computerised Personal Data Files' but the most extensive and effective form of international action has been taken by the Council of Europe. Beginning with sets of recommendations directed at public and private sector data processing adopted in 1973, the Convention for the Protection of Individuals with regard to the Automatic Processing of Personal Data was adopted in 1981 and was ratified by the UK following the enactment of the 1984 Act. As has been stated previously,[1] commercial pressure to put the UK in a position to ratify the Convention was the main factor behind the enactment of the 1984 Act. The Convention prescribed minimum standards which were to be provided in national data protection statutes. It further provided that no barriers were to be imposed on grounds of protection of privacy in respect of data flows between those states which had signed and ratified the Convention. Although the Convention makes provision for signature by states which are not members of the Council of Europe, to date this has not occurred.

----

[1] See para 1.12.

----

7.5    The Council of Europe Convention was shaped by the experiences and practices of western European states which have adopted data protection legislation. Such legislation has three major features. First, it applies to all sectors of automated data processing. Secondly, it contains substantive provisions regulating the forms of processing which can take place and the rights and remedies available to individuals. Thirdly, it provides for the establishment of some form of supervisory agency. A different approach has prevailed in other countries, notably the US. This eschews the notion of supervisory agencies which are seen as unnecessarily bureaucratic, in favour of conferring rights which are directly enforceable by individuals. Additionally, there has been criticism of the very concept of data protection and the terminology that is used. This, it is suggested, pays excessive regard to the regulation of technology and insufficient attention to the protection of privacy. It is certainly notable that the word 'privacy' does not appear in the Convention although it is used 13 times in the Directive. The approach in the US can be characterised as one of privacy protection. Laws are generally introduced on a sectoral basis, often in response to publicised instances of informational misuse. For example, the Video Privacy Protection Act 1988 was introduced following disclosure of details of videos rented by a judge containing pornographic material. The information was disclosed at the time his nomination for appointment to the Supreme Court was being considered in Congress. The result of this approach is that while some areas are well protected, others are less so. It has been suggested for example, that records of a person's video preferences are afforded greater protection than medical records.

7.6    To date, the discrepancy in the approach adopted in Europe and that in the rest of the world has been of limited practical significance. However, with the implementation of the EU Directive containing stringent provisions regulating transborder data flows this may change. The Directive's provisions in this respect have been the cause of considerable, and continuing, transatlantic controversy. The provisions will be of particular significance to the operation of multinational companies as well as to undertakings such as airlines which operate on a worldwide basis.

## Transborder data flows under the convention and the 1984 Act

7.7     The approach which has generally been adopted by states implementing data protection statutes has been to impose some form of control over the transfer of personal data, unless there can be a degree of assurance that data protection standards will be observed in the recipient country. The extent of national controls varies. In Sweden and Austria, for example, transborder data flows from countries which are not signatories to the Council of Europe Convention must be licensed by the data protection authorities. In other countries, such as the UK, data users are required to register their intent to make transfers. These may be carried out subsequently unless specifically prohibited. Experience suggests that this is an unlikely prospect. Although the 1984 Act provides that the Registrar may serve a transfer prohibition notice where he is satisfied that 'the transfer is likely to contravene, or lead to a contravention', of any of the data protection principles' (s 12(2)), to date, only one such notice has been served by the Registrar. This notice prohibited the transfer of personal data, in the form of names and addresses, to a variety of US organisations bearing such titles as the 'Astrology Society of America', 'Lourdes Water Cross Incorporated' and 'Win With Palmer Incorporated'. These companies, which had been involved in the promotion of horoscopes, religious trinkets and other products in the UK, were the subject of investigations by the US postal authorities concerning wire fraud and a variety of other unsavoury trading practices.[1]

---

[1] Details of this incident are to be found in the Seventh Report of the Data Protection Registrar, 1991, at pp 33, 34.

---

## Transborder data flows under the Directive and the 1998 Act

*Requirement for an adequate level of protection*

7.8     While the Convention is silent concerning control of transborder data flows, this topic receives extensive consideration in the Directive. Major decisions concerning the operation of the new system will be made at a Community level. To this extent, the provisions of the Directive are more important than those of the 1998 Act. The topic has been, and is expected to remain, one of the most controversial aspects of the legislation. The Directive's Preamble recognises the dilemmas arising in this area; recital (56) states—

> 'Whereas cross-border flows of personal data are necessary to the expansion of international trade; whereas the protection of individuals guaranteed in the Community by this Directive does not stand in the way of transfers of personal data to third countries which ensure an adequate level of protection . . .'.

The critical questions are what might be considered an adequate lack of protection, and can any perceived inadequacies in general legal provisions be overcome by other sources of rights and remedies?

7.9   In implementing this principle the Directive requires member states to ensure that—

> '. . . the transfer to a third country of personal data which are undergoing processing or are intended for processing may take place only if . . . the third country in question ensures an adequate level of protection.' (Art 25(1)).

Effect is given to this provision by the 1998 Act's eighth data protection principle; Sch 1, Pt I, para 8 provides that—

> 'Personal data shall not be transferred to a country or territory outside the European Economic Area unless that country or territory ensures an adequate level of protection for the rights and freedoms of data subjects in relation to the processing of personal data.'.

7.10  By addressing the matter of adequate level of protection in the principles, it follows that any breach, or anticipated breach, can be answered by service of an enforcement notice. The need therefore, for an additional transfer prohibition notice disappears. This formulation marks a significant change to the existing UK system, whereby, a data user can register an intent to transfer data on a worldwide basis and proceed with such transfers unless served with a transfer prohibition notice. The DPR has supplied guidance to data users who conduct business on the internet stating that they should register in this way.

*Determining adequacy*

7.11  The determination as to what might be considered an adequate level of protection has been the cause of considerable and continuing controversy and uncertainty. It would appear that the determination is to be made by reference to both substantive and structural provisions in the third country. Given that few non-European states have enacted data protection statutes, the effect might have been to cut the continent off from data links with the rest of the world. Even where a third country accepted a right of privacy and the notion of subject access, without a supervisory agency similar to the UK's Data Protection Commissioner, its regime may not be regarded as strict enough.

7.12  Mirroring provisions in the Directive, the interpretative provisions attached to the eighth principle provide that the issue of adequacy is to be assessed by reference to a range of factors. These include the nature of the data and of the proposed transfer, the legal position in the recipient country, including any international obligations, together with any relevant codes of practice and any provisions relating to data security (Sch 1, Pt II, para 13).

7.13  Use of the phrase 'adequate level of protection' clearly does not carry the requirement that the laws of the recipient state conform in every respect with the provisions of the Directive. It would appear unlikely, however, that a total absence of data protection legislation could be regarded as providing adequate protection. As has been discussed earlier,[1] the US has followed a very different model of privacy protection from that adopted in Europe. Although proposals have been brought forward for the introduction of a data protection statute, there appears to be little prospect that this situation will change in the near future.

---

[1] See para 7.5.

*The Commission working party*

7.14 The uniform application of the Directive would clearly be threatened if the decision as to whether third countries offered an adequate level of protection was to be made by each member state. It is provided therefore, that the member states and the Commission are to inform each other of any cases where they feel that a third country does not provide an adequate level of protection (Art 25(3)). In practice, general decisions regarding adequacy will be made at a Community level. Article 29 of the Directive establishes a 'Working Party on the Protection of Individuals with regard to the Processing of Personal Data'. Article 29(2) provides that this working party is to be—

'. . . composed of a representative of the supervisory authority or authorities designated by each Member State and of a representative of the authority or authorities established for the Community institutions and bodies, and of a representative of the Commission.'.

With regard to the functions of the working party, Art 30(1) provides that it shall—

'(a) examine any question covering the application of the national measures adopted under this Directive in order to contribute to the uniform application of such measures;

(b) give the Commission an opinion on the level of protection in the Community and in third countries;

(c) advise the Commission on any proposed amendment of this Directive, on any additional or specific measures to safeguard the rights and freedoms of natural persons with regard to the processing of personal data and on any other proposed Community measures affecting such rights and freedoms;

(d) give an opinion on codes of conduct drawn up at Community level.'.

7.15 If the working party determines that a third country does not provide an adequate level of protection, a report is to be made to a committee established under Art 31. Consisting of representatives of the member states and chaired by a representative of the Commission, the committee will consider a proposal from the Commission for action on the basis of the working party's findings and deliver an opinion. The Commission may then adopt legal measures. If these are in accord with the committee's opinion, the measures will take immediate effect. If there is any variation, application will be deferred for three months within which time the Council of Ministers may adopt a different decision. Member states are obliged to take any measures necessary to prevent data transfers to the country involved (Art 25(4)).

7.16 Within the UK, Sch 1, Pt II, para 15(1) of the 1998 Act provides that where—

'(a) in any proceedings under this Act any question arises as to whether the requirements of the eighth principle as to an adequate level of protection is met in relation to the transfer of any personal data to a country or territory outside the European Economic Area, and

(b) a Community finding has been made in relation to transfers of the kind in question,

that question is to be determined in accordance with that finding.'.

It is further provided that the Commissioner shall be obliged to comply with any decision made by the Commission under the above procedures (s 54(6)).

7.17 Utilisation of this procedure may have the result of establishing a 'black list' of countries to which data transfers will be prohibited. The Directive also provides for the procedures described to be used to identify countries which, in the opinion of the Commission, do provide an adequate level of protection. Given the reference in the Directive to the role of 'sectoral rules' and 'professional rules and security measures', it is unlikely that there will be many 'black listings' affecting all data processing activities in a particular jurisdiction.[1]

---

[1] For an indication of possible techniques for determining adequacy, see the report of the Working Party, 'First Orientations on Transfers of Personal Data to Third Countries' (XV D/5020/97-EN final WP4). This document is reproduced in the 14th Annual Report of the Data Protection Registrar.

---

*Transfers where an adequate level of protection is not provided*

7.18 As originally drafted, the Directive's prohibition of data transfers to a country where an adequate level of protection was not offered admitted of no exceptions. Even allowing for the provisions relating to acceptance of sectoral and professional rules, such an approach would have posed major problems for transborder data flows. As adopted, the Directive modifies this provision to a considerable extent, it now being provided that national implementing statutes may authorise transfers, notwithstanding the absence of adequate protection in the recipient state, where—

'(a)    the data subject has given his consent unambiguously to the proposed transfer; or

(b)    the transfer is necessary for the performance of a contract between the data subject and the controller or the implementation of precontractual measures taken in response to the data subject's request; or

(c)    the transfer is necessary for the conclusion or performance of a contract concluded in the interest of the data subject between the controller and a third party; or

(d)    the transfer is necessary or legally required on important public interest grounds, or for the establishment, exercise or defence of legal claims; or

(e)    the transfer is necessary in order to protect the vital interests of the data subject; or

(f)    the transfer is made from a register which according to laws or regulations is intended to provide information to the public and which is open to consultation either by the public in general or by any person who can demonstrate legitimate interest, to the extent that the conditions laid down in law for consultation are fulfilled in the particular case.' (Art 26(1)).

7.19 The 1998 Act makes full use of these provisions. In the main, the 1998 Act's wording follows that of the Directive but there is a divergence in respect of the exception relating to subject consent. While the Directive requires unambiguous consent, the 1998 Act refers merely to the fact that 'the data subject has given his consent to the transfer' (Sch 4, para 1). The 1998 Act also confers regulatory power on the Secretary of State to define more closely the circumstances under which transfers may, or may not, take place 'for reasons of substantial public interest' (Sch 4 para 4(2)).

7.20  Transfers coming under these headings may take place, subject to their being in conformity with any entry on the data protection register, without the need for any further permissions. Additionally, Art 26(2) of the Directive provides that—

> '. . . a Member State may authorise a transfer or a set of transfers of personal data to a third country which does not ensure an adequate level of protection . . . where the controller adduces adequate safeguards with respect to the protection of the privacy and fundamental rights and freedoms of individuals and as regards the exercise of the corresponding rights; such safeguards may in particular result from appropriate contractual clauses.'.

Any exercise of this power must be reported to the Commission and the other member states. If any party so informed objects 'on justified measures involving the protection of the privacy and the fundamental rights and freedoms of individuals', a proposal for action may be tabled before the committee by the Commission and, if approved, will require the member state involved to take necessary measures to conform (Art 26(3)).

### Transfers sanctioned by the Commissioner

7.21  In addition to the general exemptions, Sch 4, para 8 to the 1998 Act provides that transfers will be acceptable when—

> '. . . made on terms which are of a kind approved by the Commissioner as ensuring adequate safeguards for the rights and freedoms of data subjects.'.

Furthermore, Sch 4, para 9 provides that they will be acceptable when—

> '. . . authorised by the Commissioner as being made in such a manner as to ensure adequate safeguards for the rights and freedoms of data subjects.'.

Any approvals granted under these provisions shall be notified to the Commission and the supervisory authorities of the other EEA States (s 54(7)).

7.22  Authorisation may be given under the above provisions on an individual basis but may also make reference to the controller's adherence to model contractual terms and conditions. There appears to be a general acceptance that the volume of transborder data flows is such, that it is undesirable for decisions as to acceptability to be made in the context of individual transfers, and that more general provisions should be laid down. The nature of the procedures adopted by the Directive, and the open ended prospect that national measures might be challenged at the instance of any other member state, does not seem conducive to speedy resolution of the issues involved.

## CONTRACTUAL SOLUTIONS

7.23  In recent years some attention has been paid to the possible role of contract in ensuring equivalency of protection in respect of transborder data flows. The Council of Europe, in co-operation with the Commission of the European Communities and the International Chamber of Commerce (ICC), have produced a model contract which might be used by data users for this purpose.[1]

---

[1] Adopted by the Consultative Committee of the Convention for the Protection of Individuals with Regard to Automatic Processing of Personal Data (Strasbourg, 14–16 October 1992).

7.24 Paragraph 23 of the Explanatory Memorandum states that the objectives of the model contract are—

'a.    to provide an example of one way of resolving the complex problems which arise following the transfer of personal data subjected to different data protection regimes;

b.    to facilitate the free circulation of personal data in the respect of privacy;

c.    to allow the transfer of data in the interest of international commerce;

d.    to promote a climate of security and certainty of international transactions involving the transfer of personal data.'.

7.25 The contract terms are divided into five sections. The first two concern the obligations of the party initiating the transfer, the licensor, and those of the recipient, the licensee. The licensor is obliged to ensure that all domestic data protection requirements have been satisfied, while the licensee undertakes to ensure that these are complied with in the course of his or her activities. The contract also proposes a number of more detailed obligations which should be accepted by the licensee. Thus, the purpose for which the data will be used should be specified and there should generally be a prohibition on the processing of sensitive data. In addition, the data shall be used only for the licensee's own purposes and any errors subsequently notified by the licensor will be rectified immediately upon receipt.

7.26 Further provisions would hold the licensee liable for any use which may be made of the data and require that the licensor be indemnified in the event of liability arising through the licensee's breach of contract or negligent act. In the event of any dispute between the parties, the model contract contains provisions for dispute resolution. Reference is made to the possibility that disputes may be submitted to arbitration under the rules established by the ICC or United Nations Commission on International Trade Law (UNCITRAL). Finally, provision is suggested for the termination of the contract in the event of a failure by the licensee to demonstrate good faith or to observe the terms of the agreement. Any personal data held by the licensee must be destroyed in such an eventuality.

7.27 The working party produced a report in April 1998 outlining its 'preliminary views on the use of contractual terms in the context of transfers of personal data to third countries'.[1] This document identified a number of elements that must be found in any relevant contract. The contract must provide for observance of the data protection principles. While it was recognised that no system could provide a total assurance of compliance, a reasonable level of assurance would be required. Such a system should also provide support and assistance for data subjects and appropriate forms of redress.

---

[1] XVD/5009/98 final WP10; this document is reproduced in the 14th Annual Report of the Data Protection Registrar, p 133.

---

7.28 The utilisation of contractual techniques may provide what has been described as 'a sort of palliative or complement to the legal framework for data protection and transborder data flow'.[1] There remain, however, a number of objections to their widespread utilisation. A major problem concerns the enforceability of contracts at the suit of an aggrieved data subject. Under the doctrine of privity of contract, only those who are party to the instrument can rely on it in the course of legal proceedings. It might be, for example, that a data user in England would enter into a contract with a user in the US under which it is agreed that data will be transferred to the US with the recipient agreeing to observe all aspects of the data protection principles. In the event that the US party subsequently denied a request for subject access in breach of the principles, although an action for breach of contract may be available to the exporting data user, there would not appear to be any remedy for the data subject. A possible approach suggested by the working party was that the UK controller would enter into a contractual agreement with the data subject undertaking to compensate for any damage or distress suffered as a result of the data being transferred to a third country.

---

[1] Council of Europe Document T-PD(90) 13, para 8, cited in the Draft Explanatory Memorandum, para 13.

# 8  Data protection in the telecommunications sector

## INTRODUCTION

8.1   In the early days of the telephone system, a considerable quantity of personal data was recorded concerning the calls made by subscribers. All calls would be routed through operators who would record details of the numbers called and time and duration of the connection. With the development of automated exchanges, there was for some time what might be regarded as a golden age of subscriber privacy. Although meters would keep a running total of the number of units used, no information would be recorded concerning the particular calls. As was discussed in the case of *R v Gold*,[1] in situations where this information was required, typically in the course of a criminal investigation, special equipment had to be attached to the subscriber's telephone line.

---

[1] [1988] AC 1063, [1988] 2 All ER 186.

8.2   With the development of modern, digitally based networks, it has become standard practice to record considerable amounts of data concerning individual calls. The amounts of data generated are even greater where mobile networks are involved to the extent that it is possible to track a subscriber's movements around the country. All of these activities raise data protection related issues, while other forms of behaviour relating to the use of telecommunication networks fall more naturally into the wider topic of personal privacy. The increasing number of unsolicited calls received by many consumers is frequently seen as an infringement of domestic privacy. Similar considerations apply with faxes and e-mails.

8.3   Although many aspects of telecommunications networks are regulated under the general provisions of data protection law, the EU identified a need for a more specialised form of regulation; that is, one to 'particularise and complement Directive 95/46/EC'. A major factor would appear to be that network users may determine the use to which data is put. Systems such as 'caller id', for example, may be used to screen calls or to develop a marketing database. The provisions of the general data protection Directive are therefore supplemented by more specific provisions in the form of the Directive of 15 December 1997 'concerning the processing of personal data and the protection of privacy in the telecommunications sector.'[1] The provisions of this Directive will be implemented in the UK by regulations made under the provisions of the European Communities Act 1972.

---

[1] Directive 97/66/EC; OJ No L24, 30.1.98, p 1; see Appendix 2.

## SCOPE OF THE LEGISLATION

8.4   In addition to the parties identified in the general data protection regime, the Directive will apply for the benefit of 'subscribers' and 'users'. A subscriber is defined as 'any natural or legal person who or which is a party to a contract with the provider of publicly available telecommunications services for the provision of such services'. This definition, which encompasses legal as well as natural persons, marks a significant extension to the 1998 Act. As well as defining subscribers, Art 2 of the Directive refers to 'users'; these are defined as 'any natural person using a publicly available telecommunications service, for private or business purposes, without necessarily having subscribed to this service'. A call made from a public telephone box would, for example, fall within this definition.

8.5 The Directive applies to activities taking place over public telecommunications networks, defined by reference to the physical components used for the supply of a publicly available telecommunications service (Art 3). The term 'telecommunications service' is defined, again in Art 2, as consisting 'wholly or partly in the transmission and routing of signals on telecommunications networks, with the exception of radio and television broadcasting'. This definition extends to items such as e-mail and fax transmissions and also, as stated in the Directive, to 'interactive television and video on demand' (recital (10)). These definitions are a testimony to the ever extending range of services provided over what used to be referred to as the telephone network.

## SUBSTANTIVE REQUIREMENTS

### Security

8.6 The provider of a telecommunications service is obliged to take appropriate security measures (Art 4). What is appropriate will vary depending upon the nature of the system. As with the general requirements on this point, there may be conflict between maintaining a high degree of security which might involve the use of encryption technology, and complying with national laws regulating the use of such techniques. In France, for example, the use of encryption for messages passing over public networks is prohibited.

### Confidentiality

8.7 The Directive obliges member states to ensure that an appropriate legal framework exists to safeguard the confidentiality of communications transmitted over a telecommunications network. The definition, in Art 5(1), is broad referring to the prohibition of—

> '. . . listening, tapping, storage or other kinds of interception or surveillance of communications . . . except when legally authorised, in accordance with Article 14(1).'.

Article 14(1) provides that—

> 'Member States may adopt legislative measures to restrict the scope of the obligations and rights provided for in Articles 5, . . . when such restriction constitutes a necessary measure to safeguard national security, defence, public security, the prevention, investigation, detection and prosecution of criminal offences or of unauthorised use of the telecommunications system . . .'.

In the UK this has primarily taken the form of the provisions of the Interception of Communications Act 1985 which criminalises attempts to intercept communications save under the sanction of a warrant issued by the Secretary of State. This Act, however, is couched in terms of the more physical forms of 'wire tapping'. Especially where mobile networks are involved, it is possible for communications to be intercepted without the need for any form of physical contact with the network. In the case of *R v Effik*[1] the House of Lords held that calls made from a cordless telephone were not protected under the 1985 Act where interception took place between the telephone and its base unit. Such an interpretation does not comply with the requirements of the Directive.

---

[1] [1995] 1 AC 309, [1994] 3 All ER 458.

---

8.8    A further limitation with regard to UK law in this regard, is that consent to the interception of communications can be granted by the owner of equipment used. This may have a variety of implications. A hotel owner, for example, may permit interception of calls made by guests. Again, employers might monitor calls made by employees. This latter conduct was at issue before the European Court of Human Rights in the case of *Halford v United Kingdom*,[1] where it was held that the lack of appropriate legal controls placed the UK in breach of its obligations under Art 8 of the Convention. In the Directive, the requirement is that interception should not take place without the consent of 'users'. As indicated above, this is a broader term than subscriber and again the present state of UK law will not comply with the Directive's requirements. As was described by Mr Justice Sedley in *R v Broadcasting Complaints Commission, ex p Barclay*,[2] where a complaint was lodged against an alleged invasion of privacy—

> 'The law of England and Wales at present places no general constraints upon invasions of privacy as such. Section 143 of the Broadcasting Act 1990 unambiguously limits the power of the Broadcasting Complaints Commission to adjudication upon complaints of infringement of privacy against the BBC arising out of programmes which have been broadcast. If an unwarranted infringement of privacy has been committed by the BBC otherwise than in connection with the obtaining of material included in a broadcast programme—whether because the nexus is insufficient or because no programme has been broadcast—the Commission is without adjudicative power. It cannot therefore entertain an anticipatory complaint even where, once the programme is broadcast, the complaint is bound to succeed. It follows that in this field and to this extent, as elsewhere in English law, the individual is without an effective remedy before a national authority if the right to respect for his or her private and family life is violated.'.

---

[1] (1997) 24 EHRR 523.
[2] Queens Bench Division, 4 October 1996, [1997] EMLR 62.

---

8.9    It is further provided that the prohibition is not to extend to situations where communications are recorded in the course of business for evidential or other lawful purposes (Art 5(2)). Recording of calls is commonplace in organisations which contract for goods or services both by telephone, or in the growth sector of electronic commerce by e-mail. Such practices would not be considered as involving interception under the Interception of Communications Act 1985 but might fall foul of the extended provisions of the Directive.

## Billing data

8.10 Records of calls made by telephone users can reveal a great deal about the individuals concerned. The Directive provides, as a general rule, that information used to process calls must be erased or rendered anonymous at the end of a call (Art 6(1)). Such a rule must, of course, be subject to a number of exceptions. The data will need to be processed by the operator for billing purposes, and may need to be retained in case a dispute arises as to the validity of any particular charge. The Annex to the Directive lists seven categories of data which may lawfully be processed—

- '— number or identification of the subscriber station,
- — address of the subscriber and the type of station,
- — total number of units to be charged for the accounting period,
- — called subscriber number,
- — type, starting time and duration of the calls made and/or the data volume transmitted,
- — date of the call/service,
- — other information concerning payments such as advance payments, payments by instalments, disconnection and reminders.'.

It is further provided that the operators of telecommunications services may process this data for their own marketing purposes, for example, by allowing subscribers to nominate certain frequently called numbers for receipt of a discount (Art 6(3)).

## Itemised bills

8.11 The Directive provides that subscribers are to have the right to receive non-itemised bills (Art 7(1)). At first sight it is difficult to conceive of reasons why itemised bills should not be considered desirable. Once again, however, the Directive's recognition of separate categories of subscribers and users is significant. The subscriber, as the person responsible for payment of bills, is most unlikely to object to receipt of information about the nature of calls made from the equipment. However, where other parties use the equipment, they may be reluctant to have details of the calls revealed to the subscriber. While in many cases it may be accepted that the wishes and interests of the subscriber should prevail, it is not difficult to envisage circumstances where this should not be so; for example, where calls have been made to counselling or support agencies perhaps arising from the behaviour of the subscriber towards the user. The Directive requires that national implementing measures should seek to reconcile the interests of the parties involved 'by ensuring that sufficient alternative modalities for communications or payments are available to such users and subscribers' (Art 7(2)). Even by the general standards of European Directives, this formulation is opaque. In the UK there are at least three-quarters of a million pay telephones and it might be argued that this provides sufficient access to telecommunications for users who do not want details of their calls made available to third party subscribers.

**Caller ID**

8.12  These systems allow a user to identify the number from which a call originates prior to answering the call. A related system allows a user to discover details of the last call made to the telephone, typically by dialling 1471. As with itemised billing, the systems offer major benefits, not least as a means of deterring the making of hoax or harassing calls. However, they can also be used for what might be considered as less desirable purposes. Companies might, for example, use such systems to capture the details of users who contact them with an enquiry and use this information for further canvassing. The Directive, in line with current UK practice, strikes a balance by requiring that subscribers be entitled to require that the telephone service provider blocks details of their number either on a permanent basis, or for individual calls (normally attained by prefixing 141 to the number called) (Art 8(1)). In exceptional cases attempts by callers to conceal details of the number from which a communication originates can be overridden. This may take place on a temporary basis in the event a subscriber requests the assistance of the service provider in tracing the origin of malicious or nuisance calls, and on a permanent basis in respect of lines used by the emergency services. For those receiving calls, the facility has to be made available whereby incoming calls can be rejected when the caller's identifying details are withheld (Art 9).

8.13  An additional feature of modern telecommunication networks is the facility which enables a subscriber to forward calls to another number. When the caller is using a system of 'caller id', this will indicate details of the number to which the call is being forwarded. There may be situations where this would not be considered desirable, for example, a general practitioner causing calls to be forwarded from a surgery to his home. It is, therefore, a requirement of the Directive that subscribers be given the right to require that this information not be disclosed (Art 8(4)). It is further provided that a subscriber should be able to prevent third parties from forwarding calls to the subscriber's number (Art 10). In all cases, the facility is to be provided free of charge and it is further provided that service providers must take measures to inform subscribers and users of the availability of such services.

**Unsolicited calls**

8.14  For many people, one of the banes of modern life is the receipt of a seemingly endless stream of unsolicited telephone calls offering to supply double glazing, fitted kitchens or range of other goods or services. A measure of control operates at present with the Telephone Preference Service providing a mechanism through which subscribers can register their wish not to receive such calls. The system operates, however, on a voluntary basis. The Directive provides that more formal control mechanisms are to be established although a range of options are identified which are dependent, in part, on the nature of the technology used.

8.15  Where calls are made without human intervention, for example, by automatic calling machines or programmed fax machines, it is provided that these may be made to natural persons only when the recipient has given prior consent (Art 12(1)). In the case of other forms of marketing, the Directive provides that member states may operate either an 'opt out' or an 'opt in' system (Art 12(2)). In either case, the effect would be to establish a legal regime governing telephone canvassing.[1] Although the prohibitions against unsolicited calls extends only to natural persons it is provided that member states are to guarantee that the legitimate interests of legal persons are 'sufficiently protected'.

---

[1] Directive 97/7/EC on the protection of consumers in respect of distance contracts contains further provisions with regard to canvassing, OJ L144, 4.6.97, p 19. This Directive must be implemented by 4 June 2000.

---

## Telephone directories

8.16 A significant proportion of UK telephone subscribers choose to exclude their details from the telephone directory. This possibility will continue under the Directive, but a number of additional rights are also conferred upon subscribers who are natural persons. Linked to the provisions described above relating to unsolicited calls, a subscriber will be permitted to have an indication displayed in the directory to the effect that such calls are not to be made. Additionally, subscribers may require that part of their address be excluded from the directory. This might, for example, take the form of omitting a house number. Where linguistically possible a subscriber may also direct that no indication of sex is to appear in the directory entry (Art 11(1)). A reasonable charge may be levied for removal of an entry from a directory (Art 11(2)).

# Appendix 1

# Data Protection Act 1998

# Data Protection Act 1998

(1998 c 29)

## ARRANGEMENT OF SECTIONS

### PART I
### PRELIMINARY

### PART II
### RIGHTS OF DATA SUBJECTS AND OTHERS

### PART III
### NOTIFICATION BY DATA CONTROLLERS

### PART IV
### EXEMPTIONS

*An Act to make new provision for the regulation of the processing of information relating to individuals, including the obtaining, holding, use or disclosure of such information*

[16 July 1998]

**Parliamentary debates.**

House of Lords.

2nd Reading 2 February 1998: 585 HL Official Report (5th series) col 436.

Committee Stage 23 February 1998: 586 HL Official Report (5th series) CWH col 1; 25 February 1998: 586 HL Official Report (5th series) CWH col 65.

Report 16 March 1998: 587 HL Official Report (5th series) col 465.

3rd Reading 24 March 1998: 587 HL Official Report (5th series) col 1094.

Consideration of Commons' Amendments 10 July 1998: 591 HL Official Report (5th series) col 1477.

House of Commons.

2nd Reading 20 April 1998: 310 HC Official report (6th series) col 529.

Committee Stage 5 May–4 June 1998: HC Official Report; SC D (Data Protection Bill).

Remaining stages 2 July 1998: 315 HC Official Report (6th series) col 576.

## PART I
## PRELIMINARY

### 1  Basic interpretative provisions

(1) In this Act, unless the context otherwise requires—
"data" means information which—
    (a) is being processed by means of equipment operating automatically in response to instructions given for that purpose,
    (b) is recorded with the intention that it should be processed by means of such equipment,
    (c) is recorded as part of a relevant filing system or with the intention that it should form part of a relevant filing system, or
    (d) does not fall within paragraph (a), (b) or (c) but forms part of an accessible record as defined by section 68;
"data controller" means, subject to subsection (4), a person who (either alone or jointly or in common with other persons) determines the purposes for which and the manner in which any personal data are, or are to be, processed;
"data processor", in relation to personal data, means any person (other than an employee of the data controller) who processes the data on behalf of the data controller;
"data subject" means an individual who is the subject of personal data;
"personal data" means data which relate to a living individual who can be identified—
    (a) from those data, or
    (b) from those data and other information which is in the possession of, or is likely to come into the possession of, the data controller,
and includes any expression of opinion about the individual and any indication of the intentions of the data controller or any other person in respect of the individual;
"processing", in relation to information or data, means obtaining, recording or holding the information or data or carrying out any operation or set of operations on the information or data, including—
    (a) organisation, adaptation or alteration of the information or data,
    (b) retrieval, consultation or use of the information or data,
    (c) disclosure of the information or data by transmission, dissemination or otherwise making available, or
    (d) alignment, combination, blocking, erasure or destruction of the information or data;
"relevant filing system" means any set of information relating to individuals to the extent that, although the information is not processed by means of equipment operating automatically in response to instructions given for that purpose, the set is structured, either by reference to individuals or by reference to criteria relating to individuals, in such a way that specific information relating to a particular individual is readily accessible.

(2) In this Act, unless the context otherwise requires—
    (a) "obtaining" or "recording", in relation to personal data, includes obtaining or recording the information to be contained in the data, and
    (b) "using" or "disclosing", in relation to personal data, includes using or disclosing the information contained in the data.

(3)    In determining for the purposes of this Act whether any information is recorded with the intention—

(a)    that it should be processed by means of equipment operating automatically in response to instructions given for that purpose, or

(b)    that it should form part of a relevant filing system,

it is immaterial that it is intended to be so processed or to form part of such a system only after being transferred to a country or territory outside the European Economic Area.

(4)    Where personal data are processed only for purposes for which they are required by or under any enactment to be processed, the person on whom the obligation to process the data is imposed by or under that enactment is for the purposes of this Act the data controller.

**Commencement**    16 July 1998.
**Definitions**    For "enactment", see s 70(1).
**References**    See paras 2.9–2.21, 2.35–2.40.

## 2  Sensitive personal data

In this Act "sensitive personal data" means personal data consisting of information as to—

(a)    the racial or ethnic origin of the data subject,

(b)    his political opinions,

(c)    his religious beliefs or other beliefs of a similar nature,

(d)    whether he is a member of a trade union (within the meaning of the Trade Union and Labour Relations (Consolidation) Act 1992,

(e)    his physical or mental health or condition,

(f)    his sexual life,

(g)    the commission or alleged commission by him of any offence, or

(h)    any proceedings for any offence committed or alleged to have been committed by him, the disposal of such proceedings or the sentence of any court in such proceedings.

**Commencement**    16 July 1998.
**Definitions**    For "data", "data subject" and "personal data", see s 1(1).
**References**    See paras 2.22, 2.23.

## 3  The special purposes

In this Act "the special purposes" means any one or more of the following—

(a)    the purposes of journalism,

(b)    artistic purposes, and

(c)    literary purposes.

**Commencement**    16 July 1998.
**References**    See paras 6.4, 6.5.

## 4  The data protection principles

(1)    References in this Act to the data protection principles are to the principles set out in Part I of Schedule 1.

(2)    Those principles are to be interpreted in accordance with Part II of Schedule 1.

(3)    Schedule 2 (which applies to all personal data) and Schedule 3 (which applies only to sensitive personal data) set out conditions applying for the purposes of the first principle; and Schedule 4 sets out cases in which the eighth principle does not apply.

(4)   Subject to section 27(1), it shall be the duty of a data controller to comply with the data protection principles in relation to all personal data with respect to which he is the data controller.

**Commencement**   to be appointed.
**Definitions**   For "personal data", see s 1(1) (and see also as to "personal data" in connection with the data protection principles, s 27(1)); for "data controller", s 1(1), (4); for "sensitive personal data", see s 2.
**References**   See Ch 4.

## 5  Application of Act

(1)   Except as otherwise provided by or under section 54, this Act applies to a data controller in respect of any data only if—

>   (a)   the data controller is established in the United Kingdom and the data are processed in the context of that establishment, or
>   (b)   the data controller is established neither in the United Kingdom nor in any other EEA State but uses equipment in the United Kingdom for processing the data otherwise than for the purposes of transit through the United Kingdom.

(2)   A data controller falling within subsection (1)(b) must nominate for the purposes of this Act a representative established in the United Kingdom.

(3)   For the purposes of subsections (1) and (2), each of the following is to be treated as established in the United Kingdom—

>   (a)   an individual who is ordinarily resident in the United Kingdom,
>   (b)   a body incorporated under the law of, or of any part of, the United Kingdom,
>   (c)   a partnership or other unincorporated association formed under the law of any part of the United Kingdom, and
>   (d)   any person who does not fall within paragraph (a), (b) or (c) but maintains in the United Kingdom—
>> (i)   an office, branch or agency through which he carries on any activity, or
>> (ii)   a regular practice;

and the reference to establishment in any other EEA State has a corresponding meaning.

**Commencement**   to be appointed.
**Definitions**   For "data" and "processing", see s 1(1) (and note also as to "processing", s 39, Sch 8, Pt II, para 5); for "data controller", see s 1(1), (4); for "EEA State", see s 70(1).
**References**   See paras 2.41–2.46.

## 6  The Commissioner and the Tribunal

(1)   The office originally established by section 3(1)(a) of the Data Protection Act 1984 as the office of Data Protection Registrar shall continue to exist for the purposes of this Act but shall be known as the office of Data Protection Commissioner; and in this Act the Data Protection Commissioner is referred to as "the Commissioner".

(2)   The Commissioner shall be appointed by Her Majesty by Letters Patent.

(3)   For the purposes of this Act there shall continue to be a Data Protection Tribunal (in this Act referred to as "the Tribunal").

(4)   The Tribunal shall consist of—

>   (a)   a chairman appointed by the Lord Chancellor after consultation with the Lord Advocate,

(b)    such number of deputy chairmen so appointed as the Lord Chancellor may determine, and

(c)    such number of other members appointed by the Secretary of State as he may determine.

(5)    The members of the Tribunal appointed under subsection (4)(a) and (b) shall be—

(a)    persons who have a 7 year general qualification, within the meaning of section 71 of the Courts and Legal Services Act 1990,

(b)    advocates or solicitors in Scotland of at least 7 years' standing, or

(c)    members of the bar of Northern Ireland or solicitors of the Supreme Court of Northern Ireland of at least 7 years' standing.

(6)    The members of the Tribunal appointed under subsection (4)(c) shall be—

(a)    persons to represent the interests of data subjects, and

(b)    persons to represent the interests of data controllers.

(7)    Schedule 5 has effect in relation to the Commissioner and the Tribunal.

**Commencement**    to be appointed.
**Definitions**    For "data subject", see s 1(1); for "data controller", see s 1(1), (4).
**References**    See paras 3.4, 3.61, 3.62.

# PART II
## RIGHTS OF DATA SUBJECTS AND OTHERS

### 7  Right of access to personal data

(1)    Subject to the following provisions of this section and to sections 8 and 9, an individual is entitled—

(a)    to be informed by any data controller whether personal data of which that individual is the data subject are being processed by or on behalf of that data controller,

(b)    if that is the case, to be given by the data controller a description of—

(i)    the personal data of which that individual is the data subject,

(ii)    the purposes for which they are being or are to be processed, and

(iii)    the recipients or classes of recipients to whom they are or may be disclosed,

(c)    to have communicated to him in an intelligible form—

(i)    the information constituting any personal data of which that individual is the data subject, and

(ii)    any information available to the data controller as to the source of those data, and

(d)    where the processing by automatic means of personal data of which that individual is the data subject for the purpose of evaluating matters relating to him such as, for example, his performance at work, his creditworthiness, his reliability or his conduct, has constituted or is likely to constitute the sole basis for any decision significantly affecting him, to be informed by the data controller of the logic involved in that decision-taking.

(2)    A data controller is not obliged to supply any information under subsection (1) unless he has received—

(a)    a request in writing, and

(b)    except in prescribed cases, such fee (not exceeding the prescribed maximum) as he may require.

(3)    A data controller is not obliged to comply with a request under this section unless he is supplied with such information as he may reasonably require in order to

satisfy himself as to the identity of the person making the request and to locate the information which that person seeks.

(4)   Where a data controller cannot comply with the request without disclosing information relating to another individual who can be identified from that information, he is not obliged to comply with the request unless—

    (a)   the other individual has consented to the disclosure of the information to the person making the request, or

    (b)   it is reasonable in all the circumstances to comply with the request without the consent of the other individual.

(5)   In subsection (4) the reference to information relating to another individual includes a reference to information identifying that individual as the source of the information sought by the request; and that subsection is not to be construed as excusing a data controller from communicating so much of the information sought by the request as can be communicated without disclosing the identity of the other individual concerned, whether by the omission of names or other identifying particulars or otherwise.

(6)   In determining for the purposes of subsection (4)(b) whether it is reasonable in all the circumstances to comply with the request without the consent of the other individual concerned, regard shall be had, in particular, to—

    (a)   any duty of confidentiality owed to the other individual,

    (b)   any steps taken by the data controller with a view to seeking the consent of the other individual,

    (c)   whether the other individual is capable of giving consent, and

    (d)   any express refusal of consent by the other individual.

(7)   An individual making a request under this section may, in such cases as may be prescribed, specify that his request is limited to personal data of any prescribed description.

(8)   Subject to subsection (4), a data controller shall comply with a request under this section promptly and in any event before the end of the prescribed period beginning with the relevant day.

(9)   If a court is satisfied on the application of any person who has made a request under the foregoing provisions of this section that the data controller in question has failed to comply with the request in contravention of those provisions, the court may order him to comply with the request.

(10)   In this section—

    "prescribed" means prescribed by the Secretary of State by regulations;

    "the prescribed maximum" means such amount as may be prescribed;

    "the prescribed period" means forty days or such other period as may be prescribed;

    "the relevant day", in relation to a request under this section, means the day on which the data controller receives the request or, if later, the first day on which the data controller has both the required fee and the information referred to in subsection (3).

(11)   Different amounts or periods may be prescribed under this section in relation to different cases.

**Commencement**   16 July 1998 (sub-ss (7), (10), (11), in so far as conferring the power to make subordinate legislation); to be appointed (otherwise).
**Definitions**   For "data", "data subject", "personal data" and "processing", see s 1(1) (and note also as to "personal data" and the processing thereof, s 27(1), and as to "processing", s 39, Sch 8, Pt II, para 5); for "data controller", see s 1(1), (4); as to "disclosing", see s 1(2); for "recipient", see s 70(1).
**References**   See paras 5.2–5.6, 5.14–5.19.

## 8 Provisions supplementary to section 7

(1)    The Secretary of State may by regulations provide that, in such cases as may be prescribed, a request for information under any provision of subsection (1) of section 7 is to be treated as extending also to information under other provisions of that subsection.

(2)    The obligation imposed by section 7(1)(c)(i) must be complied with by supplying the data subject with a copy of the information in permanent form unless—

      (a)    the supply of such a copy is not possible or would involve disproportionate effort, or

      (b)    the data subject agrees otherwise;

and where any of the information referred to in section 7(1)(c)(i) is expressed in terms which are not intelligible without explanation the copy must be accompanied by an explanation of those terms.

(3)    Where a data controller has previously complied with a request made under section 7 by an individual, the data controller is not obliged to comply with a subsequent identical or similar request under that section by that individual unless a reasonable interval has elapsed between compliance with the previous request and the making of the current request.

(4)    In determining for the purposes of subsection (3) whether requests under section 7 are made at reasonable intervals, regard shall be had to the nature of the data, the purpose for which the data are processed and the frequency with which the data are altered.

(5)    Section 7(1)(d) is not to be regarded as requiring the provision of information as to the logic involved in any decision-taking if, and to the extent that, the information constitutes a trade secret.

(6)    The information to be supplied pursuant to a request under section 7 must be supplied by reference to the data in question at the time when the request is received, except that it may take account of any amendment or deletion made between that time and the time when the information is supplied, being an amendment or deletion that would have been made regardless of the receipt of the request.

(7)    For the purposes of section 7(4) and (5) another individual can be identified from the information being disclosed if he can be identified from that information, or from that and any other information which, in the reasonable belief of the data controller, is likely to be in, or to come into, the possession of the data subject making the request.

**Commencement**    16 July 1998 (sub-s (1), in so far as conferring the power to make subordinate legislation); to be appointed (otherwise).
**Definitions**    For "data", "data subject" and "processing", see s 1(1) (and note also as to "processing", s 39, Sch 8, Pt II, para 5); for "data controller", see s 1(1), (4); as to "disclosing", see s 1(2)(b).
**References**    See paras 5.2, 5.5.

## 9 Application of section 7 where data controller is credit reference agency

(1)    Where the data controller is a credit reference agency, section 7 has effect subject to the provisions of this section.

(2)    An individual making a request under section 7 may limit his request to personal data relevant to his financial standing, and shall be taken to have so limited his request unless the request shows a contrary intention.

(3)    Where the data controller receives a request under section 7 in a case where personal data of which the individual making the request is the data subject are being processed by or on behalf of the data controller, the obligation to supply information under that section includes an obligation to give the individual making the request a

statement, in such form as may be prescribed by the Secretary of State by regulations, of the individual's rights—

(a)    under section 159 of the Consumer Credit Act 1974, and

(b)    to the extent required by the prescribed form, under this Act.

**Commencement**   16 July 1998 (sub-s (3), in so far as conferring the power to make subordinate legislation); to be appointed (otherwise).
**Definitions**   For "data", "personal data" and "processing", see s 1(1) (and note also as to "personal data" and the processing thereof, s 27(1), and as to "processing", s 39, Sch 8, Pt II, para 5); for "data controller", see s 1(1), (4); for "credit reference agency", see s 70(1).
**References**   See para 5.7.

## 10  Right to prevent processing likely to cause damage or distress

(1)    Subject to subsection (2), an individual is entitled at any time by notice in writing to a data controller to require the data controller at the end of such period as is reasonable in the circumstances to cease, or not to begin, processing, or processing for a specified purpose or in a specified manner, any personal data in respect of which he is the data subject, on the ground that, for specified reasons—

(a)    the processing of those data or their processing for that purpose or in that manner is causing or is likely to cause substantial damage or substantial distress to him or to another, and

(b)    that damage or distress is or would be unwarranted.

(2)    Subsection (1) does not apply—

(a)    in a case where any of the conditions in paragraphs 1 to 4 of Schedule 2 is met, or

(b)    in such other cases as may be prescribed by the Secretary of State by order.

(3)    The data controller must within twenty-one days of receiving a notice under subsection (1) ("the data subject notice") give the individual who gave it a written notice—

(a)    stating that he has complied or intends to comply with the data subject notice, or

(b)    stating his reasons for regarding the data subject notice as to any extent unjustified and the extent (if any) to which he has complied or intends to comply with it.

(4)    If a court is satisfied, on the application of any person who has given a notice under subsection (1) which appears to the court to be justified (or to be justified to any extent), that the data controller in question has failed to comply with the notice, the court may order him to take such steps for complying with the notice (or for complying with it to that extent) as the court thinks fit.

(5)    The failure by a data subject to exercise the right conferred by subsection (1) or section 11(1) does not affect any other right conferred on him by this Part.

**Commencement**   16 July 1998 (sub-s (2), in so far as conferring the power to make subordinate legislation); to be appointed (otherwise).
**Definitions**   For "data subject", "personal data" and "processing", see s 1(1) (and note also as to "personal data" and the processing thereof, s 27(1), and as to "processing", s 39, Sch 8, Pt II, para 5); for "data controller", see s 1(1), (4).
**References**   See paras 5.43, 5.44.

## 11  Right to prevent processing for purposes of direct marketing

(1)    An individual is entitled at any time by notice in writing to a data controller to require the data controller at the end of such period as is reasonable in the circumstances to cease, or not to begin, processing for the purposes of direct marketing personal data in respect of which he is the data subject.

(2)    If the court is satisfied, on the application of any person who has given a notice under subsection (1), that the data controller has failed to comply with the notice, the court may order him to take such steps for complying with the notice as the court thinks fit.

(3)    In this section "direct marketing" means the communication (by whatever means) of any advertising or marketing material which is directed to particular individuals.

---

**Commencement**   to be appointed.
**Definitions**   For "data subject", "personal data" and "processing", see s 1(1) (and note also as to "personal data" and the processing thereof, s 27(1), and as to "processing", s 39, Sch 8, Pt II, para 5); for "data controller", see s 1(1), (4).
**References**   See paras 5.39–5.42.

---

## 12   Rights in relation to automated decision-taking

(1)    An individual is entitled at any time, by notice in writing to any data controller, to require the data controller to ensure that no decision taken by or on behalf of the data controller which significantly affects that individual is based solely on the processing by automatic means of personal data in respect of which that individual is the data subject for the purpose of evaluating matters relating to him such as, for example, his performance at work, his creditworthiness, his reliability or his conduct.

(2)    Where, in a case where no notice under subsection (1) has effect, a decision which significantly affects an individual is based solely on such processing as is mentioned in subsection (1)—

  (a)    the data controller must as soon as reasonably practicable notify the individual that the decision was taken on that basis, and

  (b)    the individual is entitled, within twenty-one days of receiving that notification from the data controller, by notice in writing to require the data controller to reconsider the decision or to take a new decision otherwise than on that basis.

(3)    The data controller must, within twenty-one days of receiving a notice under subsection (2)(b) ("the data subject notice") give the individual a written notice specifying the steps that he intends to take to comply with the data subject notice.

(4)    A notice under subsection (1) does not have effect in relation to an exempt decision; and nothing in subsection (2) applies to an exempt decision.

(5)    In subsection (4) "exempt decision" means any decision—

  (a)    in respect of which the condition in subsection (6) and the condition in subsection (7) are met, or

  (b)    which is made in such other circumstances as may be prescribed by the Secretary of State by order.

(6)    The condition in this subsection is that the decision—

  (a)    is taken in the course of steps taken—

    (i)    for the purpose of considering whether to enter into a contract with the data subject,

    (ii)    with a view to entering into such a contract, or

    (iii)    in the course of performing such a contract, or

  (b)    is authorised or required by or under any enactment.

(7)    The condition in this subsection is that either—

  (a)    the effect of the decision is to grant a request of the data subject, or

  (b)    steps have been taken to safeguard the legitimate interests of the data subject (for example, by allowing him to make representations).

(8)   If a court is satisfied on the application of a data subject that a person taking a decision in respect of him ("the responsible person") has failed to comply with subsection (1) or (2)(b), the court may order the responsible person to reconsider the decision, or to take a new decision which is not based solely on such processing as is mentioned in subsection (1).

(9)   An order under subsection (8) shall not affect the rights of any person other than the data subject and the responsible person.

**Commencement**  16 July 1998 (sub-s (5), in so far as conferring the power to make subordinate legislation); to be appointed (otherwise).
**Definitions**   For "data subject", "personal data" and "processing", see s 1(1) (and note also as to "personal data" and the processing thereof, s 27(1), and as to "processing", s 39, Sch 8, Pt II, para 5); for "data controller", see s 1(1), (4); for "enactment", see s 70(1).
**References**   See paras 5.54–5.59.

## [12A   Rights of data subjects in relation to exempt manual data

(1)   A data subject is entitled at any time by notice in writing—
  (a)  to require the data controller to rectify, block, erase or destroy exempt manual data which are inaccurate or incomplete, or
  (b)  to require the data controller to cease holding exempt manual data in a way incompatible with the legitimate purposes pursued by the data controller.

(2)   A notice under subsection (1)(a) or (b) must state the data subject's reasons for believing that the data are inaccurate or incomplete or, as the case may be, his reasons for believing that they are held in a way incompatible with the legitimate purposes pursued by the data controller.

(3)   If the court is satisfied, on the application of any person who has given a notice under subsection (1) which appears to the court to be justified (or to be justified to any extent) that the data controller in question has failed to comply with the notice, the court may order him to take such steps for complying with the notice (or for complying with it to that extent) as the court thinks fit.

(4)   In this section "exempt manual data" means—
  (a)  in relation to the first transitional period, as defined by paragraph 1(2) of Schedule 8, data to which paragraph 3 or 4 of that Schedule applies, and
  (b)  in relation to the second transitional period, as so defined, data to which paragraph 14 of that Schedule applies.

(5)   For the purposes of this section personal data are incomplete if, and only if, the data, although not inaccurate, are such that their incompleteness would constitute a contravention of the third or fourth data protection principles, if those principles applied to the data.]

**Commencement**   to be appointed
**Modification**   during the period beginning with the commencement of s 72 and ending with 23 October 2007, this section is inserted by s 72, Sch 13, para 1.
**Definitions**   For "data" and "data subject", see s 1(1); for "data controller", see s 1(1), (4); for "the data protection principles", see s 4; as to "inaccurate", see s 70(2).
**References**   See para 1.28.

## 13   Compensation for failure to comply with certain requirements

(1)   An individual who suffers damage by reason of any contravention by a data controller of any of the requirements of this Act is entitled to compensation from the data controller for that damage.

(2)   An individual who suffers distress by reason of any contravention by a data controller of any of the requirements of this Act is entitled to compensation from the data controller for that distress if—

(a)    the individual also suffers damage by reason of the contravention, or

(b)    the contravention relates to the processing of personal data for the special purposes.

(3)    In proceedings brought against a person by virtue of this section it is a defence to prove that he had taken such care as in all the circumstances was reasonably required to comply with the requirement concerned.

**Commencement**  to be appointed.
**Definitions**    For "personal data" and "processing", see s 1(1) (and note also as to "personal data" and the processing thereof, s 27(1), and as to "processing", s 39, Sch 8, Pt II, para 5); for "data controller", see s 1(1), (4); for "the special purposes", see s 3.
**References**    See paras 5.47, 5.48.

## 14  Rectification, blocking, erasure and destruction

(1)    If a court is satisfied on the application of a data subject that personal data of which the applicant is the subject are inaccurate, the court may order the data controller to rectify, block, erase or destroy those data and any other personal data in respect of which he is the data controller and which contain an expression of opinion which appears to the court to be based on the inaccurate data.

(2)    Subsection (1) applies whether or not the data accurately record information received or obtained by the data controller from the data subject or a third party but where the data accurately record such information, then—

(a)    if the requirements mentioned in paragraph 7 of Part II of Schedule 1 have been complied with, the court may, instead of making an order under subsection (1), make an order requiring the data to be supplemented by such statement of the true facts relating to the matters dealt with by the data as the court may approve, and

(b)    if all or any of those requirements have not been complied with, the court may, instead of making an order under that subsection, make such order as it thinks fit for securing compliance with those requirements with or without a further order requiring the data to be supplemented by such a statement as is mentioned in paragraph (a).

(3)    Where the court

(a)    makes an order under subsection (1), or

(b)    is satisfied on the application of a data subject that personal data of which he was the data subject and which have been rectified, blocked, erased or destroyed were inaccurate,

it may, where it considers it reasonably practicable, order the data controller to notify third parties to whom the data have been disclosed of the rectification, blocking, erasure or destruction.

(4)    If a court is satisfied on the application of a data subject—

(a)    that he has suffered damage by reason of any contravention by a data controller of any of the requirements of this Act in respect of any personal data, in circumstances entitling him to compensation under section 13, and

(b)    that there is a substantial risk of further contravention in respect of those data in such circumstances,

the court may order the rectification, blocking, erasure or destruction of any of those data.

(5)    Where the court makes an order under subsection (4) it may, where it considers it reasonably practicable, order the data controller to notify third parties to whom the data have been disclosed of the rectification, blocking, erasure or destruction.

(6)    In determining whether it is reasonably practicable to require such notification as is mentioned in subsection (3) or (5) the court shall have regard, in particular, to the number of persons who would have to be notified.

**Commencement**   to be appointed.
**Definitions**    For "data", "data subject" and "personal data", see s 1(1) (and note also as to "personal data", s 27(1)); for "data controller", see s 1(1), (4); as to "obtaining" data, see s 1(2)(a); as to "disclosing" data, see s 1(2)(b); for "third party", see s 70(1); as to "inaccurate", see s 70(2).
**References**    See paras 5.45, 5.46.

## 15  Jurisdiction and procedure

(1)    The jurisdiction conferred by sections 7 to 14 is exercisable by the High Court or a county court or, in Scotland, by the Court of Session or the sheriff.

(2)    For the purpose of determining any question whether an applicant under subsection (9) of section 7 is entitled to the information which he seeks (including any question whether any relevant data are exempt from that section by virtue of Part IV) a court may require the information constituting any data processed by or on behalf of the data controller and any information as to the logic involved in any decision-taking as mentioned in section 7(1)(d) to be made available for its own inspection but shall not, pending the determination of that question in the applicant's favour, require the information sought by the applicant to be disclosed to him or his representatives whether by discovery (or, in Scotland, recovery) or otherwise.

**Commencement**   to be appointed.
**Definitions**    For "data" and "processing", see s 1(1); for "data controller", see s 1(1), (4); as to "disclosing", see s 1(2)(b).

# PART III
# NOTIFICATION BY DATA CONTROLLERS

## 16  Preliminary

(1)    In this Part "the registrable particulars", in relation to a data controller, means—

    (a)    his name and address,

    (b)    if he has nominated a representative for the purposes of this Act, the name and address of the representative,

    (c)    a description of the personal data being or to be processed by or on behalf of the data controller and of the category or categories of data subject to which they relate,

    (d)    a description of the purpose or purposes for which the data are being or are to be processed,

    (e)    a description of any recipient or recipients to whom the data controller intends or may wish to disclose the data,

    (f)    the names, or a description of, any countries or territories outside the European Economic Area to which the data controller directly or indirectly transfers, or intends or may wish directly or indirectly to transfer, the data, and

    (g)    in any case where—

        (i)    personal data are being, or are intended to be, processed in circumstances in which the prohibition in subsection (1) of section 17 is excluded by subsection (2) or (3) of that section, and

        (ii)    the notification does not extend to those data,

  a statement of that fact.

(2)    In this Part—

"fees regulations" means regulations made by the Secretary of State under section 18(5) or 19(4) or (7);

"notification regulations" means regulations made by the Secretary of State under the other provisions of this Part;

"prescribed", except where used in relation to fees regulations, means prescribed by notification regulations.

(3)    For the purposes of this Part, so far as it relates to the addresses of data controllers—

(a)    the address of a registered company is that of its registered office, and

(b)    the address of a person (other than a registered company) carrying on a business is that of his principal place of business in the United Kingdom.

**Commencement**    to be appointed.

**Definitions**    For "data", "data subject", "personal data", and "processing", see s 1(1) (and note also as to "personal data" and the processing thereof, s 27(1), and as to "processing", s 39, Sch 8, Pt II, para 5); for "data controller", see s 1(1), (4); as to "disclosing", see s 1(2)(b); for "business", "recipient" and "registered company", see s 70(1).

**References**    See paras 3.25, 3.26.

## 17 Prohibition on processing without registration

(1)    Subject to the following provisions of this section, personal data must not be processed unless an entry in respect of the data controller is included in the register maintained by the Commissioner under section 19 (or is treated by notification regulations made by virtue of section 19(3) as being so included).

(2)    Except where the processing is assessable processing for the purposes of section 22, subsection (1) does not apply in relation to personal data consisting of information which falls neither within paragraph (a) of the definition of "data" in section 1(1) nor within paragraph (b) of that definition.

(3)    If it appears to the Secretary of State that processing of a particular description is unlikely to prejudice the rights and freedoms of data subjects, notification regulations may provide that, in such cases as may be prescribed, subsection (1) is not to apply in relation to processing of that description.

(4)    Subsection (1) does not apply in relation to any processing whose sole purpose is the maintenance of a public register.

**Commencement**    16 July 1998 (sub-s (3), in so far as conferring the power to make subordinate legislation); to be appointed (otherwise).

**Definitions**    For "data", "data subject", "personal data" and "processing", see s 1(1) (and note also as to "personal data" and the processing thereof, s 27(1), and as to "processing", s 39, Sch 8, Pt II, para 5); for "data controller", see s 1(1), (4); for "the Commissioner", see s 6(1); for "notification regulations" and "prescribed", see s 16(2); for "public register", see s 70(1).

**References**    See para 3.29.

## 18 Notification by data controllers

(1)    Any data controller who wishes to be included in the register maintained under section 19 shall give a notification to the Commissioner under this section.

(2)    A notification under this section must specify in accordance with notification regulations—

(a)    the registrable particulars, and

(b)    a general description of measures to be taken for the purpose of complying with the seventh data protection principle.

(3)    Notification regulations made by virtue of subsection (2) may provide for the determination by the Commissioner, in accordance with any requirements of the regulations, of the form in which the registrable particulars and the description mentioned in subsection (2)(b) are to be specified, including in particular the detail required for the purposes of section 16(1)(c), (d), (e) and (f) and subsection (2)(b).

(4)    Notification regulations may make provision as to the giving of notification—

(a)    by partnerships, or

(b)    in other cases where two or more persons are the data controllers in respect of any personal data.

(5)    The notification must be accompanied by such fee as may be prescribed by fees regulations.

(6)    Notification regulations may provide for any fee paid under subsection (5) or section 19(4) to be refunded in prescribed circumstances.

---

**Commencement**    16 July 1998 (sub-ss (2)–(6), in so far as conferring the power to make subordinate legislation); to be appointed (otherwise).

**Definitions**    For "personal data", see s 1(1); (and note s 27(1)); for "data controller", see s 1(1), (4); for "the data protection principles", see s 4; for "the Commissioner", see s 6(1); for "registrable particulars", see s 16(1); for "fees regulations", "notification regulations" and "prescribed", see s 16(2).

**References**    See paras 3.25–3.28.

## 19  Register of notifications

(1)    The Commissioner shall—

(a)    maintain a register of persons who have given notification under section 18, and

(b)    make an entry in the register in pursuance of each notification received by him under that section from a person in respect of whom no entry as data controller was for the time being included in the register.

(2)    Each entry in the register shall consist of—

(a)    the registrable particulars notified under section 18 or, as the case requires, those particulars as amended in pursuance of section 20(4), and

(b)    such other information as the Commissioner may be authorised or required by notification regulations to include in the register.

(3)    Notification regulations may make provision as to the time as from which any entry in respect of a data controller is to be treated for the purposes of section 17 as having been made in the register.

(4)    No entry shall be retained in the register for more than the relevant time except on payment of such fee as may be prescribed by fees regulations.

(5)    In subsection (4) "the relevant time" means twelve months or such other period as may be prescribed by notification regulations; and different periods may be prescribed in relation to different cases.

(6)    The Commissioner—

(a)    shall provide facilities for making the information contained in the entries in the register available for inspection (in visible and legible form) by members of the public at all reasonable hours and free of charge, and

(b)    may provide such other facilities for making the information contained in those entries available to the public free of charge as he considers appropriate.

(7)    The Commissioner shall, on payment of such fee, if any, as may be prescribed by fees regulations, supply any member of the public with a duly certified copy in writing of the particulars contained in any entry made in the register.

**Commencement**  16 July 1998 (sub-ss (3), (4), (7), in so far as conferring the power to make subordinate legislation); to be appointed (otherwise).
**Definitions**    For "data controller", see s 1(1), (4); for "the Commissioner", see s 6(1); for "registrable particulars", see s 16(1); for "fees regulations", "notification regulations" and "prescribed", see s 16(2).
**References**    See para 3.29.

## 20  Duty to notify changes

(1)    For the purpose specified in subsection (2), notification regulations shall include provision imposing on every person in respect of whom an entry as a data controller is for the time being included in the register maintained under section 19 a duty to notify to the Commissioner, in such circumstances and at such time or times and in such form as may be prescribed, such matters relating to the registrable particulars and measures taken as mentioned in section 18(2)(b) as may be prescribed.

(2)    The purpose referred to in subsection (1) is that of ensuring, so far as practicable, that at any time—

(a)    the entries in the register maintained under section 19 contain current names and addresses and describe the current practice or intentions of the data controller with respect to the processing of personal data, and

(b)    the Commissioner is provided with a general description of measures currently being taken as mentioned in section 18(2)(b).

(3)    Subsection (3) of section 18 has effect in relation to notification regulations made by virtue of subsection (1) as it has effect in relation to notification regulations made by virtue of subsection (2) of that section.

(4)    On receiving any notification under notification regulations made by virtue of subsection (1), the Commissioner shall make such amendments of the relevant entry in the register maintained under section 19 as are necessary to take account of the notification.

**Commencement**  16 July 1998 (sub-s (1), in so far as conferring the power to make subordinate legislation); to be appointed (otherwise).
**Definitions**    For "personal data" and "processing", see s 1(1) (and note also as to "personal data" and the processing thereof, s 27(1), and as to "processing", s 39, Sch 8, Pt II, para 5); for "data controller", see s 1(1), (4); for "the Commissioner", see s 6(1); for "registrable particulars", see s 16(1); for "notification regulations" and "prescribed", see s 16(2); for "address", see s 16(3).
**References**    See paras 3.27, 3.30.

## 21  Offences

(1)    If section 17(1) is contravened, the data controller is guilty of an offence.

(2)    Any person who fails to comply with the duty imposed by notification regulations made by virtue of section 20(1) is guilty of an offence.

(3)    It shall be a defence for a person charged with an offence under subsection (2) to show that he exercised all due diligence to comply with the duty.

**Commencement**  to be appointed.
**Definitions**    For "data controller", see s 1(1), (4); for "notification regulations", see s 16(2).
**References**    See para 3.29.

## 22 Preliminary assessment by Commissioner

(1)   In this section "assessable processing" means processing which is of a description specified in an order made by the Secretary of State as appearing to him to be particularly likely—

(a)   to cause substantial damage or substantial distress to data subjects, or

(b)   otherwise significantly to prejudice the rights and freedoms of data subjects.

(2)   On receiving notification from any data controller under section 18 or under notification regulations made by virtue of section 20 the Commissioner shall consider—

(a)   whether any of the processing to which the notification relates is assessable processing, and

(b)   if so, whether the assessable processing is likely to comply with the provisions of this Act.

(3)   Subject to subsection (4), the Commissioner shall, within the period of twenty-eight days beginning with the day on which he receives a notification which relates to assessable processing, give a notice to the data controller stating the extent to which the Commissioner is of the opinion that the processing is likely or unlikely to comply with the provisions of this Act.

(4)   Before the end of the period referred to in subsection (3) the Commissioner may, by reason of special circumstances, extend that period on one occasion only by notice to the data controller by such further period not exceeding fourteen days as the Commissioner may specify in the notice.

(5)   No assessable processing in respect of which a notification has been given the Commissioner as mentioned in subsection (2) shall be carried on unless either—

(a)   the period of twenty-eight days beginning with the day on which the notification is received by the Commissioner (or, in a case falling within subsection (4), that period as extended under that subsection) has elapsed, or

(b)   before the end of that period (or that period as so extended) the data controller has received a notice from the Commissioner under subsection (3) in respect of the processing.

(6)   Where subsection (5) is contravened, the data controller is guilty of an offence.

(7)   The Secretary of State may by order amend subsections (3), (4) and (5) by substituting for the number of days for the time being specified there a different number specified in the order.

**Commencement**   16 July 1998 (sub-ss (1), (7), in so far as conferring the power to make subordinate legislation); to be appointed (otherwise).
**Definitions**   For "data subject" and "processing", see s 1(1) (and note also as to "processing", s 39, Sch 8, Pt II, para 5); for "data controller", see s1(1), (4); for "the Commissioner", see s 6(1); for "notification regulations", see s 16(2).
**References**   See paras 3.32–3.35.

## 23 Power to make provision for appointment of data protection supervisors

(1)   The Secretary of State may by order—

(a)   make provision under which a data controller may appoint a person to act as a data protection supervisor responsible in particular for monitoring in an independent manner the data controller's compliance with the provisions of this Act, and

(b) provide that, in relation to any data controller who has appointed a data protection supervisor in accordance with the provisions of the order and who complies with such conditions as may be specified in the order, the provisions of this Part are to have effect subject to such exemptions or other modifications as may be specified in the order.

(2) An order under this section may—

(a) impose duties on data protection supervisors in relation to the Commissioner, and

(b) confer functions on the Commissioner in relation to data protection supervisors.

**Commencement** 16 July 1998 (in so far as conferring the power to make subordinate legislation); to be appointed (otherwise).
**Definitions** For "data controller", see s 1(1), (4); for " the Commissioner", see s 6(1).
**References** See paras 3.37, 3.38.

## 24 Duty of certain data controllers to make certain information available

(1) Subject to subsection (3), where personal data are processed in a case where—

(a) by virtue of subsection (2) or (3) of section 17, subsection (1) of that section does not apply to the processing, and

(b) the data controller has not notified the relevant particulars in respect of that processing under section 18,

the data controller must, within twenty-one days of receiving a written request from any person, make the relevant particulars available to that person in writing free of charge.

(2) In this section "the relevant particulars" means the particulars referred to in paragraphs (a) to (f) of section 16(1).

(3) This section has effect subject to any exemption conferred for the purposes of this section by notification regulations.

(4) Any data controller who fails to comply with the duty imposed by subsection (1) is guilty of an offence.

(5) It shall be a defence for a person charged with an offence under subsection (4) to show that he exercised all due diligence to comply with the duty.

**Commencement** 16 July 1998 (sub-s (3), in so far as conferring the power to make subordinate legislation); to be appointed (otherwise).
**Definitions** For "personal data" and "processing", see s 1(1) (and note also as to "personal data" and the processing thereof, s 27(1), and as to "processing", s 39, Sch 8, Pt II, para 5); for "data controller", see s 1(1), (4); for "notification regulations", see s 16(2).
**References** See para 3.36.

## 25 Functions of Commissioner in relation to making of notification regulations

(1) As soon as practicable after the passing of this Act, the Commissioner shall submit to the Secretary of State proposals as to the provisions to be included in the first notification regulations.

(2) The Commissioner shall keep under review the working of notification regulations and may from time to time submit to the Secretary of State proposals as to amendments to be made to the regulations.

(3) The Secretary of State may from time to time require the Commissioner to consider any matter relating to notification regulations and to submit to him

proposals as to amendments to be made to the regulations in connection with that matter.

(4)    Before making any notification regulations, the Secretary of State shall—

    (a)    consider any proposals made to him by the Commissioner under subsection (1), (2) or (3), and

    (b)    consult the Commissioner.

**Commencement**  16 July 1998 (sub-ss (1), (4)), (sub-ss (2), (3), in so far as conferring the power to make subordinate legislation); to be appointed (otherwise).
**Definitions**    For "the Commissioner", see s 6(1); for "notification regulations", see s 16(2).
**References**    See para 3.23.

## 26  Fees regulations

(1)    Fees regulations prescribing fees for the purposes of any provision of this Part may provide for different fees to be payable in different cases.

(2)    In making any fees regulations, the Secretary of State shall have regard to the desirability of securing that the fees payable to the Commissioner are sufficient to offset—

    (a)    the expenses incurred by the Commissioner and the Tribunal in discharging their functions and any expenses of the Secretary of State in respect of the Commissioner or the Tribunal, and

    (b)    to the extent that the Secretary of State considers appropriate—

        (i)    any deficit previously incurred (whether before or after the passing of this Act) in respect of the expenses mentioned in paragraph (a), and

        (ii)    expenses incurred or to be incurred by the Secretary of State in respect of the inclusion of any officers or staff of the Commissioner in any scheme under section 1 of the Superannuation Act 1972.

**Commencement**  16 July 1998.
**Definitions**    For "the Commissioner", see s 6(1); for "the Tribunal", see s 6(3); for "fees regulations", see s 16(2).
**References**    See para 3.24.

# PART IV
# EXEMPTIONS

## 27  Preliminary

(1)    References in any of the data protection principles or any provision of Parts II and III to personal data or to the processing of personal data do not include references to data or processing which by virtue of this Part are exempt from that principle or other provision.

(2)    In this Part "the subject information provisions" means—

    (a)    the first data protection principle to the extent to which it requires compliance with paragraph 2 of Part II of Schedule 1, and

    (b)    section 7.

(3)    In this Part "the non-disclosure provisions" means the provisions specified in subsection (4) to the extent to which they are inconsistent with the disclosure in question.

(4)    The provisions referred to in subsection (3) are—

    (a)    the first data protection principle, except to the extent to which it requires compliance with the conditions in Schedules 2 and 3,

    (b)    the second, third, fourth and fifth data protection principles, and

    (c)    sections 10 and 14(1) to (3).

(5)    Except as provided by this Part, the subject information provisions shall have effect notwithstanding any enactment or rule of law prohibiting or restricting the disclosure, or authorising the withholding, of information.

**Commencement**  to be appointed.
**Definitions**    For "data", "personal data" and "processing", see s 1(1) (and note also as to "processing", s 39, Sch 8, Pt II, para 5); as to "disclosing", see s 1(2)(b); for "the data protection principles", see s 4; for "enactment", see s 70(1).
**References**    See paras 5.10–5.12.

## 28  National security

(1)    Personal data are exempt from any of the provisions of—

    (a)    the data protection principles,

    (b)    Parts II, III and V, and

    (c)    section 55,

if the exemption from that provision is required for the purpose of safeguarding national security.

(2)    Subject to subsection (4), a certificate signed by a Minister of the Crown certifying that exemption from all or any of the provisions mentioned in subsection (1) is or at any time was required for the purpose there mentioned in respect of any personal data shall be conclusive evidence of that fact.

(3)    A certificate under subsection (2) may identify the personal data to which it applies by means of a general description and may be expressed to have prospective effect.

(4)    Any person directly affected by the issuing of a certificate under subsection (2) may appeal to the Tribunal against the certificate.

(5)    If on an appeal under subsection (4), the Tribunal finds that, applying the principles applied by the court on an application for judicial review, the Minister did not have reasonable grounds for issuing the certificate, the Tribunal may allow the appeal and quash the certificate.

(6)    Where in any proceedings under or by virtue of this Act it is claimed by a data controller that a certificate under subsection (2) which identifies the personal data to which it applies by means of a general description applies to any personal data, any other party to the proceedings may appeal to the Tribunal on the ground that the certificate does not apply to the personal data in question and, subject to any determination under subsection (7), the certificate shall be conclusively presumed so to apply.

(7)    On any appeal under subsection (6), the Tribunal may determine that the certificate does not so apply.

(8)    A document purporting to be a certificate under subsection (2) shall be received in evidence and deemed to be such a certificate unless the contrary is proved.

(9)    A document which purports to be certified by or on behalf of a Minister of the Crown as a true copy of a certificate issued by that Minister under subsection (2) shall in any legal proceedings be evidence (or, in Scotland, sufficient evidence) of that certificate.

(10)  The power conferred by subsection (2) on a Minister of the Crown shall not be exercisable except by a Minister who is a member of the Cabinet or by the Attorney General or the Lord Advocate.

(11)  No power conferred by any provision of Part V may be exercised in relation to personal data which by virtue of this section are exempt from that provision.

(12)  Schedule 6 shall have effect in relation to appeals under subsection (4) or (6) and the proceedings of the Tribunal in respect of any such appeal.

**Commencement**  to be appointed.
**Definitions**  For "personal data", see s 1(1); for "data controller", see s 1(1), (4); for "the data protection principles", see s 4; for "the Tribunal", see s 6(3); for "Minister of the Crown", see s 70(1).
**References**  See para 5.13.

## 29  Crime and taxation

(1)  Personal data processed for any of the following purposes—
    (a)  the prevention or detection of crime,
    (b)  the apprehension or prosecution of offenders, or
    (c)  the assessment or collection of any tax or duty or of any imposition of a similar nature,

are exempt from the first data protection principle (except to the extent to which it requires compliance with the conditions in Schedules 2 and 3) and section 7 in any case to the extent to which the application of those provisions to the data would be likely to prejudice any of the matters mentioned in this subsection.

(2)  Personal data which—
    (a)  are processed for the purpose of discharging statutory functions, and
    (b)  consist of information obtained for such a purpose from a person who had it in his possession for any of the purposes mentioned in subsection (1),

are exempt from the subject information provisions to the same extent as personal data processed for any of the purposes mentioned in that subsection.

(3)  Personal data are exempt from the non-disclosure provisions in any case in which—
    (a)  the disclosure is for any of the purposes mentioned in subsection (1), and
    (b)  the application of those provisions in relation to the disclosure would be likely to prejudice any of the matters mentioned in that subsection.

(4)  Personal data in respect of which the data controller is a relevant authority and which—
    (a)  consist of a classification applied to the data subject as part of a system of risk assessment which is operated by that authority for either of the following purposes—
      (i)  the assessment or collection of any tax or duty or any imposition of a similar nature, or
      (ii)  the prevention or detection of crime, or apprehension or prosecution of offenders, where the offence concerned involves any unlawful claim for any payment out of, or any unlawful application of, public funds, and
    (b)  are processed for either of those purposes,

are exempt from section 7 to the extent to which the exemption is required in the interests of the operation of the system.

(5)    In subsection (4)—
"public funds" includes funds provided by any Community institution;
"relevant authority" means—
(a)    a government department,
(b)    a local authority, or
(c)    any other authority administering housing benefit or council tax benefit.

**Commencement**   to be appointed.
**Definitions**    For "data", "data subject", "personal data" and "processing", see s 1(1) (and note also as to "processing", s 39, Sch 8, Pt II, para 5); for "data controller", see s 1(1), (4); as to "obtaining", see s 1(2)(a); as to "disclosing", see s 1(2)(b); for "the data protection principles", see s 4; for "the subject information provisions", see s 27(2); for "the non-disclosure provisions", see s 27(3); for "government department", see s 70(1).
**References**    See paras 4.70, 4.71, 5.20–5.22.

## 30  Health, education and social work

(1)    The Secretary of State may by order exempt from the subject information provisions, or modify those provisions in relation to, personal data consisting of information as to the physical or mental health or condition of the data subject.

(2)    The Secretary of State may by order exempt from the subject information provisions, or modify those provisions in relation to—
(a)    personal data in respect of which the data controller is the proprietor of, or a teacher at, a school, and which consist of information relating to persons who are or have been pupils at the school, or
(b)    personal data in respect of which the data controller is an education authority in Scotland, and which consist of information relating to persons who are receiving, or have received, further education provided by the authority.

(3)    The Secretary of State may by order exempt from the subject information provisions, or modify those provisions in relation to, personal data of such other descriptions as may be specified in the order, being information—
(a)    processed by government departments or local authorities or by voluntary organisations or other bodies designated by or under the order, and
(b)    appearing to him to be processed in the course of, or for the purposes of, carrying out social work in relation to the data subject or other individuals;
but the Secretary of State shall not under this subsection confer any exemption or make any modification except so far as he considers that the application to the data of those provisions (or of those provisions without modification) would be likely to prejudice the carrying out of social work.

(4)    An order under this section may make different provision in relation to data consisting of information of different descriptions.

(5)    In this section—
"education authority" and "further education" have the same meaning as in the Education (Scotland) Act 1980 ("the 1980 Act"), and
"proprietor"—
(a)    in relation to a school in England or Wales, has the same meaning as in the Education Act 1996,
(b)    in relation to a school in Scotland, means—
(i)    in the case of a self-governing school, the board of management within the meaning of the Self-Governing Schools etc (Scotland) Act 1989,

(ii)  in the case of an independent school, the proprietor within the meaning of the 1980 Act,

(iii)  in the case of a grant-aided school, the managers within the meaning of the 1980 Act, and

(iv)  in the case of a public school, the education authority within the meaning of the 1980 Act, and

(c)  in relation to a school in Northern Ireland, has the same meaning as in the Education and Libraries (Northern Ireland) Order 1986 and includes, in the case of a controlled school, the Board of Governors of the school.

**Commencement** 16 July 1998 (sub-ss (1)–(4), in so far as conferring the power to make subordinate legislation); to be appointed (otherwise).

**Definitions** For "data", "data subject", "personal data" and as to "processing", see s 1(1) (and note also as to "processing", s 39, Sch 8, Pt II, para 5); for "the subject information provisions", see s 27(2); for "government department", "pupil", "school" and "teacher", see s 70(1).

**References** See para 5.23.

## 31 Regulatory activity

(1)  Personal data processed for the purposes of discharging functions to which this subsection applies are exempt from the subject information provisions in any case to the extent to which the application of those provisions to the data would be likely to prejudice the proper discharge of those functions.

(2)  Subsection (1) applies to any relevant function which is designed—

(a)  for protecting members of the public against—

(i)  financial loss due to dishonesty, malpractice or other seriously improper conduct by, or the unfitness or incompetence of, persons concerned in the provision of banking, insurance, investment or other financial services or in the management of bodies corporate,

(ii)  financial loss due to the conduct of discharged or undischarged bankrupts, or

(iii)  dishonesty, malpractice or other seriously improper conduct by, or the unfitness or incompetence of, persons authorised to carry on any profession or other activity,

(b)  for protecting charities against misconduct or mismanagement (whether by trustees or other persons) in their administration,

(c)  for protecting the property of charities from loss or misapplication,

(d)  for the recovery of the property of charities,

(e)  for securing the health, safety and welfare of persons at work, or

(f)  for protecting persons other than persons at work against risk to health or safety arising out of or in connection with the actions of persons at work.

(3)  In subsection (2) "relevant function" means—

(a)  any function conferred on any person by or under any enactment,

(b)  any function of the Crown, a Minister of the Crown or a government department, or

(c)  any other function which is of a public nature and is exercised in the public interest.

(4)  Personal data processed for the purpose of discharging any function which—

(a)  is conferred by or under any enactment on—

(i)  the Parliamentary Commissioner for Administration,

(ii)   the Commission for Local Administration in England, the Commission for Local Administration in Wales or the Commissioner for Local Administration in Scotland,

(iii)  the Health Service Commissioner for England, the Health Service Commissioner for Wales or the Health Service Commissioner for Scotland,

(iv)   the Welsh Administration Ombudsman,

(v)    the Assembly Ombudsman for Northern Ireland, or

(vi)   the Northern Ireland Commissioner for Complaints, and

(b)    is designed for protecting members of the public against—

(i)    maladministration by public bodies,

(ii)   failures in services provided by public bodies, or

(iii)  a failure of a public body to provide a service which it was a function of the body to provide,

are exempt from the subject information provisions in any case to the extent to which the application of those provisions to the data would be likely to prejudice the proper discharge of that function.

(5)   Personal data processed for the purpose of discharging any function which—

(a)    is conferred by or under any enactment on the Director General of Fair Trading, and

(b)    is designed—

(i)    for protecting members of the public against conduct which may adversely affect their interests by persons carrying on a business,

(ii)   for regulating agreements or conduct which have as their object or effect the prevention, restriction or distortion of competition in connection with any commercial activity, or

(iii)  for regulating conduct on the part of one or more undertakings which amounts to the abuse of a dominant position in a market,

are exempt from the subject information provisions in any case to the extent to which the application of those provisions to the data would be likely to prejudice the proper discharge of that function.

---

**Commencement**  to be appointed.

**Definitions**   For "data" and "personal data", and as to "processed", see s 1(1) (and note also as to "processing", s 39, Sch 8, Pt II, para 5); for "the subject information provisions", see s 27(2); for "business", "enactment", "government department" and "Minister of the Crown", see s 70(1).

**References**   See para 5.24.

## 32 Journalism, literature and art

(1)   Personal data which are processed only for the special purposes are exempt from any provision to which this subsection relates if—

(a)    the processing is undertaken with a view to the publication by any person of any journalistic, literary or artistic material,

(b)    the data controller reasonably believes that, having regard in particular to the special importance of the public interest in freedom of expression, publication would be in the public interest, and

(c)    the data controller reasonably believes that, in all the circumstances, compliance with that provision is incompatible with the special purposes.

(2)   Subsection (1) relates to the provisions of—

(a)    the data protection principles except the seventh data protection principle,

(b)    section 7,

(c)    section 10,

(d)    section 12, and

(e)    section 14(1) to (3).

(3)    In considering for the purposes of subsection (1)(b) whether the belief of a data controller that publication would be in the public interest was or is a reasonable one, regard may be had to his compliance with any code of practice which—

    (a)    is relevant to the publication in question, and

    (b)    is designated by the Secretary of State by order for the purposes of this subsection.

(4)    Where at any time ("the relevant time") in any proceedings against a data controller under section 7(9), 10(4), 12(8) or 14 or by virtue of section 13 the data controller claims, or it appears to the court, that any personal data to which the proceedings relate are being processed—

    (a)    only for the special purposes, and

    (b)    with a view to the publication by any person of any journalistic, literary or artistic material which, at the time twenty-four hours immediately before the relevant time, had not previously been published by the data controller,

the court shall stay the proceedings until either of the conditions in subsection (5) is met.

(5)    Those conditions are—

    (a)    that a determination of the Commissioner under section 45 with respect to the data in question takes effect, or

    (b)    in a case where the proceedings were stayed on the making of a claim, that the claim is withdrawn.

(6)    For the purposes of this Act "publish", in relation to journalistic, literary or artistic material, means make available to the public or any section of the public.

---

**Commencement**    16 July 1998 (sub-s (3), in so far as conferring the power to make subordinate legislation); to be appointed (otherwise).

**Modification**    See s 72, Sch 13, para 2.

**Definitions**    For "personal data" and "processing", see s 1(1) (and note also as to "processing", s 39, Sch 8, Pt II, para 5); for "data controller", see s 1(1), (4); for "the special purposes", see s 3; for "the data protection principles", see s 4; for "the Commissioner", see s 6(1).

**References**    See paras 6.6–6.10.

## 33  Research, history and statistics

(1)    In this section—

    "research purposes" includes statistical or historical purposes;

    "the relevant conditions", in relation to any processing of personal data, means the conditions—

        (a)    that the data are not processed to support measures or decisions with respect to particular individuals, and

        (b)    that the data are not processed in such a way that substantial damage or substantial distress is, or is likely to be, caused to any data subject.

(2)    For the purposes of the second data protection principle, the further processing of personal data only for research purposes in compliance with the relevant conditions is not to be regarded as incompatible with the purposes for which they were obtained.

(3)    Personal data which are processed only for research purposes in compliance with the relevant conditions may, notwithstanding the fifth data protection principle, be kept indefinitely.

(4)    Personal data which are processed only for research purposes are exempt from section 7 if—

    (a)    they are processed in compliance with the relevant conditions, and

    (b)    the results of the research or any resulting statistics are not made available in a form which identifies data subjects or any of them.

(5)    For the purposes of subsections (2) to (4) personal data are not to be treated as processed otherwise than for research purposes merely because the data are disclosed—

    (a)    to any person, for research purposes only,

    (b)    to the data subject or a person acting on his behalf,

    (c)    at the request, or with the consent, of the data subject or a person acting on his behalf, or

    (d)    in circumstances in which the person making the disclosure has reasonable grounds for believing that the disclosure falls within paragraph (a), (b) or (c).

**Commencement**  to be appointed.
**Definitions**    For "data", "data subject", "personal data" and "processing", see s 1(1) (and note also as to "processing", s 39, Sch 8, Pt II, para 5); as to "obtaining", see s 1(2)(a); as to "disclosing", see s 1(2)(b) ;for "the data protection principles", see s 4.
**References**    See para 5.25.

## 34  Information available to the public by or under enactment

Personal data are exempt from—

    (a)    the subject information provisions,

    (b)    the fourth data protection principle and section 14(1) to (3), and

    (c)    the non-disclosure provisions,

if the data consist of information which the data controller is obliged by or under any enactment to make available to the public, whether by publishing it, by making it available for inspection, or otherwise and whether gratuitously or on payment of a fee.

**Commencement**  to be appointed.
**Modification**  see s 72, Sch 13, para 3.
**Definitions**    For "data" and "personal data", see s 1(1); for "data controller", see s 1(1), (4); for "the data protection principles", see s 4; for "the subject information provisions", see s 27(2); for "the non-disclosure provisions", see s 27(3); as to publishing, see s 32(6) ; for "enactment", see s 70(1).
**References**    See para 5.26.

## 35  Disclosures required by law or made in connection with legal proceedings etc

(1)    Personal data are exempt from the non-disclosure provisions where the disclosure is required by or under any enactment, by any rule of law or by the order of a court.

(2)    Personal data are exempt from the non-disclosure provisions where the disclosure is necessary—

    (a)    for the purpose of, or in connection with, any legal proceedings (including prospective legal proceedings), or

    (b)    for the purpose of obtaining legal advice,

or is otherwise necessary for the purposes of establishing, exercising or defending legal rights.

**Commencement**  to be appointed.
**Definitions**    For "personal data", see s 1(1); as to "disclosing", see s 1(2)(b); for "the non-disclosure provisions", see s 27(3); for "enactment", see s 70(1).
**References**    See para 4.72.

## 36  Domestic purposes

Personal data processed by an individual only for the purposes of that individual's personal, family or household affairs (including recreational purposes) are exempt from the data protection principles and the provisions of Parts II and III.

**Commencement**  to be appointed.
**Definitions**  For "personal data" and "processing", see s 1(1) (and note also as to "processing", s 39, Sch 8, Pt II, para 5); for "the data protection principles", see s 4.
**References**  See para 3.18.

## 37  Miscellaneous exemptions

Schedule 7 (which confers further miscellaneous exemptions) has effect.

**Commencement**  to be appointed.
**References**  See paras 5.27–5.38.

## 38  Powers to make further exemptions by order

(1)  The Secretary of State may by order exempt from the subject information provisions personal data consisting of information the disclosure of which is prohibited or restricted by or under any enactment if and to the extent that he considers it necessary for the safeguarding of the interests of the data subject or the rights and freedoms of any other individual that the prohibition or restriction ought to prevail over those provisions.

(2)  The Secretary of State may by order exempt from the non-disclosure provisions any disclosures of personal data made in circumstances specified in the order, if he considers the exemption is necessary for the safeguarding of the interests of the data subject or the rights and freedoms of any other individual.

**Commencement**  16 July 1998 (in so far as conferring the power to make subordinate legislation); to be appointed (otherwise).
**Definitions**  For "data subject" and "personal data", see s 1(1); as to "disclosing", see s 1(2)(b); for "the subject information provisions", see s 27(2); for "the non-disclosure provisions", see s 27(3); for "enactment", see s 70(1).
**References**  See para 5.27.

## 39  Transitional relief

Schedule 8 (which confers transitional exemptions) has effect.

**Commencement**  to be appointed.
**References**  See paras 1.26–1.31.

# PART V
# ENFORCEMENT

## 40  Enforcement notices

(1)  If the Commissioner is satisfied that a data controller has contravened or is contravening any of the data protection principles, the Commissioner may serve him with a notice (in this Act referred to as "an enforcement notice") requiring him, for complying with the principle or principles in question, to do either or both of the following—

      (a)   to take within such time as may be specified in the notice, or to refrain from taking after such time as may be so specified, such steps as are so specified, or

    (b)    to refrain from processing any personal data, or any personal data of a description specified in the notice, or to refrain from processing them for a purpose so specified or in a manner so specified, after such time as may be so specified.

(2)    In deciding whether to serve an enforcement notice, the Commissioner shall consider whether the contravention has caused or is likely to cause any person damage or distress.

(3)    An enforcement notice in respect of a contravention of the fourth data protection principle which requires the data controller to rectify, block, erase or destroy any inaccurate data may also require the data controller to rectify, block, erase or destroy any other data held by him and containing an expression of opinion which appears to the Commissioner to be based on the inaccurate data.

(4)    An enforcement notice in respect of a contravention of the fourth data protection principle, in the case of data which accurately record information received or obtained by the data controller from the data subject or a third party, may require the data controller either—

    (a)    to rectify, block, erase or destroy any inaccurate data and any other data held by him and containing an expression of opinion as mentioned in subsection (3), or

    (b)    to take such steps as are specified in the notice for securing compliance with the requirements specified in paragraph 7 of Part II of Schedule 1 and, if the Commissioner thinks fit, for supplementing the data with such statement of the true facts relating to the matters dealt with by the data as the Commissioner may approve.

(5)    Where—

    (a)    an enforcement notice requires the data controller to rectify, block, erase or destroy any personal data, or

    (b)    the Commissioner is satisfied that personal data which have been rectified, blocked, erased or destroyed had been processed in contravention of any of the data protection principles,

an enforcement notice may, if reasonably practicable, require the data controller to notify third parties to whom the data have been disclosed of the rectification, blocking, erasure or destruction; and in determining whether it is reasonably practicable to require such notification regard shall be had, in particular, to the number of persons who would have to be notified.

(6)    An enforcement notice must contain—

    (a)    a statement of the data protection principle or principles which the Commissioner is satisfied have been or are being contravened and his reasons for reaching that conclusion, and

    (b)    particulars of the rights of appeal conferred by section 48.

(7)    Subject to subsection (8), an enforcement notice must not require any of the provisions of the notice to be complied with before the end of the period within which an appeal can be brought against the notice and, if such an appeal is brought, the notice need not be complied with pending the determination or withdrawal of the appeal.

(8)    If by reason of special circumstances the Commissioner considers that an enforcement notice should be complied with as a matter of urgency he may include in the notice a statement to that effect and a statement of his reasons for reaching that conclusion; and in that event subsection (7) shall not apply but the notice must not require the provisions of the notice to be complied with before the end of the period of seven days beginning with the day on which the notice is served.

(9)    Notification regulations (as defined by section 16(2)) may make provision as to the effect of the service of an enforcement notice on any entry in the register maintained under section 19 which relates to the person on whom the notice is served.

(10)   This section has effect subject to section 46(1).

**Commencement**   16 July 1998 (sub-s (9), in so far as conferring the power to make subordinate legislation); to be appointed (otherwise).
**Definitions**    For "data", "data subject", "personal data" and "processing", see s 1(1) (and note also as to "processing", s 39, Sch 8, Pt II, para 5); for "data controller", see s 1(1), (4); as to "obtaining" and "recording", see s 1(2)(a); as to "disclosing", see s 1(2)(b); for "the data protection principles", see s 4; for "the Commissioner", see s 6(1) ; for "third party", see s 70(1); as to "inaccurate", see s 70(2).
**References**    See para 3.42.

## 41  Cancellation of an enforcement notice

(1)    If the Commissioner considers that all or any of the provisions of an enforcement notice need not be complied with in order to ensure compliance with the data protection principle or principles to which it relates, he may cancel or vary the notice by written notice to the person on whom it was served.

(2)    A person on whom an enforcement notice has been served may, at any time after the expiry of the period during which an appeal can be brought against that notice, apply in writing to the Commissioner for the cancellation or variation of that notice on the ground that, by reason of a change of circumstances, all or any of the provisions of that notice need not be complied with in order to ensure compliance with the data protection principle or principles to which that notice relates.

**Commencement**    to be appointed.
**Definitions**    For "the data protection principles", see s 4; for "the Commissioner", see s 6(1); for "enforcement notice", see s 40(1).
**References**    See para 3.43.

## 42  Request for assessment

(1)    A request may be made to the Commissioner by or on behalf of any person who is, or believes himself to be, directly affected by any processing of personal data for an assessment as to whether it is likely or unlikely that the processing has been or is being carried out in compliance with the provisions of this Act.

(2)    On receiving a request under this section, the Commissioner shall make an assessment in such manner as appears to him to be appropriate, unless he has not been supplied with such information as he may reasonably require in order to—
    (a)    satisfy himself as to the identity of the person making the request, and
    (b)    enable him to identify the processing in question.

(3)    The matters to which the Commissioner may have regard in determining in what manner it is appropriate to make an assessment include—
    (a)    the extent to which the request appears to him to raise a matter of substance,
    (b)    any undue delay in making the request, and
    (c)    whether or not the person making the request is entitled to make an application under section 7 in respect of the personal data in question.

(4)    Where the Commissioner has received a request under this section he shall notify the person who made the request—
    (a)    whether he has made an assessment as a result of the request, and
    (b)    to the extent that he considers appropriate, having regard in particular to any exemption from section 7 applying in relation to the personal data concerned, of any view formed or action taken as a result of the request.

**Commencement**  to be appointed.
**Definitions**  For "personal data" and "processing", see s 1(1) (and note also as to "processing", s 39, Sch 8, Pt II, para 5); for "the Commissioner", see s 6(1).
**References**  See para 3.48.

## 43  Information notices

(1)  If the Commissioner—

    (a)  has received a request under section 42 in respect of any processing of personal data, or

    (b)  reasonably requires any information for the purpose of determining whether the data controller has complied or is complying with the data protection principles,

he may serve the data controller with a notice (in this Act referred to as "an information notice") requiring the data controller, within such time as is specified in the notice, to furnish the Commissioner, in such form as may be so specified, with such information relating to the request or to compliance with the principles as is so specified.

(2)  An information notice must contain—

    (a)  in a case falling within subsection (1)(a), a statement that the Commissioner has received a request under section 42 in relation to the specified processing, or

    (b)  in a case falling within subsection (1)(b), a statement that the Commissioner regards the specified information as relevant for the purpose of determining whether the data controller has complied, or is complying, with the data protection principles and his reasons for regarding it as relevant for that purpose.

(3)  An information notice must also contain particulars of the rights of appeal conferred by section 48.

(4)  Subject to subsection (5), the time specified in an information notice shall not expire before the end of the period within which an appeal can be brought against the notice and, if such an appeal is brought, the information need not be furnished pending the determination or withdrawal of the appeal.

(5)  If by reason of special circumstances the Commissioner considers that the information is required as a matter of urgency, he may include in the notice a statement to that effect and a statement of his reasons for reaching that conclusion; and in that event subsection (4) shall not apply, but the notice shall not require the information to be furnished before the end of the period of seven days beginning with the day on which the notice is served.

(6)  A person shall not be required by virtue of this section to furnish the Commissioner with any information in respect of—

    (a)  any communication between a professional legal adviser and his client in connection with the giving of legal advice to the client with respect to his obligations, liabilities or rights under this Act, or

    (b)  any communication between a professional legal adviser and his client, or between such an adviser or his client and any other person, made in connection with or in contemplation of proceedings under or arising out of this Act (including proceedings before the Tribunal) and for the purposes of such proceedings.

(7)  In subsection (6) references to the client of a professional legal adviser include references to any person representing such a client.

(8)  A person shall not be required by virtue of this section to furnish the Commissioner with any information if the furnishing of that information would, by revealing evidence of the commission of any offence other than an offence under this Act, expose him to proceedings for that offence.

(9)    The Commissioner may cancel an information notice by written notice to the person on whom it was served.

(10)    This section has effect subject to section 46(3).

---

**Commencement**    to be appointed.
**Definitions**    For "personal data" and "processing", see s 1(1) (and note also as to "processing", s 39, Sch 8, Pt II, para 5); for "data controller", see s 1(1), (4); for "the data protection principles", see s 4; for "the Commissioner", see s 6(1); for "the Tribunal", see s 6(3).
**References**    See paras 3.45–3.47.

## 44  Special information notices

If the Commissioner—
    (a)    has received a request under section 42 in respect of any processing of personal data, or
    (b)    has reasonable grounds for suspecting that, in a case in which proceedings have been stayed under section 32, the personal data to which the proceedings relate—
        (i)    are not being processed only for the special purposes, or
        (ii)    are not being processed with a view to the publication by any person of any journalistic, literary or artistic material which has not previously been published by the data controller,

he may serve the data controller with a notice (in this Act referred to as a "special information notice") requiring the data controller, within such time as is specified in the notice, to furnish the Commissioner, in such form as may be so specified, with such information as is so specified for the purpose specified in subsection (2).

(2)    That purpose is the purpose of ascertaining—
    (a)    whether the personal data are being processed only for the special purposes, or
    (b)    whether they are being processed with a view to the publication by any person of any journalistic, literary or artistic material which has not previously been published by the data controller.

(3)    A special information notice must contain—
    (a)    in a case falling within paragraph (a) of subsection (1), a statement that the Commissioner has received a request under section 42 in relation to the specified processing, or
    (b)    in a case falling within paragraph (b) of that subsection, a statement of the Commissioner's grounds for suspecting that the personal data are not being processed as mentioned in that paragraph.

(4)    A special information notice must also contain particulars of the rights of appeal conferred by section 48.

(5)    Subject to subsection (6), the time specified in a special information notice shall not expire before the end of the period within which an appeal can be brought against the notice and, if such an appeal is brought, the information need not be furnished pending the determination or withdrawal of the appeal.

(6)    If by reason of special circumstances the Commissioner considers that the information is required as a matter of urgency, he may include in the notice a statement to that effect and a statement of his reasons for reaching that conclusion; and in that event subsection (5) shall not apply, but the notice shall not require the information to be furnished before the end of the period of seven days beginning with the day on which the notice is served.

(7)    A person shall not be required by virtue of this section to furnish the Commissioner with any information in respect of—

(a)   any communication between a professional legal adviser and his client in connection with the giving of legal advice to the client with respect to his obligations, liabilities or rights under this Act, or

(b)   any communication between a professional legal adviser and his client, or between such an adviser or his client and any other person, made in connection with or in contemplation of proceedings under or arising out of this Act (including proceedings before the Tribunal) and for the purposes of such proceedings.

(8)   In subsection (7) references to the client of a professional legal adviser include references to any person representing such a client.

(9)   A person shall not be required by virtue of this section to furnish the Commissioner with any information if the furnishing of that information would, by revealing evidence of the commission of any offence other than an offence under this Act, expose him to proceedings for that offence.

(10)   The Commissioner may cancel a special information notice by written notice to the person on whom it was served.

**Commencement**   to be appointed.
**Definitions**   For "personal data" and "processing", see s 1(1) (and note also as to "processing", s 39, Sch 8, Pt II, para 5); for "data controller", see s 1(1), (4); for "the special purposes", see s 3; for "publish", see s 31(6); for "the Commissioner", see s 6(1); for "the Tribunal", see s 6(3); as to publications see s 32(6).
**References**   See paras 6.13, 6.14.

## 45  Determination by Commissioner as to the special purposes

(1)   Where at any time it appears to the Commissioner (whether as a result of the service of a special information notice or otherwise) that any personal data—

(a)   are not being processed only for the special purposes, or

(b)   are not being processed with a view to the publication by any person of any journalistic, literary or artistic material which has not previously been published by the data controller,

he may make a determination in writing to that effect.

(2)   Notice of the determination shall be given to the data controller; and the notice must contain particulars of the right of appeal conferred by section 48.

(3)   A determination under subsection (1) shall not take effect until the end of the period within which an appeal can be brought and, where an appeal is brought, shall not take effect pending the determination or withdrawal of the appeal.

**Commencement**   to be appointed.
**Definitions**   For "personal data" and "processing", see s 1(1) (and note also as to "processing", s 39, Sch 8, Pt II, para 5); for "data controller", see s 1(1), (4); for "the special purposes", see s 3; for "the Commissioner", see s 6(1); as to publication, see s 32(6); for "special information notices", see s 44(1).
**References**   See para 6.12.

## 46  Restriction on enforcement in case of processing for the special purposes

(1)   The Commissioner may not at any time serve an enforcement notice on a data controller with respect to the processing of personal data for the special purposes unless—

(a)   a determination under section 45(1) with respect to those data has taken effect, and

(b)   the court has granted leave for the notice to be served.

(2)    The court shall not grant leave for the purposes of subsection (1)(b) unless it is satisfied—

(a)    that the Commissioner has reason to suspect a contravention of the data protection principles which is of substantial public importance, and

(b)    except where the case is one of urgency, that the data controller has been given notice, in accordance with rules of court, of the application for leave.

(3)    The Commissioner may not serve an information notice on a data controller with respect to the processing of personal data for the special purposes unless a determination under section 45(1) with respect to those data has taken effect.

**Commencement**  to be appointed.
**Definitions**    For "data", "personal data" and "processing", see s 1(1) (and note also as to "processing", s 39, Sch 8, Pt II, para 5); for "data controller", see s 1(1), (4); for "the special purposes", see s 3; for "the data protection principles", see s 4; for "the Commissioner", see s 6(1); for "enforcement notice", see s 40(1); for "information notice", see s 43(1).
**References**    See para 6.15.

## 47  Failure to comply with notice

(1)    A person who fails to comply with an enforcement notice, an information notice or a special information notice is guilty of an offence.

(2)    A person who, in purported compliance with an information notice or a special information notice—

(a)    makes a statement which he knows to be false in a material respect, or

(b)    recklessly makes a statement which is false in a material respect,

is guilty of an offence.

(3)    It is a defence for a person charged with an offence under subsection (1) to prove that he exercised all due diligence to comply with the notice in question.

**Commencement**  to be appointed.
**Definitions**    For "enforcement notice", see s 40(1); for "information notice", see s 43(1); for "special information notice", see s 44(1).
**References**    See paras 3.43, 3.45.

## 48  Rights of appeal

(1)    A person on whom an enforcement notice, an information notice or a special information notice has been served may appeal to the Tribunal against the notice.

(2)    A person on whom an enforcement notice has been served may appeal to the Tribunal against the refusal of an application under section 41(2) for cancellation or variation of the notice.

(3)    Where an enforcement notice, an information notice or a special information notice contains a statement by the Commissioner in accordance with section 40(8), 43(5) or 44(6) then, whether or not the person appeals against the notice, he may appeal against—

(a)    the Commissioner's decision to include the statement in the notice, or

(b)    the effect of the inclusion of the statement as respects any part of the notice.

(4)    A data controller in respect of whom a determination has been made under section 45 may appeal to the Tribunal against the determination.

(5)    Schedule 6 has effect in relation to appeals under this section and the proceedings of the Tribunal in respect of any such appeal.

**Commencement**  to be appointed.
**Definitions**    For "data controller", see s 1(1), (4); for "the Commissioner", see s 6(1); for "the Tribunal", see s 6(3); for "enforcement notice", see s 40(1); for "information notice", see s 43(1); for "special information notice", see s 44(1).
**References**    See paras 3.43, 3.45.

## 49  Determination of appeals

(1)    If on an appeal under section 48(1) the Tribunal considers—
    (a)    that the notice against which the appeal is brought is not in accordance with the law, or
    (b)    to the extent that the notice involved an exercise of discretion by the Commissioner, that he ought to have exercised his discretion differently,

the Tribunal shall allow the appeal or substitute such other notice or decision as could have been served or made by the Commissioner; and in any other case the Tribunal shall dismiss the appeal.

(2)    On such an appeal, the Tribunal may review any determination of fact on which the notice in question was based.

(3)    If on an appeal under section 48(2) the Tribunal considers that the enforcement notice ought to be cancelled or varied by reason of a change in circumstances, the Tribunal shall cancel or vary the notice.

(4)    On an appeal under subsection (3) of section 48 the Tribunal may direct—
    (a)    that the notice in question shall have effect as if it did not contain any such statement as is mentioned in that subsection, or
    (b)    that the inclusion of the statement shall not have effect in relation to any part of the notice,

and may make such modifications in the notice as may be required for giving effect to the direction.

(5)    On an appeal under section 48(4), the Tribunal may cancel the determination of the Commissioner.

(6)    Any party to an appeal to the Tribunal under section 48 may appeal from the decision of the Tribunal on a point of law to the appropriate court; and that court shall be—
    (a)    the High Court of Justice in England if the address of the person who was the appellant before the Tribunal is in England or Wales,
    (b)    the Court of Session if that address is in Scotland, and
    (c)    the High Court of Justice in Northern Ireland if that address is in Northern Ireland.

(7)    For the purposes of subsection (6)—
    (a)    the address of a registered company is that of its registered office, and
    (b)    the address of a person (other than a registered company) carrying on a business is that of his principal place of business in the United Kingdom.

**Commencement**  to be appointed.
**Definitions**    For "the Commissioner", see s 6(1); for "the Tribunal", see s 6(3); for "enforcement notice", see s 40(1); for "business" and "registered company", see s 70(1).
**References**    See para 3.61.

## 50  Powers of entry and inspection

Schedule 9 (powers of entry and inspection) has effect.

**Commencement**  to be appointed.
**References**  See para 3.40.

# PART VI
# MISCELLANEOUS AND GENERAL

*Functions of Commissioner*

## 51 General duties of Commissioner

(1)   It shall be the duty of the Commissioner to promote the following of good practice by data controllers and, in particular, so to perform his functions under this Act as to promote the observance of the requirements of this Act by data controllers.

(2)   The Commissioner shall arrange for the dissemination in such form and manner as he considers appropriate of such information as it may appear to him expedient to give to the public about the operation of this Act, about good practice, and about other matters within the scope of his functions under this Act, and may give advice to any person as to any of those matters.

(3)   Where—
    (a)   the Secretary of State so directs by order, or
    (b)   the Commissioner considers it appropriate to do so,
the Commissioner shall, after such consultation with trade associations, data subjects or persons representing data subjects as appears to him to be appropriate, prepare and disseminate to such persons as he considers appropriate codes of practice for guidance as to good practice.

(4)   The Commissioner shall also—
    (a)   where he considers it appropriate to do so, encourage trade associations to prepare, and to disseminate to their members, such codes of practice, and
    (b)   where any trade association submits a code of practice to him for his consideration, consider the code and, after such consultation with data subjects or persons representing data subjects as appears to him to be appropriate, notify the trade association whether in his opinion the code promotes the following of good practice.

(5)   An order under subsection (3) shall describe the personal data or processing to which the code of practice is to relate, and may also describe the persons or classes of persons to whom it is to relate.

(6)   The Commissioner shall arrange for the dissemination in such form and manner as he considers appropriate of—
    (a)   any Community finding as defined by paragraph 15(2) of Part II of Schedule 1,
    (b)   any decision of the European Commission, under the procedure provided for in Article 31(2) of the Data Protection Directive, which is made for the purposes of Article 26(3) or (4) of the Directive, and
    (c)   such other information as it may appear to him to be expedient to give to data controllers in relation to any personal data about the protection of the rights and freedoms of data subjects in relation to the processing of personal data in countries and territories outside the European Economic Area.

(7)   The Commissioner may, with the consent of the data controller, assess any processing of personal data for the following of good practice and shall inform the data controller of the results of the assessment.

(8)   The Commissioner may charge such sums as he may with the consent of the Secretary of State determine for any services provided by the Commissioner by virtue of this Part.

(9)   In this section—

"good practice" means such practice in the processing of personal data as appears to the Commissioner to be desirable having regard to the interests of data subjects and others, and includes (but is not limited to) compliance with the requirements of this Act;

"trade association" includes any body representing data controllers.

**Commencement**   16 July 1998 (sub-ss (3), (5), in so far as conferring the power to make subordinate legislation); to be appointed (otherwise).
**Definitions**   For "data subject", "personal data" and "processing", see s 1(1) (and note also as to "processing", s 39, Sch 8, Pt II, para 5); for "data controller", see s 1(1), (4); for "the Commissioner", see s 6(1); for "the Data Protection Directive", see s 70(1).
**References**   See paras 3.6, 3.50, 3.55.

## 52   Reports and codes of practice to be laid before Parliament

(1)   The Commissioner shall lay annually before each House of Parliament a general report on the exercise of his functions under this Act.

(2)   The Commissioner may from time to time lay before each House of Parliament such other reports with respect to those functions as he thinks fit.

(3)   The Commissioner shall lay before each House of Parliament any code of practice prepared under section 51(3) for complying with a direction of the Secretary of State, unless the code is included in any report laid under subsection (1) or (2).

**Commencement**   to be appointed.
**Definitions**   For "the Commissioner", see s 6(1).
**References**   See para 3.54.

## 53   Assistance by Commissioner in cases involving processing for the special purposes

(1)   An individual who is an actual or prospective party to any proceedings under section 7(9), 10(4), 12(8) or 14 or by virtue of section 13 which relate to personal data processed for the special purposes may apply to the Commissioner for assistance in relation to those proceedings.

(2)   The Commissioner shall, as soon as reasonably practicable after receiving an application under subsection (1), consider it and decide whether and to what extent to grant it, but he shall not grant the application unless, in his opinion, the case involves a matter of substantial public importance.

(3)   If the Commissioner decides to provide assistance, he shall, as soon as reasonably practicable after making the decision, notify the applicant, stating the extent of the assistance to be provided.

(4)   If the Commissioner decides not to provide assistance, he shall, as soon as reasonably practicable after making the decision, notify the applicant of his decision and, if he thinks fit, the reasons for it.

(5)　In this section—

    (a)　references to "proceedings" include references to prospective proceedings, and

    (b)　"applicant", in relation to assistance under this section, means an individual who applies for assistance.

(6)　Schedule 10 has effect for supplementing this section.

---

**Commencement**　to be appointed.
**Modification**　see s 72, Sch 13, para 4.
**Definitions**　For "personal data" and as to "processing", see s 1(1) (and note also as to "processing", s 39, Sch 8, Pt II, para 5); for "the special purposes", see s 3; for "the Commissioner", see s 6(1).
**References**　See para 6.17.

## 54 International co-operation

(1)　The Commissioner—

    (a)　shall continue to be the designated authority in the United Kingdom for the purposes of Article 13 of the Convention, and

    (b)　shall be the supervisory authority in the United Kingdom for the purposes of the Data Protection Directive.

(2)　The Secretary of State may by order make provision as to the functions to be discharged by the Commissioner as the designated authority in the United Kingdom for the purposes of Article 13 of the Convention.

(3)　The Secretary of State may by order make provision as to co-operation by the Commissioner with the European Commission and with supervisory authorities in other EEA States in connection with the performance of their respective duties and, in particular, as to—

    (a)　the exchange of information with supervisory authorities in other EEA States or with the European Commission, and

    (b)　the exercise within the United Kingdom at the request of a supervisory authority in another EEA State, in cases excluded by section 5 from the application of the other provisions of this Act, of functions of the Commissioner specified in the order.

(4)　The Commissioner shall also carry out any data protection functions which the Secretary of State may by order direct him to carry out for the purpose of enabling Her Majesty's Government in the United Kingdom to give effect to any international obligations of the United Kingdom.

(5)　The Commissioner shall, if so directed by the Secretary of State, provide any authority exercising data protection functions under the law of a colony specified in the direction with such assistance in connection with the discharge of those functions as the Secretary of State may direct or approve, on such terms (including terms as to payment) as the Secretary of State may direct or approve.

(6)　Where the European Commission makes a decision for the purposes of Article 26(3) or (4) of the Data Protection Directive under the procedure provided for in Article 31(2) of the Directive, the Commissioner shall comply with that decision in exercising his functions under paragraph 9 of Schedule 4 or, as the case may be, paragraph 8 of that Schedule.

(7)　The Commissioner shall inform the European Commission and the supervisory authorities in other EEA States—

    (a)　of any approvals granted for the purposes of paragraph 8 of Schedule 4, and

    (b)　of any authorisations granted for the purposes of paragraph 9 of that Schedule.

(8)     In this section—

"the Convention" means the Convention for the Protection of Individuals with regard to Automatic Processing of Personal Data which was opened for signature on 28th January 1981;

"data protection functions" means functions relating to the protection of individuals with respect to the processing of personal information.

**Commencement**  16 July 1998 (sub-ss (2)–(4), in so far as conferring the power to make subordinate legislation); to be appointed (otherwise).
**Definitions**     As to "processing", see s 1(1) (and note s 39, Sch 8, Pt II, para 5); for "the Commissioner", see s 6(1); for "the Data Protection Directive" and "EEA State", see s 70(1).
**References**     See paras 3.56, 3.57.

*Unlawful obtaining etc of personal data*

## 55  Unlawful obtaining etc of personal data

(1)     A person must not knowingly or recklessly, without the consent of the data controller—

(a)     obtain or disclose personal data or the information contained in personal data, or

(b)     procure the disclosure to another person of the information contained in personal data.

(2)     Subsection (1) does not apply to a person who shows—

(a)     that the obtaining, disclosing or procuring—

(i)     was necessary for the purpose of preventing or detecting crime, or

(ii)    was required or authorised by or under any enactment, by any rule of law or by the order of a court,

(b)     that he acted in the reasonable belief that he had in law the right to obtain or disclose the data or information or, as the case may be, to procure the disclosure of the information to the other person,

(c)     that he acted in the reasonable belief that he would have had the consent of the data controller if the data controller had known of the obtaining, disclosing or procuring and the circumstances of it, or

(d)     that in the particular circumstances the obtaining, disclosing or procuring was justified as being in the public interest.

(3)     A person who contravenes subsection (1) is guilty of an offence.

(4)     A person who sells personal data is guilty of an offence if he has obtained the data in contravention of subsection (1).

(5)     A person who offers to sell personal data is guilty of an offence if—

(a)     he has obtained the data in contravention of subsection (1), or

(b)     he subsequently obtains the data in contravention of that subsection.

(6)     For the purposes of subsection (5), an advertisement indicating that personal data are or may be for sale is an offer to sell the data.

(7)     Section 1(2) does not apply for the purposes of this section; and for the purposes of subsections (4) to (6), "personal data" includes information extracted from personal data.

(8)     References in this section to personal data do not include references to personal data which by virtue of section 28 are exempt from this section.

**Commencement**   to be appointed.
**Definitions**     For "data" and "personal data", see s 1(1), and note also as to "personal data", sub-ss (7), (8) above; for "data controller", see s 1(1), (4); for "enactment", see s 70(1).
**References**     See paras 4.80–4.83.

*Records obtained under data subject's right of access*

## 56 Prohibition of requirement as to production of certain records

(1)    A person must not, in connection with—
    (a)   the recruitment of another person as an employee,
    (b)   the continued employment of another person, or
    (c)   any contract for the provision of services to him by another person,

require that other person or a third party to supply him with a relevant record or to produce a relevant record to him.

(2)    A person concerned with the provision (for payment or not) of goods, facilities or services to the public or a section of the public must not, as a condition of providing or offering to provide any goods, facilities or services to another person, require that other person or a third party to supply him with a relevant record or to produce a relevant record to him.

(3)    Subsections (1) and (2) do not apply to a person who shows—
    (a)   that the imposition of the requirement was required or authorised by or under any enactment, by any rule of law or by the order of a court, or
    (b)   that in the particular circumstances the imposition of the requirement was justified as being in the public interest.

(4)    Having regard to the provisions of Part V of the Police Act 1997 (certificates of criminal records etc), the imposition of the requirement referred to in subsection (1) or (2) is not to be regarded as being justified as being in the public interest on the ground that it would assist in the prevention or detection of crime.

(5)    A person who contravenes subsection (1) or (2) is guilty of an offence.

(6)    In this section "a relevant record" means any record which—
    (a)   has been or is to be obtained by a data subject from any data controller specified in the first column of the Table below in the exercise of the right conferred by section 7, and
    (b)   contains information relating to any matter specified in relation to that data controller in the second column,

and includes a copy of such a record or a part of such a record.

## TABLE

| Data controller | Subject-matter |
| --- | --- |
| 1. Any of the following persons— | (a) Convictions. |
| (a) a chief officer of police of a police force in England and Wales. | (b) Cautions. |
| (b) a chief constable of a police force in Scotland. | |
| (c) the Chief Constable of the Royal Ulster Constabulary. | |
| (d) the Director General of the National Criminal Intelligence Service. | |
| (e) the Director General of the National Crime Squad. | |

| Data controller | Subject-matter |
|---|---|
| 2. The Secretary of State. | (a) Convictions. |
| | (b) Cautions. |
| | (c) His functions under section 53 of the Children and Young Persons Act 1933, section 205(2) or 208 of the Criminal Procedure (Scotland) Act 1995 or section 73 of the Children and Young Persons Act (Northern Ireland) 1968 in relation to any person sentenced to detention. |
| | (d) His functions under the Prison Act 1952, the Prisons (Scotland) Act 1989 or the Prison Act (Northern Ireland) 1953 in relation to any person imprisoned or detained. |
| | (e) His functions under the Social Security Contributions and Benefits Act 1992, the Social Security Administration Act 1992 or the Jobseekers Act 1995. |
| | (f) His functions under Part V of the Police Act 1997. |
| 3. The Department of Health and Social Services for Northern Ireland. | Its functions under the Social Security Contributions and Benefits (Northern Ireland) Act 1992, the Social Security Administration (Northern Ireland) Act 1992 or the Jobseekers (Northern Ireland) Order 1995. |

(7)    In the Table in subsection (6)—
"caution" means a caution given to any person in England and Wales or Northern Ireland in respect of an offence which, at the time when the caution is given, is admitted;
"conviction" has the same meaning as in the Rehabilitation of Offenders Act 1974 or the Rehabilitation of Offenders (Northern Ireland) Order 1978.

(8)    The Secretary of State may by order amend—
(a)    the Table in subsection (6), and
(b)    subsection (7).

(9)    For the purposes of this section a record which states that a data controller is not processing any personal data relating to a particular matter shall be taken to be a record containing information relating to that matter.

(10)   In this section "employee" means an individual who—
(a)    works under a contract of employment, as defined by section 230(2) of the Employment Rights Act 1996, or
(b)    holds any office,
whether or not he is entitled to remuneration; and "employment" shall be construed accordingly.

**Commencement** 16 July 1998 (sub-s (8), in so far as conferring the power to make subordinate legislation); to be appointed (otherwise).
**Definitions** For "data subject", "personal data" and "processing", see s 1(1) (and note also as to "processing", s 39, Sch 8, Pt II, para 5); for "data controller", see s 1(1), (4); as to obtaining data, see s 1(2)(a); for "third party", see s 70(1).
**References** See paras 5.49–5.53.

## 57 Avoidance of certain contractual terms relating to health records

(1)    Any term or condition of a contract is void in so far as it purports to require an individual—

(a)    to supply any other person with a record to which this section applies, or with a copy of such a record or a part of such a record, or

(b)    to produce to any other person such a record, copy or part.

(2)    This section applies to any record which—

(a)    has been or is to be obtained by a data subject in the exercise of the right conferred by section 7, and

(b)    consists of the information contained in any health record as defined by section 68(2).

**Commencement** to be appointed.
**Definitions** For "data subject", see s 1(1); as to obtaining data, see s 1(2)(a).
**References** See para 5.51.

*Information provided to Commissioner or Tribunal*

## 58 Disclosure of information

No enactment or rule of law prohibiting or restricting the disclosure of information shall preclude a person from furnishing the Commissioner or the Tribunal with any information necessary for the discharge of their functions under this Act.

**Commencement** to be appointed.
**Definitions** As to "disclosure", see s 1(2)(b); for "the Commissioner", see s 6(1); for "the Tribunal", see s 6(3); for "enactment", see s 70(1).

## 59 Confidentiality of information

(1)    No person who is or has been the Commissioner, a member of the Commissioner's staff or an agent of the Commissioner shall disclose any information which—

(a)    has been obtained by, or furnished to, the Commissioner under or for the purposes of this Act,

(b)    relates to an identified or identifiable individual or business, and

(c)    is not at the time of the disclosure, and has not previously been, available to the public from other sources,

unless the disclosure is made with lawful authority.

(2)    For the purposes of subsection (1) a disclosure of information is made with lawful authority only if, and to the extent that—

(a)    the disclosure is made with the consent of the individual or of the person for the time being carrying on the business,

(b)    the information was provided for the purpose of its being made available to the public (in whatever manner) under any provision of this Act,

(c)    the disclosure is made for the purposes of, and is necessary for, the discharge of—

      (i)    any functions under this Act, or

      (ii)    any Community obligation,

(d)    the disclosure is made for the purposes of any proceedings, whether criminal or civil and whether arising under, or by virtue of, this Act or otherwise, or

(e)    having regard to the rights and freedoms or legitimate interests of any person, the disclosure is necessary in the public interest.

(3)    Any person who knowingly or recklessly discloses information in contravention of subsection (1) is guilty of an offence.

---

**Commencement**    to be appointed.
**Definitions**    As to "obtaining", see s 1(2)(a); as to "disclosing", see s 1(2)(b); for "the Commissioner", see s 6(1); for "business", see s 70(1).
**References**    See paras 5.58–5.60.

*General provisions relating to offences*

## 60 Prosecutions and penalties

(1)    No proceedings for an offence under this Act shall be instituted—

(a)    in England or Wales, except by the Commissioner or by or with the consent of the Director of Public Prosecutions;

(b)    in Northern Ireland, except by the Commissioner or by or with the consent of the Director of Public Prosecutions for Northern Ireland.

(2)    A person guilty of an offence under any provision of this Act other than paragraph 12 of Schedule 9 is liable—

(a)    on summary conviction, to a fine not exceeding the statutory maximum, or

(b)    on conviction on indictment, to a fine.

(3)    A person guilty of an offence under paragraph 12 of Schedule 9 is liable on summary conviction to a fine not exceeding level 5 on the standard scale.

(4)    Subject to subsection (5), the court by or before which a person is convicted of—

(a)    an offence under section 21(1), 22(6), 55 or 56,

(b)    an offence under section 21(2) relating to processing which is assessable processing for the purposes of section 22, or

(c)    an offence under section 47(1) relating to an enforcement notice,

may order any document or other material used in connection with the processing of personal data and appearing to the court to be connected with the commission of the offence to be forfeited, destroyed or erased.

(5)    The court shall not make an order under subsection (4) in relation to any material where a person (other than the offender) claiming to be the owner of or otherwise interested in the material applies to be heard by the court, unless an opportunity is given to him to show cause why the order should not be made.

---

**Commencement**    to be appointed.
**Definitions**    For "personal data" and "processing", see s 1(1) (and note also as to "processing", s 39, Sch 8, Pt II, para 5); for "the Commissioner", see s 6(1); for "enforcement notice", see s 40(1).
**References**    See para 3.39.

## 61 Liability of directors etc

(1)    Where an offence under this Act has been committed by a body corporate and is proved to have been committed with the consent or connivance of or to be attributable to any neglect on the part of any director, manager, secretary or similar officer of the body corporate or any person who was purporting to act in any such capacity, he as well as the body corporate shall be guilty of that offence and be liable to be proceeded against and punished accordingly.

(2)    Where the affairs of a body corporate are managed by its members subsection (1) shall apply in relation to the acts and defaults of a member in connection with his functions of management as if he were a director of the body corporate.

(3)    Where an offence under this Act has been committed by a Scottish partnership and the contravention in question is proved to have occurred with the consent or connivance of, or to be attributable to any neglect on the part of, a partner, he as well as the partnership shall be guilty of that offence and shall be liable to be proceeded against and punished accordingly.

**Commencement**    to be appointed.
**Definitions**    As to offences generally, see s 60; for powers of entry and seizure, see s 50, Sch 9.

*Amendments of Consumer Credit Act 1974*

## 62 Amendments of Consumer Credit Act 1974

(1)    In section 158 of the Consumer Credit Act 1974 (duty of agency to disclose filed information)—
>    (a)    in subsection (1)—
>>    (i)    in paragraph (a) for "individual" there is substituted "partnership or other unincorporated body of persons not consisting entirely of bodies corporate", and
>>    (ii)    for "him" there is substituted "it",
>    (b)    in subsection (2), for "his" there is substituted "the consumer's", and
>    (c)    in subsection (3), for "him" there is substituted "the consumer".

(2)    In section 159 of that Act (correction of wrong information) for subsection (1) there is substituted—

>    "(1)    Any individual (the "objector") given—
>>    (a)    information under section 7 of the Data Protection Act 1998 by a credit reference agency, or
>>    (b)    information under section 158,

>    who considers that an entry in his file is incorrect, and that if it is not corrected he is likely to be prejudiced, may give notice to the agency requiring it either to remove the entry from the file or amend it.".

(3)    In subsections (2) to (6) of that subsection—
>    (a)    for "consumer", wherever occurring, there is substituted "objector", and
>    (b)    for "Director", wherever occurring, there is substituted "the relevant authority".

(4)    After subsection (6) of that section there is inserted—

>    "(7)    The Data Protection Commissioner may vary or revoke any order made by him under this section.

(8)   In this section "the relevant authority" means—
    (a)   where the objector is a partnership or other unincorporated body of persons, the Director, and
    (b)   in any other case, the Data Protection Commissioner.".

(5)   In section 160 of that Act (alternative procedure for business consumers)—
    (a)   in subsection (4)—
       (i)   for "him" there is substituted "to the consumer", and
      (ii)   in paragraphs (a) and (b) for "he" there is substituted "the consumer" and for "his" there is substituted "the consumer's", and
    (b)   after subsection (6) there is inserted—

"(7)   In this section "consumer" has the same meaning as in section 158.".

**Commencement**   to be appointed.
**Definitions**   For "credit reference agency", see the Consumer Credit Act 1974, s 145(8); for "consumer", see s 158(1) of that Act; for "file", see s 158(5) thereof; for "give", "individual" and "notice", see s 158(1) thereof; for "objector", see s 159(1) thereof, as substituted by sub-s (2) above.
**References**   See para 5.7.

## *General*

## 63  Application to Crown

(1)   This Act binds the Crown.

(2)   For the purposes of this Act each government department shall be treated as a person separate from any other government department.

(3)   Where the purposes for which and the manner in which any personal data are, or are to be, processed are determined by any person acting on behalf of the Royal Household, the Duchy of Lancaster or the Duchy of Cornwall, the data controller in respect of those data for the purposes of this Act shall be—
    (a)   in relation to the Royal Household, the Keeper of the Privy Purse,
    (b)   in relation to the Duchy of Lancaster, such person as the Chancellor of the Duchy appoints, and
    (c)   in relation to the Duchy of Cornwall, such person as the Duke of Cornwall, or the possessor for the time being of the Duchy of Cornwall, appoints.

(4)   Different persons may be appointed under subsection (3)(b) or (c) for different purposes.

(5)   Neither a government department nor a person who is a data controller by virtue of subsection (3) shall be liable to prosecution under this Act, but section 55 and paragraph 12 of Schedule 9 shall apply to a person in the service of the Crown as they apply to any other person.

**Commencement**   to be appointed.
**Definitions**   For "data", "personal data" and "processing", see s 1(1) (and note also as to "processing", s 39, Sch 8, Pt II, para 5); for "data controller", see s 1(1), (4); for "government department", see s 70(1).

## 64  Transmission of notices etc by electronic or other means

(1)   This section applies to
    (a)   a notice or request under any provision of Part II,
    (b)   a notice under subsection (1) of section 24 or particulars made available under that subsection, or
    (c)   an application under section 41(2),

but does not apply to anything which is required to be served in accordance with rules of court.

(2)    The requirement that any notice, request, particulars or application to which this section applies should be in writing is satisfied where the text of the notice, request, particulars or application—

      (a)   is transmitted by electronic means,

      (b)   is received in legible form, and

      (c)   is capable of being used for subsequent reference.

(3)    The Secretary of State may by regulations provide that any requirement that any notice, request, particulars or application to which this section applies should be in writing is not to apply in such circumstances as may be prescribed by the regulations.

**Commencement**  16 July 1998 (sub-s (3), in so far as conferring the power to make subordinate legislation); to be appointed (otherwise).
**References**  See para 5.4.

## 65  Service of notices by Commissioner

(1)    Any notice authorised or required by this Act to be served on or given to any person by the Commissioner may—

      (a)   if that person is an individual, be served on him—

          (i)   by delivering it to him, or

          (ii)   by sending it to him by post addressed to him at his usual or last-known place of residence or business, or

          (iii)   by leaving it for him at that place;

      (b)   if that person is a body corporate or unincorporate, be served on that body—

          (i)   by sending it by post to the proper officer of the body at its principal office, or

          (ii)   by addressing it to the proper officer of the body and leaving it at that office;

      (c)   if that person is a partnership in Scotland, be served on that partnership—

          (i)   by sending it by post to the principal office of the partnership, or

          (ii)   by addressing it to that partnership and leaving it at that office.

(2)    In subsection (1)(b) "principal office", in relation to a registered company, means its registered office and "proper officer", in relation to any body, means the secretary or other executive officer charged with the conduct of its general affairs.

(3)    This section is without prejudice to any other lawful method of serving or giving a notice.

**Commencement**  to be appointed.
**Definitions**  For "the Commissioner", see s 6(1); for "business" and "registered company", see s 70(1).

## 66  Exercise of rights in Scotland by children

(1)    Where a question falls to be determined in Scotland as to the legal capacity of a person under the age of sixteen years to exercise any right conferred by any provision of this Act, that person shall be taken to have that capacity where he has a general understanding of what it means to exercise that right.

(2)    Without prejudice to the generality of subsection (1), a person of twelve years of age or more shall be presumed to be of sufficient age and maturity to have such understanding as is mentioned in that subsection.

**Commencement**  to be appointed.

## 67  Orders, regulations and rules

(1)    Any power conferred by this Act on the Secretary of State to make an order, regulations or rules shall be exercisable by statutory instrument.

(2)    Any order, regulations or rules made by the Secretary of State under this Act may—

    (a)    make different provision for different cases, and

    (b)    make such supplemental, incidental, consequential or transitional provision or savings as the Secretary of State considers appropriate;

and nothing in section 7(11), 19(5), 26(1) or 30(4) limits the generality of paragraph (a).

(3)    Before making—

    (a)    an order under any provision of this Act other than section 75(3),

    (b)    any regulations under this Act other than notification regulations (as defined by section 16(2)),

the Secretary of State shall consult the Commissioner.

(4)    A statutory instrument containing (whether alone or with other provisions) an order under—

    section 10(2)(b),
    section 12(5)(b),
    section 22(1),
    section 30,
    section 32(3),
    section 38,
    section 56(8),
    paragraph 10 of Schedule 3, or
    paragraph 4 of Schedule 7,

shall not be made unless a draft of the instrument has been laid before and approved by a resolution of each House of Parliament.

(5)    A statutory instrument which contains (whether alone or with other provisions)—

    (a)    an order under—
    section 22(7),
    section 23,
    section 51(3),
    section 54(2), (3) or (4),
    paragraph 3, 4 or 14 of Part II of Schedule 1,
    paragraph 6 of Schedule 2,
    paragraph 2, 7 or 9 of Schedule 3,
    paragraph 4 of Schedule 4,
    paragraph 6 of Schedule 7,

    (b)    regulations under section 7 which—

      (i)    prescribe cases for the purposes of subsection (2)(b),

      (ii)    are made by virtue of subsection (7), or

      (iii)    relate to the definition of "the prescribed period",

    (c)    regulations under section 8(1) or 9(3),

    (d)    regulations under section 64,

    (e)    notification regulations (as defined by section 16(2)), or

    (f)    rules under paragraph 7 of Schedule 6,

and which is not subject to the requirement in subsection (4) that a draft of the instrument be laid before and approved by a resolution of each House of Parliament, shall be subject to annulment in pursuance of a resolution of either House of Parliament.

(6)    A statutory instrument which contains only—
      (a)    regulations prescribing fees for the purposes of any provision of this Act, or
      (b)    regulations under section 7 prescribing fees for !he purposes of any other enactment,

shall be laid before Parliament after being made.

**Commencement**   16 July 1998.
**Definitions**     For "the Commissioner", see s 6(1); for "notification regulations", see s 16(2); for "enactment", see s 70(1).

## 68  Meaning of "accessible record"

(1)    In this Act "accessible record" means—
      (a)    a health record as defined by subsection (2),
      (b)    an educational record as defined by Schedule 11, or
      (c)    an accessible public record as defined by Schedule 12.

(2)    In subsection (1)(a) "health record" means any record which—
      (a)    consists of information relating to the physical or mental health or condition of an individual, and
      (b)    has been made by or on behalf of a health professional in connection with the care of that individual.

**Commencement**   16 July 1998.
**References**     See para 1.28.

## 69  Meaning of "health professional"

(1)    In this Act "health professional" means any of the following—
      (a)    a registered medical practitioner,
      (b)    a registered dentist as defined by section 53(1) of the Dentists Act 1984,
      (c)    a registered optician as defined by section 36(1) of the Opticians Act 1989,
      (d)    a registered pharmaceutical chemist as defined by section 24(1) of the Pharmacy Act 1954 or a registered person as defined by Article 2(2) of the Pharmacy (Northern Ireland) Order 1976,
      (e)    a registered nurse, midwife or health visitor,
      (f)    a registered osteopath as defined by section 41 of the Osteopaths Act 1993,
      (g)    a registered chiropractor as defined by section 43 of the Chiropractors Act 1994,
      (h)    any person who is registered as a member of a profession to which the Professions Supplementary to Medicine Act 1960 for the time being extends,
      (i)    a clinical psychologist, child psychotherapist or speech therapist,
      (j)    a music therapist employed by a health service body, and
      (k)    a scientist employed by such a body as head of a department.

(2)    In subsection (1)(a) "registered medical practitioner" includes any person who is provisionally registered under section 15 or 21 of the Medical Act 1983 and is engaged in such employment as is mentioned in subsection (3) of that section.

(3)  In subsection (1) "health service body" means—
- (a)  a Health Authority established under section 8 of the National Health Service Act 1977,
- (b)  a Special Health Authority established under section 11 of that Act,
- (c)  a Health Board within the meaning of the National Health Service (Scotland) Act 1978,
- (d)  a Special Health Board within the meaning of that Act,
- (e)  the managers of a State Hospital provided under section 102 of that Act,
- (f)  a National Health Service trust first established under section 5 of the National Health Service and Community Care Act 1990 or section 12A of the National Health Service (Scotland) Act 1978,
- (g)  a Health and Social Services Board established under Article 16 of the Health and Personal Social Services (Northern Ireland) Order 1972,
- (h)  a special health and social services agency established under the Health and Personal Social Services (Special Agencies) (Northern Ireland) Order 1990, or
- (i)  a Health and Social Services trust established under Article 10 of the Health and Personal Social Services (Northern Ireland) Order 1991.

---

**Commencement**  16 July 1998.

## 70  Supplementary definitions

(1)  In this Act, unless the context otherwise requires—
"business" includes any trade or profession;
"the Commissioner" means the Data Protection Commissioner;
"credit reference agency" has the same meaning as in the Consumer Credit Act 1974;
"the Data Protection Directive" means Directive 95/46/EC on the protection of individuals with regard to the processing of personal data and on the free movement of such data;
"EEA State" means a State which is a contracting party to the Agreement on the European Economic Area signed at Oporto on 2nd May 1992 as adjusted by the Protocol signed at Brussels on 17th March 1993;
"enactment" includes an enactment passed after this Act;
"government department" includes a Northern Ireland department and any body or authority exercising statutory functions on behalf of the Crown;
"Minister of the Crown" has the same meaning as in the Ministers of the Crown Act 1975;
"public register" means any register which pursuant to a requirement imposed—
- (a)  by or under any enactment, or
- (b)  in pursuance of any international agreement,

is open to public inspection or open to inspection by any person having a legitimate interest;
"pupil"—
- (a)  in relation to a school in England and Wales, means a registered pupil within the meaning of the Education Act 1996,
- (b)  in relation to a school in Scotland, means a pupil within the meaning of the Education (Scotland) Act 1980, and
- (c)  in relation to a school in Northern Ireland, means a registered pupil within the meaning of the Education and Libraries (Northern Ireland) Order 1986;

"recipient", in relation to any personal data, means any person to whom the data are disclosed, including any person (such as an employee or agent of the data controller, a data processor or an employee or agent of a data processor) to whom they are disclosed in the course of processing the data for the data controller, but does not include any person to whom disclosure is or may be made as a result of, or with a view to, a particular inquiry by or on behalf of that person made in the exercise of any power conferred by law;

"registered company" means a company registered under the enactments relating to companies for the time being in force in the United Kingdom;

"school"—

(a)  in relation to England and Wales, has the same meaning as in the Education Act 1996,

(b)  in relation to Scotland, has the same meaning as in the Education (Scotland) Act 1980, and

(c)  in relation to Northern Ireland, has the same meaning as in the Education and Libraries (Northern Ireland) Order 1986;

"teacher" includes—

(a)  in Great Britain, head teacher, and

(b)  in Northern Ireland, the principal of a school;

"third party", in relation to personal data, means any person other than—

(a)  the data subject,

(b)  the data controller, or

(c)  any data processor or other person authorised to process data for the data controller or processor;

"the Tribunal" means the Data Protection Tribunal.

(2)  For the purposes of this Act data are inaccurate if they are incorrect or misleading as to any matter of fact.

---

**Commencement**  16 July 1998.

**Definitions**  For "data", "data processor", "data subject", "personal data" and "processing", see s 1(1) (and note also as to "processing", s 39, Sch 8, Pt II, para 5); for "data controller", see s 1(1), (4); as to "disclosing", see s 1(2)(b).

## 71  Index of defined expressions

The following Table shows provisions defining or otherwise explaining expressions used in this Act (other than provisions defining or explaining an expression only used in the same section or Schedule)—

| | |
|---|---|
| accessible record | section 68 |
| address (in Part III) | section 16(3) |
| business | section 70(1) |
| the Commissioner | section 70(1) |
| credit reference agency | section 70(1) |
| data | section 1(1) |
| data controller | sections 1(1) and (4) and 63(3) |
| data processor | section 1(1) |
| the Data Protection Directive | section 70(1) |
| data protection principles | section 4 and Schedule 1 |

| | |
|---|---|
| data subject | section 1(1) |
| disclosing (of personal data) | section 1(2)(b) |
| EEA State | section 70(1) |
| enactment | section 70(1) |
| enforcement notice | section 40(1) |
| fees regulations (in Part III) | section 16(2) |
| government department | section 70(1) |
| health professional | section 69 |
| inaccurate (in relation to data) | section 70(2) |
| information notice | section 43(1) |
| Minister of the Crown | section 70(1) |
| the non-disclosure provisions (in Part IV) | section 27(3) |
| notification regulations (in Part III) | section 16(2) |
| obtaining (of personal data) | section 1(2)(a) |
| personal data | section 1(1) |
| prescribed (in Part III) | section 16(2) |
| processing (of information or data) | section 1(1) and paragraph 5 of Schedule 8 |
| public register | section 70(1) |
| publish (in relation to journalistic, literary or artistic material) | section 32(6) |
| pupil (in relation to a school) | section 70(1) |
| recipient (in relation to personal data) | section 70(1) |
| recording (of personal data) | section 1(2)(a) |
| registered company | section 70(1) |
| registrable particulars (in Part III) | section 16(1) |
| relevant filing system | section 1(1) |
| school | section 70(1) |
| sensitive personal data | section 2 |
| special information notice | section 44(1) |
| the special purposes | section 3 |
| the subject information provisions (in Part IV) | section 27(2) |
| teacher | section 70(1) |
| third party (in relation to processing of personal data) | section 70(1) |
| the Tribunal | section 70(1) |
| using (of personal data) | section 1(2)(b). |

**Commencement**    16 July 1998.

### 72 Modifications of Act

During the period beginning with the commencement of this section and ending with 23rd October 2007, the provisions of this Act shall have effect subject to the modifications set out in Schedule 13.

**Commencement** to be appointed.

### 73 Transitional provisions and savings

Schedule 14 (which contains transitional provisions and savings) has effect.

**Commencement** to be appointed.

### 74 Minor and consequential amendments and repeals and revocations

(1)  Schedule 15 (which contains minor and consequential amendments) has effect.

(2)  The enactments and instruments specified in Schedule 16 are repealed or revoked to the extent specified.

**Commencement** to be appointed.
**Definitions** For "enactment", see s 70(1).

### 75 Short title, commencement and extent

(1)  This Act may be cited as the Data Protection Act 1998.

(2)  The following provisions of this Act—
    (a)  sections 1 to 3,
    (b)  section 25(1) and (4),
    (c)  section 26,
    (d)  sections 67 to 71,
    (e)  this section,
    (f)  paragraph 17 of Schedule 5,
    (g)  Schedule 11,
    (h)  Schedule 12, and
    (i)  so much of any other provision of this Act as confers any power to make subordinate legislation,
shall come into force on the day on which this Act is passed.

(3)  The remaining provisions of this Act shall come into force on such day as the Secretary of State may by order appoint; and different days may be appointed for different purposes.

(4)  The day appointed under subsection (3) for the coming into force of section 56 must not be earlier than the first day on which sections 112, 113 and 115 of the Police Act 1997 (which provide for the issue by the Secretary of State of criminal conviction certificates, criminal record certificates and enhanced criminal record certificates) are all in force.

(5)  Subject to subsection (6), this Act extends to Northern Ireland.

(6)  Any amendment, repeal or revocation made by Schedule 15 or 16 has the same extent as that of the enactment or instrument to which it relates.

**Commencement** 16 July 1998.
**Definitions** For "enactment", see s 70(1).

# SCHEDULES

## SCHEDULE 1

Section 4(1) and (2)

## THE DATA PROTECTION PRINCIPLES

### PART I
### THE PRINCIPLES

1.  Personal data shall be processed fairly and lawfully and, in particular, shall not be processed unless—

    (a)    at least one of the conditions in Schedule 2 is met, and

    (b)    in the case of sensitive personal data, at least one of the conditions in Schedule 3 is also met.

2.  Personal data shall be obtained only for one or more specified and lawful purposes, and shall not be further processed in any manner incompatible with that purpose or those purposes.

3.  Personal data shall be adequate, relevant and not excessive in relation to the purpose or purposes for which they are processed.

4.  Personal data shall be accurate and, where necessary, kept up to date.

5.  Personal data processed for any purpose or purposes shall not be kept for longer than is necessary for that purpose or those purposes.

6.  Personal data shall be processed in accordance with the rights of data subjects under this Act.

7.  Appropriate technical and organisational measures shall be taken against unauthorised or unlawful processing of personal data and against accidental loss or destruction of, or damage to, personal data.

8.  Personal data shall not be transferred to a country or territory outside the European Economic Area unless that country or territory ensures an adequate level of protection for the rights and freedoms of data subjects in relation to the processing of personal data.

---

**Commencement**  to be appointed.
**Definitions**    For "data", "data subject", "personal data" and "processed", see s 1(1) (and note also as to "personal data" and the processing thereof, s 27(1), and as to "processing", s 39, Sch 8, Pt II, para 5); as to "obtaining" data, see s 1(2)(a); for "sensitive personal data", see s 2.
**References**    See Ch 4.

### PART II
### INTERPRETATION OF THE PRINCIPLES IN PART I

*The first principle*

1.—(1) In determining for the purposes of the first principle whether personal data are processed fairly, regard is to be had to the method by which they are obtained, including in particular whether any person from whom they are obtained is deceived or misled as to the purpose or purposes for which they are to be processed.

(2) Subject to paragraph 2, for the purposes of the first principle data are to be treated as obtained fairly if they consist of information obtained from a person who—

    (a)    is authorised by or under any enactment to supply it, or

    (b)    is required to supply it by or under any enactment or by any convention or other instrument imposing an international obligation on the United Kingdom.

2.—(1) Subject to paragraph 3, for the purposes of the first principle personal data are not to be treated as processed fairly unless—

    (a)    in the case of data obtained from the data subject, the data controller ensures so far as practicable that the data subject has, is provided with, or has made readily available to him, the information specified in sub-paragraph (3), and

(b) in any other case, the data controller ensures so far as practicable that, before the relevant time or as soon as practicable after that time, the data subject has, is provided with, or has made readily available to him, the information specified in sub-paragraph (3).

(2) In sub-paragraph (1)(b) "the relevant time" means—
    (a) the time when the data controller first processes the data, or
    (b) in a case where at that time disclosure to a third party within a reasonable period is envisaged—
        (i) if the data are in fact disclosed to such a person within that period, the time when the data are first disclosed,
        (ii) if within that period the data controller becomes, or ought to become, aware that the data are unlikely to be disclosed to such a person within that period, the time when the data controller does become, or ought to become, so aware, or
        (iii) in any other case, the end of that period.

(3) The information referred to in sub-paragraph (1) is as follows, namely—
    (a) the identity of the data controller,
    (b) if he has nominated a representative for the purposes of this Act, the identity of that representative,
    (c) the purpose or purposes for which the data are intended to be processed, and
    (d) any further information which is necessary, having regard to the specific circumstances in which the data are or are to be processed, to enable processing in respect of the data subject to be fair.

3.—(1) Paragraph 2(1)(b) does not apply where either of the primary conditions in sub-paragraph (2), together with such further conditions as may be prescribed by the Secretary of State by order, are met.

(2) The primary conditions referred to in sub-paragraph (1) are—
    (a) that the provision of that information would involve a disproportionate effort, or
    (b) that the recording of the information to be contained in the data by, or the disclosure of the data by, the data controller is necessary for compliance with any legal obligation to which the data controller is subject, other than an obligation imposed by contract.

4.—(1) Personal data which contain a general identifier falling within a description prescribed by the Secretary of State by order are not to be treated as processed fairly and lawfully unless they are processed in compliance with any conditions so prescribed in relation to general identifiers of that description.

(2) In sub-paragraph (1) "a general identifier" means any identifier (such as, for example, a number or code used for identification purposes) which—
    (a) relates to an individual, and
    (b) forms part of a set of similar identifiers which is of general application.

## *The second principle*

5. The purpose or purposes for which personal data are obtained may in particular be specified—
    (a) in a notice given for the purposes of paragraph 2 by the data controller to the data subject, or
    (b) in a notification given to the Commissioner under Part III of this Act.

6. In determining whether any disclosure of personal data is compatible with the purpose or purposes for which the data were obtained, regard is to be had to the purpose or purposes for which the personal data are intended to be processed by any person to whom they are disclosed.

## *The fourth principle*

7. The fourth principle is not to be regarded as being contravened by reason of any inaccuracy in personal data which accurately record information obtained by the data controller from the data subject or a third party in a case where—
    (a) having regard to the purpose or purposes for which the data were obtained and further processed, the data controller has taken reasonable steps to ensure the accuracy of the data, and

(b)   if the data subject has notified the data controller of the data subject's view that the data are inaccurate, the data indicate that fact.

*The sixth principle*

8.   A person is to be regarded as contravening the sixth principle if, but only if—
    (a)   he contravenes section 7 by failing to supply information in accordance with that section,
    (b)   he contravenes section 10 by failing to comply with a notice given under subsection (1) of that section to the extent that the notice is justified or by failing to give a notice under subsection (3) of that section,
    (c)   he contravenes section 11 by failing to comply with a notice given under subsection (1) of that section, or
    (d)   he contravenes section 12 by failing to comply with a notice given under subsection (1) or (2)(b) of that section or by failing to give a notification under subsection (2)(a) of that section or a notice under subsection (3) of that section.

*The seventh principle*

9.   Having regard to the state of technological development and the cost of implementing any measures, the measures must ensure a level of security appropriate to—
    (a)   the harm that might result from such unauthorised or unlawful processing or accidental loss, destruction or damage as are mentioned in the seventh principle, and
    (b)   the nature of the data to be protected.

10. The data controller must take reasonable steps to ensure the reliability of any employees of his who have access to the personal data.

11. Where processing of personal data is carried out by a data processor on behalf of a data controller, the data controller must in order to comply with the seventh principle—
    (a)   choose a data processor providing sufficient guarantees in respect of the technical and organisational security measures governing the processing to be carried out, and
    (b)   take reasonable steps to ensure compliance with those measures.

12. Where processing of personal data is carried out by a data processor on behalf of a data controller, the data controller is not to be regarded as complying with the seventh principle unless—
    (a)   the processing is carried out under a contract—
        (i)   which is made or evidenced in writing, and
        (ii)  under which the data processor is to act only on instructions from the data controller, and
    (b)   the contract requires the data processor to comply with obligations equivalent to those imposed on a data controller by the seventh principle.

*The eighth principle*

13. An adequate level of protection is one which is adequate in all the circumstances of the case, having regard in particular to—
    (a)   the nature of the personal data,
    (b)   the country or territory of origin of the information contained in the data,
    (c)   the country or territory of final destination of that information,
    (d)   the purposes for which and period during which the data are intended to be processed,
    (e)   the law in force in the country or territory in question,
    (f)   the international obligations of that country or territory,
    (g)   any relevant codes of conduct or other rules which are enforceable in that country or territory (whether generally or by arrangement in particular cases), and
    (h)   any security measures taken in respect of the data in that country or territory.

14. The eighth principle does not apply to a transfer falling within any paragraph of Schedule 4, except in such circumstances and to such extent as the Secretary of State may by order provide.

15.—(1) Where—

    (a)  in any proceedings under this Act any question arises as to whether the requirement of the eighth principle as to an adequate level of protection is met in relation to the transfer of any personal data to a country or territory outside the European Economic Area, and

    (b)  a Community finding has been made in relation to transfers of the kind in question,

that question is to be determined in accordance with that finding.

(2) In sub-paragraph (1) "Community finding" means a finding of the European Commission, under the procedure provided for in Article 31(2) of the Data Protection Directive, that a country or territory outside the European Economic Area does, or does not, ensure an adequate level of protection within the meaning of Article 25(2) of the Directive.

**Commencement**  to be appointed.
**Modification**  see s 72, Sch 13, para 5.
**Definitions**  For "data", "data processor", "data subject", "personal data" and "processed", see s 1(1) (and note also as to processing, s 39, Sch 8, Pt II, para 5); for "data controller", see s 1(1), (4); as to "obtaining" and "recording" data, see s 1(2)(a); as to "disclosing" data, see s 1(2)(b); for "the Commissioner", see s 6(1); for "the Data Protection Directive", "enactment" and "third party", see s 70(1); as to "inaccurate", see s 70(2).
**References**  See Ch 4.

# SCHEDULE 2

Section 4(3)

## CONDITIONS RELEVANT FOR PURPOSES OF THE FIRST PRINCIPLE: PROCESSING OF ANY PERSONAL DATA

1.  The data subject has given his consent to the processing.

2.  The processing is necessary—

    (a)  for the performance of a contract to which the data subject is a party, or

    (b)  for the taking of steps at the request of the data subject with a view to entering into a contract.

3.  The processing is necessary for compliance with any legal obligation to which the data controller is subject, other than an obligation imposed by contract.

4.  The processing is necessary in order to protect the vital interests of the data subject.

5.  The processing is necessary—

    (a)  for the administration of justice,

    (b)  for the exercise of any functions conferred on any person by or under any enactment,

    (c)  for the exercise of any functions of the Crown, a Minister of the Crown or a government department, or

    (d)  for the exercise of any other functions of a public nature exercised in the public interest by any person.

6.—(1)  The processing is necessary for the purposes of legitimate interests pursued by the data controller or by the third party or parties to whom the data are disclosed, except where the processing is unwarranted in any particular case by reason of prejudice to the rights and freedoms or legitimate interests of the data subject.

(2)  The Secretary of State may by order specify particular circumstances in which this condition is, or is not, to be taken to be satisfied.

**Commencement**  16 July 1998 (in so far as conferring the power to make subordinate legislation); to be appointed (otherwise).
**Definitions**  For "data subject" and "processed", see s 1(1) (and note also as to processing, s 39, Sch 8, Pt II, para 5); for "data controller", see s 1(1), (4); as to "disclosing" data, see s 1(2)(b); for "enactment", "government department", "Minister of the Crown" and "third party", see s 70(1).
**References**  See paras 4.6–4.14.

## SCHEDULE 3

Section 4(3)

## CONDITIONS RELEVANT FOR PURPOSES OF THE FIRST PRINCIPLE: PROCESSING OF SENSITIVE PERSONAL DATA

1.  The data subject has given his explicit consent to the processing of the personal data.

2.—(1)  The processing is necessary for the purposes of exercising or performing any right or obligation which is conferred or imposed by law on the data controller in connection with employment.

(2)  The Secretary of State may by order—
  (a)  exclude the application of sub-paragraph (1) in such cases as may be specified, or
  (b)  provide that, in such cases as may be specified, the condition in subparagraph (1) is not to be regarded as satisfied unless such further conditions as may be specified in the order are also satisfied.

3.  The processing is necessary—
  (a)  in order to protect the vital interests of the data subject or another person, in a case where—
    (i)  consent cannot be given by or on behalf of the data subject, or
    (ii)  the data controller cannot reasonably be expected to obtain the consent of the data subject, or
  (b)  in order to protect the vital interests of another person, in a case where consent by or on behalf of the data subject has been unreasonably withheld.

4.  The processing—
  (a)  is carried out in the course of its legitimate activities by any body or association which—
    (i)  is not established or conducted for profit, and
    (ii)  exists for political, philosophical religious or trade-union purposes,
  (b)  is carried out with appropriate safeguards for the rights and freedoms of data subjects,
  (c)  relates only to individuals who either are members of the body or association or have regular contact with it in connection with its purposes, and
  (d)  does not involve disclosure of the personal data to a third party without the consent of the data subject.

5.  The information contained in the personal data has been made public as a result of steps deliberately taken by the data subject.

6.  The processing—
  (a)  is necessary for the purpose of, or in connection with, any legal proceedings (including prospective legal proceedings),
  (b)  is necessary for the purpose of obtaining legal advice, or
  (c)  is otherwise necessary for the purposes of establishing, exercising or defending legal rights.

7.—(1)  The processing is necessary—
  (a)  for the administration of justice,
  (b)  for the exercise of any functions conferred on any person by or under an enactment, or
  (c)  for the exercise of any functions of the Crown, a Minister of the Crown or a government department.

(2)  The Secretary of State may by order—
  (a)  exclude the application of sub-paragraph (1) in such cases as may be specified, or
  (b)  provide that, in such cases as may be specified, the condition in subparagraph (1) is not to be regarded as satisfied unless such further conditions as may be specified in the order are also satisfied.

8.—(1)  The processing is necessary for medical purposes and is undertaken by—

    (a)  a health professional, or

    (b)  a person who in the circumstances owes a duty of confidentiality which is equivalent to that which would arise if that person were a health professional.

(2)  In this paragraph "medical purposes" includes the purposes of preventative medicine, medical diagnosis, medical research, the provision of care and treatment and the management of healthcare services.

9.—(1)  The processing—

    (a)  is of sensitive personal data consisting of information as to racial or ethnic origin,

    (b)  is necessary for the purpose of identifying or keeping under review the existence or absence of equality of opportunity or treatment between persons of different racial or ethnic origins, with a view to enabling such equality to be promoted or maintained, and

    (c)  is carried out with appropriate safeguards for the rights and freedoms of data subjects.

(2)  The Secretary of State may by order specify circumstances in which processing falling within sub-paragraph (1)(a) and (b) is, or is not, to be taken for the purposes of sub-paragraph (1)(c) to be carried out with appropriate safeguards for the rights and freedoms of data subjects.

10.  The personal data are processed in circumstances specified in an order made by the Secretary of State for the purposes of this paragraph.

---

**Commencement**  16 July 1998 (in so far as conferring the power to make subordinate legislation); to be appointed (otherwise).

**Definitions**  For "data subject", "personal data" and "processed", see s 1(1) (and note also as to processing, s 39, Sch 8, Pt II, para 5); for "data controller", see s 1(1), (4); as to "disclosing" data, see s 1(2)(b); for "sensitive personal data", see s 2; for "health professional", see s 69; for "enactment", "government department", "Minister of the Crown" and "third party", see s 70(1).

**References**  See paras 2.25–2.34.

---

# SCHEDULE 4

Section 4(3)

## CASES WHERE THE EIGHTH PRINCIPLE DOES NOT APPLY

1.  The data subject has given his consent to the transfer.

2.  The transfer is necessary—

    (a)  for the performance of a contract between the data subject and the data controller, or

    (b)  for the taking of steps at the request of the data subject with a view to his entering into a contract with the data controller.

3.  The transfer is necessary—

    (a)  for the conclusion of a contract between the data controller and a person other than the data subject which—

        (i)  is entered into at the request of the data subject, or

        (ii)  is in the interests of the data subject, or

    (b)  for the performance of such a contract.

4.—(1)  The transfer is necessary for reasons of substantial public interest.

(2)  The Secretary of State may by order specify—

    (a)  circumstances in which a transfer is to be taken for the purposes of subparagraph (1) to be necessary for reasons of substantial public interest, and

    (b)  circumstances in which a transfer which is not required by or under an enactment is not to be taken for the purpose of sub-paragraph (1) to be necessary for reasons of substantial public interest.

5. The transfer—
    (a)  is necessary for the purpose of, or in connection with, any legal proceedings (including prospective legal proceedings),
    (b)  is necessary for the purpose of obtaining legal advice, or
    (c)  is otherwise necessary for the purposes of establishing, exercising or defending legal rights.

6. The transfer is necessary in order to protect the vital interests of the data subject.

7. The transfer is of part of the personal data on a public register and any conditions subject to which the register is open to inspection are complied with by any person to whom the data are or may be disclosed after the transfer.

8. The transfer is made on terms which are of a kind approved by the Commissioner as ensuring adequate safeguards for the rights and freedoms of data subjects.

9. The transfer has been authorised by the Commissioner as being made in such a manner as to ensure adequate safeguards for the rights and freedoms of data subjects.

---

**Commencement**  16 July 1998 (in so far as conferring the power to make subordinate legislation); to be appointed (otherwise).
**Definitions**  For "data", "data subject" and "personal data", see s 1(1); for "data controller", see s 1(1), (4); as to "disclosing" data, see s 1(2)(b); for "the Commissioner", see s 6(1); for "enactment" and "public register", see s 70(1).
**References**  See paras 7.8–7.26.

---

## SCHEDULE 5
Section 6(7)

## THE DATA PROTECTION COMMISSIONER
## AND THE DATA PROTECTION TRIBUNAL

### PART I
### THE COMMISSIONER

*Status and capacity*

1.—(1) The corporation sole by the name of the Data Protection Registrar established by the Data Protection Act 1984 shall continue in existence by the name of the Data Protection Commissioner.

(2) The Commissioner and his officers and staff are not to be regarded as servants or agents of the Crown.

*Tenure of office*

2.—(1) Subject to the provisions of this paragraph, the Commissioner shall hold office for such term not exceeding five years as may be determined at the time of his appointment.

(2) The Commissioner may be relieved of his office by Her Majesty at his own request.

(3) The Commissioner may be removed from office by Her Majesty in pursuance of an Address from both Houses of Parliament.

(4) The Commissioner shall in any case vacate his office—
    (a)  on completing the year of service in which he attains the age of sixty-five years, or
    (b)  if earlier, on completing his fifteenth year of service.

(5) Subject to sub-paragraph (4), a person who ceases to be Commissioner on the expiration of his term of office shall be eligible for re-appointment, but a person may not be re-appointed for a third or subsequent term as Commissioner unless, by reason of special circumstances, the person's re-appointment for such a term is desirable in the public interest.

*Salary etc*

3.—(1)  There shall be paid—

    (a)   to the Commissioner such salary, and

    (b)   to or in respect of the Commissioner such pension,

as may be specified by a resolution of the House of Commons.

    (2)  A resolution for the purposes of this paragraph may—

    (a)   specify the salary or pension,

    (b)   provide that the salary or pension is to be the same as, or calculated on the same basis as, that payable to, or to or in respect of, a person employed in a specified office under, or in a specified capacity in the service of, the Crown, or

    (c)   specify the salary or pension and provide for it to be increased by reference to such variables as may be specified in the resolution.

    (3)  A resolution for the purposes of this paragraph may take effect from the date on which it is passed or from any earlier or later date specified in the resolution.

    (4)  A resolution for the purposes of this paragraph may make different provision in relation to the pension payable to or in respect of different holders of the office of Commissioner.

    (5)  Any salary or pension payable under this paragraph shall be charged on and issued out of the Consolidated Fund.

    (6)  In this paragraph "pension" includes an allowance or gratuity and any reference to the payment of a pension includes a reference to the making of payments towards the provision of a pension.

*Officers and staff*

4.—(1)  The Commissioner—

    (a)   shall appoint a deputy commissioner, and

    (b)   may appoint such number of other officers and staff as he may determine.

    (2)  The remuneration and other conditions of service of the persons appointed under this paragraph shall be determined by the Commissioner.

    (3)  The Commissioner may pay such pensions, allowances or gratuities to or in respect of the persons appointed under this paragraph, or make such payments towards the provision of such pensions, allowances or gratuities, as he may determine.

    (4)  The references in sub-paragraph (3) to pensions, allowances or gratuities to or in respect of the persons appointed under this paragraph include references to pensions, allowances or gratuities by way of compensation to or in respect of any of those persons who suffer loss of office or employment.

    (5)  Any determination under sub-paragraph (1)(b), (2) or (3) shall require the approval of the Secretary of State.

    (6)  The Employers' Liability (Compulsory Insurance) Act 1969 shall not require insurance to be effected by the Commissioner.

5.—(1)  The deputy commissioner shall perform the functions conferred by this Act on the Commissioner during any vacancy in that office or at any time when the Commissioner is for any reason unable to act.

    (2)  Without prejudice to sub-paragraph (1), any functions of the Commissioner under this Act may, to the extent authorised by him, be performed by any of his officers or staff.

*Authentication of seal of the Commissioner*

6.  The application of the seal of the Commissioner shall be authenticated by his signature or by the signature of some other person authorised for the purpose.

*Presumption of authenticity of documents issued by the Commissioner*

7.  Any document purporting to be an instrument issued by the Commissioner and to be duly executed under the Commissioner's seal or to be signed by or on behalf of the Commissioner shall be received in evidence and shall be deemed to be such an instrument unless the contrary is shown.

*Money*

8. The Secretary of State may make payments to the Commissioner out of money provided by Parliament.

9.—(1) All fees and other sums received by the Commissioner in the exercise of his functions under this Act or section 159 of the Consumer Credit Act 1974 shall be paid by him to the Secretary of State.

(2) Sub-paragraph (1) shall not apply where the Secretary of State, with the consent of the Treasury, otherwise directs.

(3) Any sums received by the Secretary of State under sub-paragraph (1) shall be paid into the Consolidated Fund.

*Accounts*

10.—(1) It shall be the duty of the Commissioner—

    (a) to keep proper accounts and other records in relation to the accounts,

    (b) to prepare in respect of each financial year a statement of account in such form as the Secretary of State may direct, and

    (c) to send copies of that statement to the Comptroller and Auditor General on or before 31st August next following the end of the year to which the statement relates or on or before such earlier date after the end of that year as the Treasury may direct.

(2) The Comptroller and Auditor General shall examine and certify any statement sent to him under this paragraph and lay copies of it together with his report thereon before each House of Parliament.

(3) In this paragraph "financial year" means a period of twelve months beginning with 1st April.

*Application of Part I in Scotland*

11. Paragraphs 1(1), 6 and 7 do not extend to Scotland.

---

**Commencement**  to be appointed.
**Definitions**  For "the Commissioner", see s 6(1).
**References**  See paras 3.4, 3.5.

---

# PART II
# THE TRIBUNAL

*Tenure of office*

12.—(1) Subject to the following provisions of this paragraph, a member of the Tribunal shall hold and vacate his office in accordance with the terms of his appointment and shall, on ceasing to hold office, be eligible for re-appointment.

(2) Any member of the Tribunal may at any time resign his office by notice in writing to the Lord Chancellor (in the case of the chairman or a deputy chairman) or to the Secretary of State (in the case of any other member).

(3) A person who is the chairman or deputy chairman of the Tribunal shall vacate his office on the day on which he attains the age of seventy years; but this sub-paragraph is subject to section 26(4) to (6) of the Judicial Pensions and Retirement Act 1993 (power to authorise continuance in office up to the age of seventy-five years).

*Salary etc*

13. The Secretary of State shall pay to the members of the Tribunal out of money provided by Parliament such remuneration and allowances as he may determine.

*Officers and staff*

14. The Secretary of State may provide the Tribunal with such officers and staff as he thinks necessary for the proper discharge of its functions.

*Expenses*

15. Such expenses of the Tribunal as the Secretary of State may determine shall be defrayed by the Secretary of State out of money provided by Parliament.

---

**Commencement** to be appointed.
**Definitions** For "the Tribunal", see s 6(3).
**References** See paras 5.61, 5.62.

---

# PART III
# TRANSITIONAL PROVISIONS

16. Any reference in any enactment, instrument or other document to the Data Protection Registrar shall be construed, in relation to any time after the commencement of section 6(1), as a reference to the Commissioner.

17. Any reference in this Act or in any instrument under this Act to the Commissioner shall be construed, in relation to any time before the commencement of section 6(1), as a reference to the Data Protection Registrar.

---

**Commencement** 16 July 1998 (para 17); to be appointed (otherwise).
**Definitions** For "the Commissioner", see s 6(1); for "enactment", see s 70(1).

---

# SCHEDULE 6

Sections 28(12), 48(5)

# APPEAL PROCEEDINGS

*Hearing of appeals*

1. For the purpose of hearing and determining appeals or any matter preliminary or incidental to an appeal the Tribunal shall sit at such times and in such places as the chairman or a deputy chairman may direct and may sit in two or more divisions.

*Constitution of Tribunal in national security cases*

2.—(1) The Lord Chancellor shall from time to time designate, from among the chairman and deputy chairmen appointed by him under section 6(4)(a) and (b), those persons who are to be capable of hearing appeals under section 28(4) or (6).

(2) A designation under sub-paragraph (1) may at any time be revoked by the Lord Chancellor.

3. In any case where the application of paragraph 6(1) is excluded by rules under paragraph 7, the Tribunal shall be duly constituted for an appeal under section 28(4) or (6) if it consists of three of the persons designated under paragraph 2(1), of whom one shall be designated by the Lord Chancellor to preside.

*Constitution of Tribunal in other cases*

4.—(1) Subject to any rules made under paragraph 7, the Tribunal shall be duly constituted for an appeal under section 48(1), (2) or (4) if it consists of—
    (a)   the chairman or a deputy chairman (who shall preside), and
    (b)   an equal number of the members appointed respectively in accordance with paragraphs (a) and (b) of section 6(6).

(2) The members who are to constitute the Tribunal in accordance with subparagraph (1) shall be nominated by the chairman or, if he is for any reason unable to act, by a deputy chairman.

*Determination of questions by full Tribunal*

5. The determination of any question before the Tribunal when constituted in accordance with paragraph 3 or 4 shall be according to the opinion of the majority of the members hearing the appeal.

*Ex parte proceedings*

6.—(1) Subject to any rules made under paragraph 7, the jurisdiction of the Tribunal in respect of an appeal under section 28(4) or (6) shall be exercised ex parte by one or more persons designated under paragraph 2(1).

(2) Subject to any rules made under paragraph 7, the jurisdiction of the Tribunal in respect of an appeal under section 48(3) shall be exercised ex parte by the chairman or a deputy chairman sitting alone.

*Rules of procedure*

7.—(1) The Secretary of State may make rules for regulating the exercise of the rights of appeal conferred by sections 28(4) or (6) and 48 and the practice and procedure of the Tribunal.

(2) Rules under this paragraph may in particular make provision—
   (a) with respect to the period within which an appeal can be brought and the burden of proof on an appeal,
   (b) for the summoning (or, in Scotland, citation) of witnesses and the administration of oaths,
   (c) for securing the production of documents and material used for the processing of personal data,
   (d) for the inspection, examination, operation and testing of any equipment or material used in connection with the processing of personal data,
   (e) for the hearing of an appeal wholly or partly in camera,
   (f) for hearing an appeal in the absence of the appellant or for determining an appeal without a hearing,
   (g) for enabling an appeal under section 48(1) against an information notice to be determined by the chairman or a deputy chairman,
   (h) for enabling any matter preliminary or incidental to an appeal to be dealt with by the chairman or a deputy chairman,
   (i) for the awarding of costs or, in Scotland, expenses,
   (j) for the publication of reports of the Tribunal's decisions, and
   (k) for conferring on the Tribunal such ancillary powers as the Secretary of State thinks necessary for the proper discharge of its functions.

(3) In making rules under this paragraph which relate to appeals under section 28(4) or (6) the Secretary of State shall have regard, in particular, to the need to secure that information is not disclosed contrary to the public interest.

*Obstruction etc*

8.—(1) If any person is guilty of any act or omission in relation to proceedings before the Tribunal which, if those proceedings were proceedings before a court having power to commit for contempt, would constitute contempt of court, the Tribunal may certify the offence to the High Court or, in Scotland, the Court of Session.

(2) Where an offence is so certified, the court may inquire into the matter and, after hearing any witness who may be produced against or on behalf of the person charged with the offence, and after hearing any statement that may be offered in defence, deal with him in any manner in which it could deal with him if he had committed the like offence in relation to the court.

---

**Commencement**   16 July 1998 (in so far as conferring the power to make subordinate legislation); to be appointed (otherwise).

**Definitions**   For "personal data" and "processing", see s 1(1) (and note also as to "processing", s 39, Sch 8, Pt II, para 5); as to "disclosing", see s 1(2)(b); for "the Tribunal", see s 6(3); for "information notices", see s 43(1).

## SCHEDULE 7

Section 37

## MISCELLANEOUS EXEMPTIONS

*Confidential references given by the data controller*

1. Personal data are exempt from section 7 if they consist of a reference given or to be given in confidence by the data controller for the purposes of—
   (a) the education, training or employment, or prospective education, training or employment, of the data subject,
   (b) the appointment, or prospective appointment, of the data subject to any office, or
   (c) the provision, or prospective provision, by the data subject of any service.

*Armed forces*

2. Personal data are exempt from the subject information provisions in any case to the extent to which the application of those provisions would be likely to prejudice the combat effectiveness of any of the armed forces of the Crown.

*Judicial appointments and honours*

3. Personal data processed for the purposes of—
   (a) assessing any person's suitability for judicial office or the office of Queen's Counsel, or
   (b) the conferring by the Crown of any honour,

are exempt from the subject information provisions.

*Crown employment and Crown or Ministerial appointments*

4. The Secretary of State may by order exempt from the subject information provisions personal data processed for the purposes of assessing any person's suitability for—
   (a) employment by or under the Crown, or
   (b) any office to which appointments are made by Her Majesty, by a Minister of the Crown or by a Northern Ireland department.

*Management forecasts etc*

5. Personal data processed for the purposes of management forecasting or management planning to assist the data controller in the conduct of any business or other activity are exempt from the subject information provisions in any case to the extent to which the application of those provisions would be likely to prejudice the conduct of that business or other activity.

*Corporate finance*

6.—(1) Where personal data are processed for the purposes of, or in connection with, a corporate finance service provided by a relevant person—
   (a) the data are exempt from the subject information provisions in any case to the extent to which either—
       (i) the application of those provisions to the data could affect the price of any instrument which is already in existence or is to be or may be created, or
       (ii) the data controller reasonably believes that the application of those provisions to the data could affect the price of any such instrument, and
   (b) to the extent that the data are not exempt from the subject information provisions by virtue of paragraph (a), they are exempt from those provisions if the exemption is required for the purpose of safeguarding an important economic or financial interest of the United Kingdom.

(2) For the purposes of sub-paragraph (1)(b) the Secretary of State may by order specify—
   (a) matters to be taken into account in determining whether exemption from the subject information provisions is required for the purpose of safeguarding an important economic or financial interest of the United Kingdom, or
   (b) circumstances in which exemption from those provisions is, or is not, to be taken to be required for that purpose.

(3) In this paragraph—
   "corporate finance service" means a service consisting in—
       (a) underwriting in respect of issues of, or the placing of issues of, any instrument,

(b)  advice to undertakings on capital structure, industrial strategy and related matters and advice and service relating to mergers and the purchase of undertakings, or

(c)  services relating to such underwriting as is mentioned in paragraph (a);

"instrument" means any instrument listed in section B of the Annex to the Council Directive on investment services in the securities field (93/22/EEC), as set out in Schedule 1 to the Investment Services Regulations 1995;

"price" includes value;

"relevant person" means—

(a)  any person who is authorised under Chapter III of Part I of the Financial Services Act 1986 or is an exempted person under Chapter IV of Part I of that Act,

(b)  any person who, but for Part III or IV of Schedule 1 to that Act, would require authorisation under that Act,

(c)  any European investment firm within the meaning given by Regulation 3 of the Investment Services Regulations 1995,

(d)  any person who, in the course of his employment, provides to his employer a service falling within paragraph (b) or (c) of the definition of "corporate finance service", or

(e)  any partner who provides to other partners in the partnership a service falling within either of those paragraphs.

*Negotiations*

7.  Personal data which consist of records of the intentions of the data controller in relation to any negotiations with the data subject are exempt from the subject information provisions in any case to the extent to which the application of those provisions would be likely to prejudice those negotiations.

*Examination marks*

8.—(1)  Section 7 shall have effect subject to the provisions of sub-paragraphs (2) to (4) in the case of personal data consisting of marks or other information processed by a data controller—

(a)  for the purpose of determining the results of an academic, professional or other examination or of enabling the results of any such examination to be determined, or

(b)  in consequence of the determination of any such results.

(2)  Where the relevant day falls before the day on which the results of the examination are announced, the period mentioned in section 7(8) shall be extended until—

(a)  the end of five months beginning with the relevant day, or

(b)  the end of forty days beginning with the date of the announcement,

whichever is the earlier.

(3)  Where by virtue of sub-paragraph (2) a period longer than the prescribed period elapses after the relevant day before the request is complied with, the information to be supplied pursuant to the request shall be supplied both by reference to the data in question at the time when the request is received and (if different) by reference to the data as from time to time held in the period beginning when the request is received and ending when it is complied with.

(4)  For the purposes of this paragraph the results of an examination shall be treated as announced when they are first published or (if not published) when they are first made available or communicated to the candidate in question.

(5)  In this paragraph—

"examination" includes any process for determining the knowledge, intelligence, skill or ability of a candidate by reference to his performance in any test, work or other activity;

"the prescribed period" means forty days or such other period as is for the time being prescribed under section 7 in relation to the personal data in question;

"relevant day" has the same meaning as in section 7.

*Examination scripts etc*

9.—(1) Personal data consisting of information recorded by candidates during an academic, professional or other examination are exempt from section 7.

(2) In this paragraph "examination" has the same meaning as in paragraph 8.

*Legal professional privilege*

10. Personal data are exempt from the subject information provisions if the data consist of information in respect of which a claim to legal professional privilege or, in Scotland, to confidentiality as between client and professional legal adviser, could be maintained in legal proceedings.

*Self-incrimination*

11.—(1) A person need not comply with any request or order under section 7 to the extent that compliance would, by revealing evidence of the commission of any offence other than an offence under this Act, expose him to proceedings for that offence.

(2) Information disclosed by any person in compliance with any request or order under section 7 shall not be admissible against him in proceedings for an offence under this Act.

---

**Commencement**  16 July 1998 (in so far as conferring the power to make subordinate legislation); to be appointed (otherwise).
**Definitions**  For "data", "data subject", "personal data" and "processing", see s 1(1) (and note also as to "processing", s 39, Sch 8, Pt II, para 5); for "data controller", see s 1(1), (4); as to "recording", see s 1(2)(a); as to "disclosing", see s 1(2)(b); for "the subject information provisions", see s 27(2); as to "published", see s 32(6); for "business" and "Minister of the Crown", see s 70(1).
**References**  See paras 5.27–5.38.

# SCHEDULE 8

Section 39

## TRANSITIONAL RELIEF

### PART I
### INTERPRETATION OF SCHEDULE

1.—(1)  For the purposes of this Schedule, personal data are "eligible data" at any time if, and to the extent that, they are at that time subject to processing which was already under way immediately before 24th October 1998.

(2)  In this Schedule—
> "eligible automated data" means eligible data which fall within paragraph (a) or (b) of the definition of "data" in section 1(1);
> "eligible manual data" means eligible data which are not eligible automated data;
> "the first transitional period" means the period beginning with the commencement of this Schedule and ending with 23rd October 2001;
> "the second transitional period" means the period beginning with 24th October 2001 and ending with 23rd October 2007.

---

**Commencement**  to be appointed.
**Definitions**  For "data", "personal data" and as to "processing", see s 1(1).

### PART II
### EXEMPTIONS AVAILABLE BEFORE 24TH OCTOBER 2001

*Manual data*

2.—(1)  Eligible manual data, other than data forming part of an accessible record, are exempt from the data protection principles and Parts II and III of this Act during the first transitional period.

(2)  This paragraph does not apply to eligible manual data to which paragraph 4 applies.

3.—(1)  This paragraph applies to—
   (a)  eligible manual data forming part of an accessible record, and
   (b)  personal data which fall within paragraph (d) of the definition of "data" in section 1(1) but which, because they are not subject to processing which was already under way immediately before 24th October 1998, are not eligible data for the purposes of this Schedule.

(2)  During the first transitional period, data to which this paragraph applies are exempt from—
   (a)  the data protection principles, except the sixth principle so far as relating to sections 7 and 12A,
   (b)  Part II of this Act, except—
      (i)  section 7 (as it has effect subject to section 8) and section 12A, and
      (ii)  section 15 so far as relating to those sections, and
   (c)  Part III of this Act.

4.—(1)  This paragraph applies to eligible manual data which consist of information relevant to the financial standing of the data subject and in respect of which the data controller is a credit reference agency.

(2)  During the first transitional period, data to which this paragraph applies are exempt from—
   (a)  the data protection principles, except the sixth principle so far as relating to sections 7 and 12A,
   (b)  Part II of this Act, except—
      (i)  section 7 (as it has effect subject to sections 8 and 9) and section 12A, and
      (ii)  section 15 so far as relating to those sections, and
   (c)  Part III of this Act.

*Processing otherwise than by reference to the data subject*

5.  During the first transitional period, for the purposes of this Act (apart from paragraph 1), eligible automated data are not to be regarded as being "processed" unless the processing is by reference to the data subject.

*Payrolls and accounts*

6.—(1)  Subject to sub-paragraph (2), eligible automated data processed by a data controller for one or more of the following purposes—
   (a)  calculating amounts payable by way of remuneration or pensions in respect of service in any employment or office or making payments of, or of sums deducted from, such remuneration or pensions, or
   (b)  keeping accounts relating to any business or other activity carried on by the data controller or keeping records of purchases, sales or other transactions for the purpose of ensuring that the requisite payments are made by or to him in respect of those transactions or for the purpose of making financial or management forecasts to assist him in the conduct of any such business or activity,

are exempt from the data protection principles and Parts II and III of this Act during the first transitional period.

(2)  It shall be a condition of the exemption of any eligible automated data under this paragraph that the data are not processed for any other purpose, but the exemption is not lost by any processing of the eligible data for any other purpose if the data controller shows that he had taken such care to prevent it as in all the circumstances was reasonably required.

(3)  Data processed only for one or more of the purposes mentioned in subparagraph (1)(a) may be disclosed—
   (a)  to any person, other than the data controller, by whom the remuneration or pensions in question are payable,
   (b)  for the purpose of obtaining actuarial advice,
   (c)  for the purpose of giving information as to the persons in any employment or office for use in medical research into the health of, or injuries suffered by, persons engaged in particular occupations or working in particular places or areas,

- (d) if the data subject (or a person acting on his behalf) has requested or consented to the disclosure of the data either generally or in the circumstances in which the disclosure in question is made, or
- (e) if the person making the disclosure has reasonable grounds for believing that the disclosure falls within paragraph (d).

(4) Data processed for any of the purposes mentioned in sub-paragraph (1) may be disclosed—
- (a) for the purpose of audit or where the disclosure is for the purpose only of giving information about the data controller's financial affairs, or
- (b) in any case in which disclosure would be permitted by any other provision of this Part of this Act if sub-paragraph (2) were included among the non-disclosure provisions.

(5) In this paragraph "remuneration" includes remuneration in kind and "pensions" includes gratuities or similar benefits.

### Unincorporated members' clubs and mailing lists

7. Eligible automated data processed by an unincorporated members' club and relating only to the members of the club are exempt from the data protection principles and Parts II and III of this Act during the first transitional period.

8. Eligible automated data processed by a data controller only for the purposes of distributing, or recording the distribution of, articles or information to the data subjects and consisting only of their names, addresses or other particulars necessary for effecting the distribution, are exempt from the data protection principles and Parts II and III of this Act during the first transitional period.

9. Neither paragraph 7 nor paragraph 8 applies to personal data relating to any data subject unless he has been asked by the club or data controller whether he objects to the data relating to him being processed as mentioned in that paragraph and has not objected.

10. It shall be a condition of the exemption of any data under paragraph 7 that the data are not disclosed except as permitted by paragraph 11 and of the exemption under paragraph 8 that the data are not processed for any purpose other than that mentioned in that paragraph or as permitted by paragraph 11, but—
- (a) the exemption under paragraph 7 shall not be lost by any disclosure in breach of that condition, and
- (b) the exemption under paragraph 8 shall not be lost by any processing in breach of that condition,

if the data controller shows that he had taken such care to prevent it as in all the circumstances was reasonably required.

11. Data to which paragraph 10 applies may be disclosed—
- (a) if the data subject (or a person acting on his behalf) has requested or consented to the disclosure of the data either generally or in the circumstances in which the disclosure in question is made,
- (b) if the person making the disclosure has reasonable grounds for believing that the disclosure falls within paragraph (a), or
- (c) in any case in which disclosure would be permitted by any other provision of this Part of this Act if paragraph 8 were included among the non-disclosure provisions.

### Back-up data

12. Eligible automated data which are processed only for the purpose of replacing other data in the event of the latter being lost, destroyed or impaired are exempt from section 7 during the first transitional period.

### Exemption of all eligible automated data from certain requirements

13.—(1) During the first transitional period, eligible automated data are exempt from the following provisions—
- (a) the first data protection principle to the extent to which it requires compliance with—
  - (i) paragraph 2 of Part II of Schedule 1,
  - (ii) the conditions in Schedule 2, and
  - (iii) the conditions in Schedule 3,
- (b) the seventh data protection principle to the extent to which it requires compliance with paragraph 12 of Part II of Schedule 1;

  (c)   the eighth data protection principle,
  (d)   in section 7(1), paragraphs (b), (c)(ii) and (d),
  (e)   sections 10 and 11,
  (f)   section 12, and
  (g)   section 13, except so far as relating to—
    (i)  any contravention of the fourth data protection principle,
   (ii)  any disclosure without the consent of the data controller,
  (iii)  loss or destruction of data without the consent of the data controller, or
  (iv)  processing for the special purposes.

(2)  The specific exemptions conferred by sub-paragraph (1)(a), (c) and (e) do not limit the data controller's general duty under the first data protection principle to ensure that processing is fair.

**Commencement**  to be appointed.
**Definitions**  For "data", "data subject", "personal data" and "processed", see s 1(1); for "data controller", see s 1(1), (4); as to "disclosing" data, see s 1(2)(b); for "the data protection principles", see s 4; for "accessible record", see s 68; for "business" and "credit reference agency", see s 70(1); for "eligible data", see para 1(1) of Pt I of this Schedule; for "eligible automated data", "eligible manual data" and "the first transitional period", see para 1(2) of Pt I of this Schedule.
**References**  See paras 1.28, 1.29, 1.31.

## PART III
### EXEMPTIONS AVAILABLE AFTER 23RD OCTOBER 2001 BUT BEFORE 24TH OCTOBER 2007

14.—(1)  This paragraph applies to—
  (a)   eligible manual data which were held immediately before 24th October 1998, and
  (b)   personal data which fall within paragraph (d) of the definition of "data" in section 1(1) but do not fall within paragraph (a) of this subparagraph,

but does not apply to eligible manual data to which the exemption in paragraph 16 applies.

(2)  During the second transitional period, data to which this paragraph applies are exempt from the following provisions—
  (a)   the first data protection principle except to the extent to which it requires compliance with paragraph 2 of Part II of Schedule 1,
  (b)   the second, third, fourth and fifth data protection principles, and
  (c)   section 14(1) to (3).

**Commencement**  to be appointed.
**Definitions**  For "data" and "personal data", see s 1(1); for "the data protection principles", see s 4; for "eligible manual data" and "the second transitional period", see para 1(2) of Pt I of this Schedule.
**References**  See para 1.30.

## PART IV
### EXEMPTIONS AFTER 23RD OCTOBER 2001 FOR HISTORICAL RESEARCH

15.  In this Part of this Schedule "the relevant conditions" has the same meaning as in section 33.

16.—(1)  Eligible manual data which are processed only for the purpose of historical research in compliance with the relevant conditions are exempt from the provisions specified in sub-paragraph (2) after 23rd October 2001.

(2)  The provisions referred to in sub-paragraph (1) are—
  (a)   the first data protection principle except in so far as it requires compliance with paragraph 2 of Part II of Schedule 1,
  (b)   the second, third, fourth and fifth data protection principles, and
  (c)   section 14(1) to (3).

17.—(1) After 23rd October 2001 eligible automated data which are processed only for the purpose of historical research in compliance with the relevant conditions are exempt from the first data protection principle to the extent to which it requires compliance with the conditions in Schedules 2 and 3.

(2) Eligible automated data which are processed—
  (a)  only for the purpose of historical research,
  (b)  in compliance with the relevant conditions, and
  (c)  otherwise than by reference to the data subject,

are also exempt from the provisions referred to in sub-paragraph (3) after 23rd October 2001.

(3) The provisions referred to in sub-paragraph (2) are—
  (a)  the first data protection principle except in so far as it requires compliance with paragraph 2 of Part II of Schedule 1,
  (b)  the second, third, fourth and fifth data protection principles, and
  (c)  section 14(1) to (3).

18. For the purposes of this Part of this Schedule personal data are not to be treated as processed otherwise than for the purpose of historical research merely because the data are disclosed—
  (a)  to any person, for the purpose of historical research only,
  (b)  to the data subject or a person acting on his behalf,
  (c)  at the request, or with the consent, of the data subject or a person acting on his behalf, or
  (d)  in circumstances in which the person making the disclosure has reasonable grounds for believing that the disclosure falls within paragraph (a), (b) or (c).

**Commencement**  to be appointed.
**Definitions**    For "data", "data subject", "personal data" and "processed", see s 1(1); as to "disclosing" data, see s 1(2)(b); for "the data protection principles", see s 4; for "eligible automated data" and "eligible manual data", see para 1(2) of Pt I of this Schedule.

## PART V
## EXEMPTION FROM SECTION 22

19. Processing which was already under way immediately before 24th October 1998 is not assessable processing for the purposes of section 22.

**Commencement**  to be appointed.
**Definitions**    As to "processed", see s 1(1).

## SCHEDULE 9
Section 50

## POWERS OF ENTRY AND INSPECTION

*Issue of warrants*

1.—(1) If a circuit judge is satisfied by information on oath supplied by the Commissioner that there are reasonable grounds for suspecting—
  (a)  that a data controller has contravened or is contravening any of the data protection principles, or
  (b)  that an offence under this Act has been or is being committed,

and that evidence of the contravention or of the commission of the offence is to be found on any premises specified in the information, he may, subject to subparagraph (2) and paragraph 2, grant a warrant to the Commissioner.

(2) A judge shall not issue a warrant under this Schedule in respect of any personal data processed for the special purposes unless a determination by the Commissioner under section 45 with respect to those data has taken effect.

(3)   A warrant issued under sub-paragraph (1) shall authorise the Commissioner or any of his officers or staff at any time within seven days of the date of the warrant to enter the premises, to search them, to inspect, examine, operate and test any equipment found there which is used or intended to be used for the processing of personal data and to inspect and seize any documents or other material found there which may be such evidence as is mentioned in that sub-paragraph.

2.—(1)   A judge shall not issue a warrant under this Schedule unless he is satisfied—

(a)   that the Commissioner has given seven days' notice in writing to the occupier of the premises in question demanding access to the premises, and

(b)   that either—

    (i)   access was demanded at a reasonable hour and was unreasonably refused, or

    (ii)   although entry to the premises was granted, the occupier unreasonably refused to comply with a request by the Commissioner or any of the Commissioner's officers or staff to permit the Commissioner or the officer or member of staff to do any of the things referred to in paragraph 1(3), and

(c)   that the occupier, has, after the refusal, been notified by the Commissioner of the application for the warrant and has had an opportunity of being heard by the judge on the question whether or not it should be issued.

(2)   Sub-paragraph (1) shall not apply if the judge is satisfied that the case is one of urgency or that compliance with those provisions would defeat the object of the entry.

3.   A judge who issues a warrant under this Schedule shall also issue two copies of it and certify them clearly as copies.

### Execution of warrants

4.   A person executing a warrant issued under this Schedule may use such reasonable force as may be necessary.

5.   A warrant issued under this Schedule shall be executed at a reasonable hour unless it appears to the person executing it that there are grounds for suspecting that the evidence in question would not be found if it were so executed.

6.   If the person who occupies the premises in respect of which a warrant is issued under this Schedule is present when the warrant is executed, he shall be shown the warrant and supplied with a copy of it; and if that person is not present a copy of the warrant shall be left in a prominent place on the premises.

7.—(1)   A person seizing anything in pursuance of a warrant under this Schedule shall give a receipt for it if asked to do so.

(2)   Anything so seized may be retained for so long as is necessary in all the circumstances but the person in occupation of the premises in question shall be given a copy of anything that is seized if he so requests and the person executing the warrant considers that it can be done without undue delay.

### Matters exempt from inspection and seizure

8.   The powers of inspection and seizure conferred by a warrant issued under this Schedule shall not be exercisable in respect of personal data which by virtue of section 28 are exempt from any of the provisions of this Act.

9.—(1)   Subject to the provisions of this paragraph, the powers of inspection and seizure conferred by a warrant issued under this Schedule shall not be exercisable in respect of—

(a)   any communication between a professional legal adviser and his client in connection with the giving of legal advice to the client with respect to his obligations, liabilities or rights under this Act, or

(b)   any communication between a professional legal adviser and his client, or between such an adviser or his client and any other person, made in connection with or in contemplation of proceedings under or arising out of this Act (including proceedings before the Tribunal) and for the purposes of such proceedings.

(2) Sub-paragraph (1) applies also to—

(a) any copy or other record of any such communication as is there mentioned, and

(b) any document or article enclosed with or referred to in any such communication if made in connection with the giving of any advice or, as the case may be, in connection with or in contemplation of and for the purposes of such proceedings as are there mentioned.

(3) This paragraph does not apply to anything in the possession of any person other than the professional legal adviser or his client or to anything held with the intention of furthering a criminal purpose.

(4) In this paragraph references to the client of a professional legal adviser include references to any person representing such a client.

10. If the person in occupation of any premises in respect of which a warrant is issued under this Schedule objects to the inspection or seizure under the warrant of any material on the grounds that it consists partly of matters in respect of which those powers are not exercisable, he shall, if the person executing the warrant so requests, furnish that person with a copy of so much of the material as is not exempt from those powers.

### Return of warrants

11. A warrant issued under this Schedule shall be returned to the court from which it was issued—

(a) after being executed, or

(b) if not executed within the time authorised for its execution;

and the person by whom any such warrant is executed shall make an endorsement on it stating what powers have been exercised by him under the warrant.

### Offences

12. Any person who—

(a) intentionally obstructs a person in the execution of a warrant issued under this Schedule, or

(b) fails without reasonable excuse to give any person executing such a warrant such assistance as he may reasonably require for the execution of the warrant,

is guilty of an offence.

### Vessels, vehicles etc

13. In this Schedule "premises" includes any vessel, vehicle, aircraft or hovercraft, and references to the occupier of any premises include references to the person in charge of any vessel, vehicle, aircraft or hovercraft.

### Scotland and Northern Ireland

14. In the application of this Schedule to Scotland—

(a) for any reference to a circuit judge there is substituted a reference to the sheriff,

(b) for any reference to information on oath there is substituted a reference to evidence on oath, and

(c) for the reference to the court from which the warrant was issued there is substituted a reference to the sheriff clerk.

15. In the application of this Schedule to Northern Ireland—

(a) for any reference to a circuit judge there is substituted a reference to a county court judge, and

(b) for any reference to information on oath there is substituted a reference to a complaint on oath.

---

**Commencement** to be appointed.

**Definitions** For "data", "personal data" and "processing", see s 1(1) (and note also as to "processing", s 39, Sch 8, Pt II, para 5); for "the special purposes", see s 3; for "the data protection principles", see s 4; for "the Commissioner", see s 6(1); for "the Tribunal", see s 6(3).

**References** See paras 3.40, 3.41.

# SCHEDULE 10

Section 53(6)

## FURTHER PROVISIONS RELATING TO
## ASSISTANCE UNDER SECTION 53

1.  In this Schedule "applicant" and "proceedings" have the same meaning as in section 53.

2.  The assistance provided under section 53 may include the making of arrangements for, or for the Commissioner to bear the costs of—

   (a)   the giving of advice or assistance by a solicitor or counsel, and
   (b)   the representation of the applicant, or the provision to him of such assistance as is usually given by a solicitor or counsel—
      (i)   in steps preliminary or incidental to the proceedings, or
      (ii)   in arriving at or giving effect to a compromise to avoid or bring an end to the proceedings.

3.  Where assistance is provided with respect to the conduct of proceedings—

   (a)   it shall include an agreement by the Commissioner to indemnify the applicant (subject only to any exceptions specified in the notification) in respect of any liability to pay costs or expenses arising by virtue of any judgment or order of the court in the proceedings,
   (b)   it may include an agreement by the Commissioner to indemnify the applicant in respect of any liability to pay costs or expenses arising by virtue of any compromise or settlement arrived at in order to avoid the proceedings or bring the proceedings to an end, and
   (c)   it may include an agreement by the Commissioner to indemnify the applicant in respect of any liability to pay damages pursuant to an undertaking given on the grant of interlocutory relief (in Scotland, an interim order) to the applicant.

4.  Where the Commissioner provides assistance in relation to any proceedings, he shall do so on such terms, or make such other arrangements, as will secure that a person against whom the proceedings have been or are commenced is informed that assistance has been or is being provided by the Commissioner in relation to them.

5.  In England and Wales or Northern Ireland, the recovery of expenses incurred by the Commissioner in providing an applicant with assistance (as taxed or assessed in such manner as may be prescribed by rules of court) shall constitute a first charge for the benefit of the Commissioner—

   (a)   on any costs which, by virtue of any judgment or order of the court, are payable to the applicant by any other person in respect of the matter in connection with which the assistance is provided, and
   (b)   on any sum payable to the applicant under a compromise or settlement arrived at in connection with that matter to avoid or bring to an end any proceedings.

6.  In Scotland, the recovery of such expenses (as taxed or assessed in such manner as may be prescribed by rules of court) shall be paid to the Commissioner, in priority to other debts—

   (a)   out of any expenses which, by virtue of any judgment or order of the court, are payable to the applicant by any other person in respect of the matter in connection with which the assistance is provided, and
   (b)   out of any sum payable to the applicant under a compromise or settlement arrived at in connection with that matter to avoid or bring to an end any proceedings.

---

**Commencement**  to be appointed.
**Definitions**    For "the Commissioner", see s 6(1).

---

# SCHEDULE 11

Section 68(1), (6)

## EDUCATIONAL RECORDS

### *Meaning of "educational record"*

1.  For the purposes of section 68 "educational record" means any record to which paragraph 2, 5 or 7 applies.

*England and Wales*

2. This paragraph applies to any record of information which—
    (a) is processed by or on behalf of the governing body of, or a teacher at, any school in England and Wales specified in paragraph 3,
    (b) relates to any person who is or has been a pupil at the school, and
    (c) originated from or was supplied by or on behalf of any of the persons specified in paragraph 4,

other than information which is processed by a teacher solely for the teacher's own use.

3. The schools referred to in paragraph 2(a) are—
    (a) a school maintained by a local education authority, and
    (b) a special school, as defined by section 6(2) of the Education Act 1996, which is not so maintained.

\*4. The persons referred to in paragraph 2(c) are—
    (a) an employee of the local education authority which maintains the school,
    (b) in the case of—
        (i) a voluntary aided, foundation or foundation special school (within the meaning of the School Standards and Framework Act 1998), or
        (ii) a special school which is not maintained by a local education authority,
    a teacher or other employee at the school (including an educational psychologist engaged by the governing body under a contract for services),
    (c) the pupil to whom the record relates, and
    (d) a parent, as defined by section 576(1) of the Education Act 1996, of that pupil.

*Scotland*

5. This paragraph applies to any record of information which is processed—
    (a) by an education authority in Scotland, and
    (b) for the purpose of the relevant function of the authority,

other than information which is processed by a teacher solely for the teacher's own use.

6. For the purposes of paragraph 5—
    (a) "education authority" means an education authority within the meaning of the Education (Scotland) Act 1980 ("the 1980 Act") or, in relation to a self-governing school, the board of management within the meaning of the Self-Governing Schools etc (Scotland) Act 1989 ("the 1989 Act"),
    (b) "the relevant function" means, in relation to each of those authorities, their function under section 1 of the 1980 Act and section 7(1) of the 1989 Act, and
    (c) information processed by an education authority is processed for the purpose of the relevant function of the authority if the processing relates to the discharge of that function in respect of a person—
        (i) who is or has been a pupil in a school provided by the authority, or
        (ii) who receives, or has received, further education (within the meaning of the 1980 Act) so provided.

*Northern Ireland*

7.—(1) This paragraph applies to any record of information which—
    (a) is processed by or on behalf of the Board of Governors of, or a teacher at, any grant-aided school in Northern Ireland,
    (b) relates to any person who is or has been a pupil at the school, and
    (c) originated from or was supplied by or on behalf of any of the persons specified in paragraph 8,

other than information which is processed by a teacher solely for the teacher's own use.

(2) In sub-paragraph (1) "grant-aided school" has the same meaning as in the Education and Libraries (Northern Ireland) Order 1986.

8. The persons referred to in paragraph 7(1) are—
    (a) a teacher at the school,
    (b) an employee of an education and library board, other than such a teacher,
    (c) the pupil to whom the record relates, and

(d)    a parent (as defined by Article 2(2) of the Education and Libraries (Northern Ireland) Order 1986) of that pupil.

*England and Wales: transitory provisions*

9.—(1) Until the appointed day within the meaning of section 20 of the School Standards and Framework Act 1998, this Schedule shall have effect subject to the following modifications.

(2) Paragraph 3 shall have effect as if for paragraph (b) and the "and" immediately preceding it there were substituted—

"(aa)  a grant-maintained school, as defined by section 183(1) of the Education Act 1996,

(ab)  a grant-maintained special school, as defined by section 337(4) of that Act, and

(b)    a special school, as defined by section 6(2) of that Act, which is neither a maintained special school, as defined by section 337(3) of that Act, nor a grant-maintained special school.".

(3) Paragraph 4(b)(i) shall have effect as if for the words from "foundation", in the first place where it occurs, to "1998)" there were substituted "or grant-maintained school".

**Commencement**  16 July 1998.
**Definitions**    For "processing", see s 1(1) (and note also as to "processing", s 39, Sch 8, Pt II, para 5); for "pupil", "school" and "teacher", see s 70(1).

## SCHEDULE 12

Section 68(1)(c)

### ACCESSIBLE PUBLIC RECORDS

*Meaning of "accessible public record"*

1. For the purposes of section 68 "accessible public record" means any record which is kept by an authority specified—
(a)    as respects England and Wales, in the Table in paragraph 2,
(b)    as respects Scotland, in the Table in paragraph 4, or
(c)    as respects Northern Ireland, in the Table in paragraph 6,

and is a record of information of a description specified in that Table in relation to that authority.

*Housing and social services records: England and Wales*

2. The following is the Table referred to in paragraph 1(a).

### TABLE OF AUTHORITIES AND INFORMATION

| The authorities | The accessible information |
| --- | --- |
| Housing Act local authority. | Information held for the purpose of any of the authority's tenancies. |
| Local social services authority. | Information held for any purpose of the authority's social services functions. |

3.—(1) The following provisions apply for the interpretation of the Table in paragraph 2.

(2) Any authority which, by virtue of section 4(e) of the Housing Act 1985, is a local authority for the purpose of any provision of that Act is a "Housing Act local authority" for the purposes of this Schedule, and so is any housing action trust established under Part III of the Housing Act 1988.

(3) Information contained in records kept by a Housing Act local authority is "held for the purpose of any of the authority's tenancies" if it is held for any purpose of the relationship of landlord and tenant of a dwelling which subsists, has subsisted or may subsist between the authority and any individual who is, has been or, as the case may be, has applied to be, a tenant of the authority.

(4) Any authority which, by virtue of section 1 or 12 of the Local Authority Social Services Act 1970, is or is treated as a local authority for the purposes of that Act is a "local social services authority" for the purposes of this Schedule; and information contained in records kept by such an authority is "held for any purpose of the authority's social services functions" if it is held for the purpose of any past, current or proposed exercise of such a function in any case.

(5) Any expression used in paragraph 2 or this paragraph and in Part II of the Housing Act 1985 or the Local Authority Social Services Act 1970 has the same meaning as in that Act.

*Housing and social services records: Scotland*

4. The following is the Table referred to in paragraph 1(b).

## TABLE OF AUTHORITIES AND INFORMATION

| The authorities | The accessible information |
| --- | --- |
| Local authority. | Information held for any purpose of any of the body's tenancies. |
| Scottish Homes. | |
| Social work authority. | Information held for any purpose of the authority's functions under the Social Work (Scotland) Act 1968 and the enactments referred to in section 5(1B) of that Act. |

5.—(1) The following provisions apply for the interpretation of the Table in paragraph 4.

(2) "Local authority" means—
   (a) a council constituted under section 2 of the Local Government etc (Scotland) Act 1994,
   (b) a joint board or joint committee of two or more of those councils, or
   (c) any trust under the control of such a council.

(3) Information contained in records kept by a local authority or Scottish Homes is held for the purpose of any of their tenancies if it is held for any purpose of the relationship of landlord and tenant of a dwelling-house which subsists, has subsisted or may subsist between the authority or, as the case may be, Scottish Homes and any individual who is, has been or, as the case may be, has applied to be a tenant of theirs.

(4) "Social work authority" means a local authority for the purposes of the Social Work (Scotland) Act 1968; and information contained in records kept by such an authority is held for any purpose of their functions if it is held for the purpose of any past, current or proposed exercise of such a function in any case.

*Housing and social services records: Northern Ireland*

6. The following is the Table referred to in paragraph 1(c).

## TABLE OF AUTHORITIES AND INFORMATION

| The authorities | The accessible information |
| --- | --- |
| The Northern Ireland Housing Executive. | Information held for the purpose of any of the Executive's tenancies. |

| The authorities | The accessible information |
|---|---|
| A Health and Social Services Board. | Information held for the purpose of any past, current or proposed exercise by the Board of any function exercisable, by virtue of directions under Article 17(1) of the Health and Personal Social Services (Northern Ireland) Order 1972, by the Board on behalf of the Department of Health and Social Services with respect to the administration of personal social services under— |
| | (a) the Children and Young Persons Act (Northern Ireland) 1968; |
| | (b) the Health and Personal Social Services (Northern Ireland) Order 1972; |
| | (c) Article 47 of the Matrimonial Causes (Northern Ireland) Order 1978; |
| | (d) Article 11 of the Domestic Proceedings (Northern Ireland) Order 1980; |
| | (e) the Adoption (Northern Ireland) Order 1987; or |
| | (f) the Children (Northern Ireland) Order 1995. |
| An HSS trust. | Information held for the purpose of any past, current or proposed exercise by the trust of any function exercisable, by virtue of an authorisation under Article 3(1) of the Health and Personal Social Services (Northern Ireland) Order 1994, by the trust on behalf of a Health and Social Services Board with respect to the administration of personal social services under any statutory provision mentioned in the last preceding entry. |

7.—(1) This paragraph applies for the interpretation of the Table in paragraph 6.

(2) Information contained in records kept by the Northern Ireland Housing Executive is "held for the purpose of any of the Executive's tenancies" if it is held for any purpose of the relationship of landlord and tenant of a dwelling which subsists, has subsisted or may subsist between the Executive and any individual who is, has been or, as the case may be, has applied to be, a tenant of the Executive.

**Commencement** 16 July 1998.
**Definitions** For "enactment" see s 70(1).

## SCHEDULE 13

Section 72

## MODIFICATIONS OF ACT HAVING EFFECT BEFORE 24TH OCTOBER 2007

1. After section 12 there is inserted—

**"12A  Rights of data subjects in relation to exempt manual data**

(1) A data subject is entitled at any time by notice in writing—
   (a) to require the data controller to rectify, block, erase or destroy exempt manual data which are inaccurate or incomplete, or
   (b) to require the data controller to cease holding exempt manual data in a way incompatible with the legitimate purposes pursued by the data controller.

(2)     A notice under subsection (1)(a) or (b) must state the data subject's reasons for believing that the data are inaccurate or incomplete or, as the case may be, his reasons for believing that they are held in a way incompatible with the legitimate purposes pursued by the data controller.

(3)     If the court is satisfied, on the application of any person who has given a notice under subsection (1) which appears to the court to be justified (or to be justified to any extent) that the data controller in question has failed to comply with the notice, the court may order him to take such steps for complying with the notice (or for complying with it to that extent) as the court thinks fit.

(4)     In this section "exempt manual data" means—
   (a)   in relation to the first transitional period, as defined by paragraph 1(2) of Schedule 8, data to which paragraph 3 or 4 of that Schedule applies, and
   (b)   in relation to the second transitional period, as so defined, data to which paragraph 14 of that Schedule applies.

(5)     For the purposes of this section personal data are incomplete if, and only if, the data, although not inaccurate, are such that their incompleteness would constitute a contravention of the third or fourth data protection principles, if those principles applied to the data.".

2.   In section 32—
   (a)   in subsection (2) after "section 12" there is inserted—
         "(dd) section 12A,", and
   (b)   in subsection (4) after "12(8)" there is inserted ", 12A(3)".

3.   In section 34 for "section 14(1) to (3)" there is substituted "sections 12A and 14(1) to (3)."

4.   In section 53(1) after "12(8)" there is inserted ", 12A(3)".

5.   In paragraph 8 of Part II of Schedule 1, the word "or" at the end of paragraph (c) is omitted and after paragraph (d) there is inserted
         "or
   (e)   he contravenes section 12A by failing to comply with a notice given under subsection (1) of that section to the extent that the notice is justified.".

---

**Commencement**   to be appointed.
**Definitions**         For "data" and "data subject", see s 1(1); for "data controller", see s 1(1), (4); for "the data protection principles", see s 4; as to "inaccurate", see s 70(2).

# SCHEDULE 14

Section 73

## TRANSITIONAL PROVISIONS AND SAVINGS

*Interpretation*

1.   In this Schedule—
   "the 1984 Act" means the Data Protection Act 1984;
   "the old principles" means the data protection principles within the meaning of the 1984 Act;
   "the new principles" means the data protection principles within the meaning of this Act.

*Effect of registration under Part II of 1984 Act*

2.—(1)   Subject to sub-paragraphs (4) and (5) any person who, immediately before the commencement of Part III of this Act—
   (a)   is registered as a data user under Part II of the 1984 Act, or
   (b)   is treated by virtue of section 7(6) of the 1984 Act as so registered,

is exempt from section 17(1) of this Act until the end of the registration period or, if earlier, 24th October 2001.

(2) In sub-paragraph (1) "the registration period", in relation to a person, means—

    (a)   where there is a single entry in respect of that person as a data user, the period at the end of which, if section 8 of the 1984 Act had remained in force, that entry would have fallen to be removed unless renewed, and

    (b)   where there are two or more entries in respect of that person as a data user, the period at the end of which, if that section had remained in force, the last of those entries to expire would have fallen to be removed unless renewed.

(3) Any application for registration as a data user under Part II of the 1984 Act which is received by the Commissioner before the commencement of Part III of this Act (including any appeal against a refusal of registration) shall be determined in accordance with the old principles and the provisions of the 1984 Act.

(4) If a person falling within paragraph (b) of sub-paragraph (1) receives a notification under section 7(1) of the 1984 Act of the refusal of his application, sub-paragraph (1) shall cease to apply to him—

    (a)   if no appeal is brought, at the end of the period within which an appeal can be brought against the refusal, or

    (b)   on the withdrawal or dismissal of the appeal.

(5) If a data controller gives a notification under section 18(1) at a time when he is exempt from section 17(1) by virtue of sub-paragraph (1), he shall cease to be so exempt.

(6) The Commissioner shall include in the register maintained under section 19 an entry in respect of each person who is exempt from section 17(1) by virtue of sub-paragraph (1); and each entry shall consist of the particulars which, immediately before the commencement of Part III of this Act, were included (or treated as included) in respect of that person in the register maintained under section 4 of the 1984 Act.

(7) Notification regulations under Part III of this Act may make provision modifying the duty referred to in section 20(1) in its application to any person in respect of whom an entry in the register maintained under section 19 has been made under sub-paragraph (6).

(8) Notification regulations under Part III of this Act may make further transitional provision in connection with the substitution of Part III of this Act for Part II of the 1984 Act (registration), including provision modifying the application of provisions of Part III in transitional cases.

*Rights of data subjects*

3.—(1) The repeal of section 21 of the 1984 Act (right of access to personal data) does not affect the application of that section in any case in which the request (together with the information referred to in paragraph (a) of subsection (4) of that section and, in a case where it is required, the consent referred to in paragraph (b) of that subsection) was received before the day on which the repeal comes into force.

(2) Sub-paragraph (1) does not apply where the request is made by reference to this Act.

(3) Any fee paid for the purposes of section 21 of the 1984 Act before the commencement of section 7 in a case not falling within sub-paragraph (1) shall be taken to have been paid for the purposes of section 7.

4. The repeal of section 22 of the 1984 Act (compensation for inaccuracy) and the repeal of section 23 of that Act (compensation for loss or unauthorised disclosure) do not affect the application of those sections in relation to damage or distress suffered at any time by reason of anything done or omitted to be done before the commencement of the repeals.

5. The repeal of section 24 of the 1984 Act (rectification and erasure) does not affect any case in which the application to the court was made before the day on which the repeal comes into force.

6. Subsection (3)(b) of section 14 does not apply where the rectification, blocking, erasure or destruction occurred before the commencement of that section.

*Enforcement and transfer prohibition notices served under Part V of 1984 Act*

7.—(1)  If, immediately before the commencement of section 40—

    (a)   an enforcement notice under section 10 of the 1984 Act has effect, and

    (b)   either the time for appealing against the notice has expired or any appeal has been determined,

then, after that commencement, to the extent mentioned in sub-paragraph (3), the notice shall have effect for the purposes of sections 41 and 47 as if it were an enforcement notice under section 40.

(2)  Where an enforcement notice has been served under section 10 of the 1984 Act before the commencement of section 40 and immediately before that commencement either—

    (a)   the time for appealing against the notice has not expired, or

    (b)   an appeal has not been determined,

the appeal shall be determined in accordance with the provisions of the 1984 Act and the old principles and, unless the notice is quashed on appeal, to the extent mentioned in sub-paragraph (3) the notice shall have effect for the purposes of sections 41 and 47 as if it were an enforcement notice under section 40.

(3)  An enforcement notice under section 10 of the 1984 Act has the effect described in sub-paragraph (1) or (2) only to the extent that the steps specified in the notice for complying with the old principle or principles in question are steps which the data controller could be required by an enforcement notice under section 40 to take for complying with the new principles or any of them.

8.—(1)  If, immediately before the commencement of section 40—

    (a)   a transfer prohibition notice under section 12 of the 1984 Act has effect, and

    (b)   either the time for appealing against the notice has expired or any appeal has been determined,

then, on and after that commencement, to the extent specified in sub-paragraph (3), the notice shall have effect for the purposes of sections 41 and 47 as if it were an enforcement notice under section 40.

(2)  Where a transfer prohibition notice has been served under section 12 of the 1984 Act and immediately before the commencement of section 40 either—

    (a)   the time for appealing against the notice has not expired, or

    (b)   an appeal has not been determined,

the appeal shall be determined in accordance with the provisions of the 1984 Act and the old principles and, unless the notice is quashed on appeal, to the extent mentioned in sub-paragraph (3) the notice shall have effect for the purposes of sections 41 and 47 as if it were an enforcement notice under section 40.

(3)  A transfer prohibition notice under section 12 of the 1984 Act has the effect described in sub-paragraph (1) or (2) only to the extent that the prohibition imposed by the notice is one which could be imposed by an enforcement notice under section 40 for complying with the new principles or any of them.

*Notices under new law relating to matters in relation to which 1984 Act had effect*

9.  The Commissioner may serve an enforcement notice under section 40 on or after the day on which that section comes into force if he is satisfied that, before that day, the data controller contravened the old principles by reason of any act or omission which would also have constituted a contravention of the new principles if they had applied before that day.

10. Subsection (5)(b) of section 40 does not apply where the rectification, blocking, erasure or destruction occurred before the commencement of that section.

11. The Commissioner may serve an information notice under section 43 on or after the day on which that section comes into force if he has reasonable grounds for suspecting that, before that day, the data controller contravened the old principles by reason of any act or omission which would also have constituted a contravention of the new principles if they had applied before that day.

12. Where by virtue of paragraph 11 an information notice is served on the basis of anything done or omitted to be done before the day on which section 43 comes into force, subsection (2)(b) of that section shall have effect as if the reference to the data controller having

complied, or complying, with the new principles were a reference to the data controller having contravened the old principles by reason of any such act or omission as is mentioned in paragraph 11.

*Self-incrimination, etc*

13.—(1) In section 43(8), section 44(9) and paragraph 11 of Schedule 7, any reference to an offence under this Act includes a reference to an offence under the 1984 Act.

(2) In section 34(9) of the 1984 Act, any reference to an offence under that Act includes a reference to an offence under this Act.

*Warrants issued under 1984 Act*

14. The repeal of Schedule 4 to the 1984 Act does not affect the application of that Schedule in any case where a warrant was issued under that Schedule before the commencement of the repeal.

*Complaints under section 36(2) of 1984 Act and requests for assessment under section 42*

15. The repeal of section 36(2) of the 1984 Act does not affect the application of that provision in any case where the complaint was received by the Commissioner before the commencement of the repeal.

16. In dealing with a complaint under section 36(2) of the 1984 Act or a request for an assessment under section 42 of this Act, the Commissioner shall have regard to the provisions from time to time applicable to the processing, and accordingly—
- (a) in section 36(2) of the 1984 Act, the reference to the old principles and the provisions of that Act includes, in relation to any time when the new principles and the provisions of this Act have effect, those principles and provisions, and
- (b) in section 42 of this Act, the reference to the provisions of this Act includes, in relation to any time when the old principles and the provisions of the 1984 Act had effect, those principles and provisions.

*Applications under Access to Health Records Act 1990 or corresponding Northern Ireland legislation*

17.—(1) The repeal of any provision of the Access to Health Records Act 1990 does not affect—
- (a) the application of section 3 or 6 of that Act in any case in which the application under that section was received before the day on which the repeal comes into force, or
- (b) the application of section 8 of that Act in any case in which the application to the court was made before the day on which the repeal comes into force.

(2) Sub-paragraph (1)(a) does not apply in relation to an application for access to information which was made by reference to this Act.

18.—(1) The revocation of any provision of the Access to Health Records (Northern Ireland) Order 1993 does not affect—
- (a) the application of Article 5 or 8 of that Order in any case in which the application under that Article was received before the day on which the repeal comes into force, or
- (b) the application of Article 10 of that Order in any case in which the application to the court was made before the day on which the repeal comes into force.

(2) Sub-paragraph (1)(a) does not apply in relation to an application for access to information which was made by reference to this Act.

*Applications under regulations under Access to Personal Files Act 1987 or corresponding Northern Ireland legislation*

19.—(1) The repeal of the personal files enactments does not affect the application of regulations under those enactments in relation to—
- (a) any request for information,
- (b) any application for rectification or erasure, or
- (c) any application for review of a decision,

which was made before the day on which the repeal comes into force.

(2) Sub-paragraph (1)(a) does not apply in relation to a request for information which was made by reference to this Act.

    (3)  In sub–paragraph (1) "the personal files enactments" means—

        (a)  in relation to Great Britain, the Access to Personal Files Act 1987, and

        (b)  in relation to Northern Ireland, Part II of the Access to Personal Files and Medical Reports (Northern Ireland) Order 1991.

*Applications under section 158 of Consumer Credit Act 1974*

20. Section 62 does not affect the application of section 158 of the Consumer Credit Act 1974 in any case where the request was received before the commencement of section 62, unless the request is made by reference to this Act.

---

**Commencement**  to be appointed.

**Definitions**  For "processing", see s 1(1); for "data controller", see s 1(1), (4); for "the data protection principles", see s 4; for "the Commissioner", see s 6(1); for "notification regulations", see s 16(2); for "enforcement notice", see s 40(1); for "information notice", see s 43(1).

---

# SCHEDULE 15

Section 74(1)

## MINOR AND CONSEQUENTIAL AMENDMENTS

### Public Records Act 1958 (c 51)

1.—(1)  In Part II of the Table in paragraph 3 of Schedule 1 to the Public Records Act 1958 (definition of public records) for "the Data Protection Registrar" there is substituted "the Data Protection Commissioner".

    (2)  That Schedule shall continue to have effect with the following amendment (originally made by paragraph 14 of Schedule 2 to the Data Protection Act 1984).

    (3)  After paragraph 4(1)(n) there is inserted—

        "(nn)  records of the Data Protection Tribunal".

### Parliamentary Commissioner Act 1967 (c 13)

2.  In Schedule 2 to the Parliamentary Commissioner Act 1967 (departments etc subject to investigation) for "Data Protection Registrar" there is substituted "Data Protection Commissioner".

3.  In Schedule 4 to that Act (tribunals exercising administrative functions), in the entry relating to the Data Protection Tribunal, for "section 3 of the Data Protection Act 1984" there is substituted "section 6 of the Data Protection Act 1998".

### Superannuation Act 1972 (c 11)

4.  In Schedule 1 to the Superannuation Act 1972, for "Data Protection Registrar" there is substituted "Data Protection Commissioner".

### House of Commons Disqualification Act 1975 (c 24)

5.—(1)  Part II of Schedule 1 to the House of Commons Disqualification Act 1975 (bodies whose members are disqualified) shall continue to include the entry "The Data Protection Tribunal" (originally inserted by paragraph 12(1) of Schedule 2 to the Data Protection Act 1984).

    (2)  In Part III of that Schedule (disqualifying offices) for "The Data Protection Registrar" there is substituted "The Data Protection Commissioner".

### Northern Ireland Assembly Disqualification Act 1975 (c 25)

6.—(1)  Part II of Schedule 1 to the Northern Ireland Assembly Disqualification Act 1975 (bodies whose members are disqualified) shall continue to include the entry "The Data Protection Tribunal" (originally inserted by paragraph 12(3) of Schedule 2 to the Data Protection Act 1984).

    (2)  In Part III of that Schedule (disqualifying offices) for "The Data Protection Registrar" there is substituted "The Data Protection Commissioner".

*Representation of the People Act 1983 (c 2)*

7. In Schedule 2 of the Representation of the People Act 1983 (provisions which may be included in regulations as to registration etc), in paragraph 11A(2)—

    (a)   for "data user" there is substituted "data controller", and

    (b)   for "the Data Protection Act 1984" there is substituted "the Data Protection Act 1998".

*Access to Medical Reports Act 1988 (c 28)*

8. In section 2(1) of the Access to Medical Reports Act 1988 (interpretation), in the definition of "health professional", for "the Data Protection (Subject Access Modification) Order 1987" there is substituted "the Data Protection Act 1998".

*Football Spectators Act 1989 (c 37)*

9.—(1) Section 5 of the Football Spectators Act 1989 (national membership scheme: contents and penalties) is amended as follows.

(2) In subsection (5), for "paragraph 1(2) of Part II of Schedule 1 to the Data Protection Act 1984" there is substituted "paragraph 1(2) of Part II of Schedule 1 to the Data Protection Act 1998".

(3) In subsection (6), for "section 28(1) and (2) of the Data Protection Act 1984" there is substituted "section 29(1) and (2) of the Data Protection Act 1998".

*Education (Student Loans) Act 1990 (c 6)*

10. Schedule 2 to the Education (Student Loans) Act 1990 (loans for students) so far as that Schedule continues in force shall have effect as if the reference in paragraph 4(2) to the Data Protection Act 1984 were a reference to this Act.

*Access to Health Records Act 1990 (c 23)*

11. For section 2 of the Access to Health Records Act 1990 there is substituted—

"Health professionals.    2. In this Act "health professional" has the same meaning as in the Data Protection Act 1998."

12. In section 3(4) of that Act (cases where fee may be required) in paragraph (a), for "the maximum prescribed under section 21 of the Data Protection Act 1984" there is substituted "such maximum as may be prescribed for the purposes of this section by regulations under section 7 of the Data Protection Act 1998".

13. In section 5(3) of that Act (cases where right of access may be partially excluded) for the words from the beginning to "record" in the first place where it occurs there is substituted "Access shall not be given under section 3(2) to any part of a health record".

*Access to Personal Files and Medical Reports (Northern Ireland) Order 1991 (1991/1707 (NI 14))*

14. In Article 4 of the Access to Personal Files and Medical Reports (Northern Ireland) Order 1991 (obligation to give access), in paragraph (2) (exclusion of information to which individual entitled under section 21 of the Data Protection Act 1984) for "section 21 of the Data Protection Act 1984" there is substituted "section 7 of the Data Protection Act 1998".

15. In Article 6(1) of that Order (interpretation), in the definition of "health professional", for "the Data Protection (Subject Access Modification) (Health) Order 1987" there is substituted "the Data Protection Act 1998".

*Tribunals and Inquiries Act 1992 (c 53)*

16. In Part 1 of Schedule 1 to the Tribunals and Inquiries Act 1992 (tribunals under direct supervision of Council on Tribunals), for paragraph 14 there is substituted—

"Data protection    14. (a)   The Data Protection Commissioner appointed under section 6 of the Data Protection Act 1998;

    (b)   the Data Protection Tribunal constituted under that section, in respect of its jurisdiction under section 48 of that Act."

17. For paragraphs (1) and (2) of Article 4 of the Access to Health Records (Northern Ireland) Order 1993 there is substituted—

"(1) In this Order "health professional" has the same meaning as in the Data Protection Act 1998.".

18. In Article 5(4) of that Order (cases where fee may be required) in subparagraph (a), for "the maximum prescribed under section 21 of the Data Protection Act 1984" there is substituted "such maximum as may be prescribed for the purposes of this Article by regulations under section 7 of the Data Protection Act 1998".

19. In Article 7 of that Order (cases where right of access may be partially excluded) for the words from the beginning to "record" in the first place where it occurs there is substituted "Access shall not be given under Article 5(2) to any part of a health record".

**Commencement** to be appointed.

## SCHEDULE 16

Section 74(2)

## REPEALS AND REVOCATIONS

## PART I
## REPEALS

| Chapter | Short title | Extent of repeal |
|---------|-------------|------------------|
| 1984 c 35. | The Data Protection Act 1984. | The whole Act. |
| 1986 c 60. | The Financial Services Act 1986. | Section 190. |
| 1987 c 37. | The Access to Personal Files Act 1987. | The whole Act. |
| 1988 c 40. | The Education Reform Act 1988. | Section 223. |
| 1988 c 50. | The Housing Act 1988. | In Schedule 17, paragraph 80. |
| 1990 c 23. | The Access to Health Records Act 1990. | In section 1(1), the words from "but does not" to the end. |
| | | In section 3, subsection (1)(a) to (e) and, in subsection (6)(a), the words "in the case of an application made otherwise than by the patient". |
| | | Section 4(1) and (2). |
| | | In section 5(1)(a)(i), the words "of the patient or" and the word "other". |
| | | In section 10, in subsection (2) the words "or orders" and in subsection (3) the words "or an order under section 2(3) above". |
| | | In section 11, the definitions of "child" and "parental responsibility". |
| 1990 c 37. | The Human Fertilisation and Embryology Act 1990. | Section 33(8). |
| 1990 c 41. | The Courts and Legal Services Act 1990. | In Schedule 10, paragraph 58. |

| Chapter | Short title | Extent of repeal |
|---------|-------------|------------------|
| 1992 c 13. | The Further and Higher Education Act 1992. | Section 86. |
| 1992 c 37. | The Further and Higher Education (Scotland) Act 1992. | Section 59. |
| 1993 c 8. | The Judicial Pensions and Retirement Act 1993. | In Schedule 6, paragraph 50. |
| 1993 c 10. | The Charities Act 1993. | Section 12. |
| 1993 c 21. | The Osteopaths Act 1993. | Section 38. |
| 1994 c 17. | The Chiropractors Act 1994. | Section 38. |
| 1994 c 19. | The Local Government (Wales) Act 1994. | In Schedule 13, paragraph 30. |
| 1994 c 33. | The Criminal Justice and Public Order Act 1994. | Section 161. |
| 1994 c 39. | The Local Government etc (Scotland) Act 1994. | In Schedule 13, paragraph 154. |

**Commencement** to be appointed.

## PART II
## REVOCATIONS

| Number | Title | Extent of revocation |
|--------|-------|---------------------|
| SI 1991/1142. | The Data Protection Registration Fee Order 1991. | The Whole Order. |
| SI 1991/1707 (NI 14). | The Access to Personal Files and Medical Reports (Northern Ireland) Order 1991. | Part II.<br><br>The Schedule. |
| SI 1992/3218. | The Banking Co-ordination (Second Council Directive) Regulations 1992. | In Schedule 10, paragraphs 15 and 40. |
| SI 1993/1250 (NI 4). | The Access to Health Records (Northern Ireland) Order 1993. | In Article 2(2), the definitions of "child" and "parental responsibility".<br><br>In Article 3(1), the words from "but does not include" to the end.<br><br>In Article 5, paragraph (1)(a) to (d) and, in paragraph (6)(a), the words "in the case of an application made otherwise than by the patient".<br><br>Article 6(1) and (2).<br><br>In Article 7(1)(a)(i), the words "of the patient or" and the word "other". |

| Number | Title | Extent of revocation |
|---|---|---|
| SI 1994/429 (NI 2). | The Health and Personal Social Services (Northern Ireland) Order 1994. | In Schedule 1, the entries relating to the Access to Personal Files and Medical Reports (Northern Ireland) Order 1991. |
| SI 1994/1696. | The Insurance Companies Third Insurance Directives) Regulations 1994. | In Schedule 8, paragraph 8. |
| SI 1995/755 (NI 2). | The Children (Northern Ireland) Order 1995. | In Schedule 9, paragraphs 177 and 191. |
| SI 1995/3275. | The Investment Services Regulations 1995. | In Schedule 10, paragraphs 3 and 15. |
| SI 1996/2827. | The Open-Ended Investment Companies (Investment Companies with Variable Capital) Regulations 1996. | In Schedule 8, paragraphs 3 and 26. |

**Commencement**  to be appointed.

# Appendix 2

Directive of the European Parliament and of the Council
95/46/EC

Directive of the European Parliament and of the Council
97/66/EC

# DIRECTIVE OF THE EUROPEAN PARLIAMENT AND OF THE COUNCIL

## of 24 October 1995

**on the protection of individuals with regard to the processing of personal data and on the free movement of such data**

(95/46/EC)

NOTES

Date of publication in OJ: OJ L281, 23.11.95, p 31.

THE EUROPEAN PARLIAMENT AND THE COUNCIL OF THE EUROPEAN UNION,

Having regard to the Treaty establishing the European Community, and in particular Article 100a thereof,

Having regard to the proposal from the Commission,[1]

Having regard to the opinion of the Economic and Social Committee,[2]

Acting in accordance with the procedure referred to in Article 189b of the Treaty,

(1) Whereas the objectives of the Community, as laid down in the Treaty, as amended by the Treaty on European Union, include creating an ever closer union among the peoples of Europe, fostering closer relations between the States belonging to the Community, ensuring economic and social progress by common action to eliminate the barriers which divide Europe, encouraging the constant improvement of the living conditions of its peoples, preserving and strengthening peace and liberty and promoting democracy on the basis of the fundamental rights recognised in the constitution and laws of the Member States and in the European Convention for the Protection of Human Rights and Fundamental Freedoms;

(2) Whereas data-processing systems are designed to serve man; whereas they must, whatever the nationality or residence of natural persons, respect their fundamental rights and freedoms, notably the right to privacy, and contribute to economic and social progress, trade expansion and the well-being of individuals;

(3) Whereas the establishment and functioning of an internal market in which, in accordance with Article 7a of the Treaty, the free movement of goods, persons, services and capital is ensured require not only that personal data should be able to flow freely from one Member State to another, but also that the fundamental rights of individuals should be safeguarded;

(4) Whereas increasingly frequent recourse is being had in the Community to the processing of personal data in the various spheres of economic and social activity; whereas the progress made in information technology is making the processing and exchange of such data considerably easier;

(5) Whereas the economic and social integration resulting from the establishment and functioning of the internal market within the meaning of Article 7a of the Treaty will necessarily lead to a substantial increase in cross-border flows of personal data between all those involved in a private or public capacity in economic and social activity in the Member States; whereas the exchange of personal data between undertakings in different Member States is set to increase; whereas the national authorities in the various Member States are being called upon by virtue of Community law to collaborate and exchange personal data so as to be able to perform their duties or carry out tasks on behalf of an authority in another Member State within the context of the area without internal frontiers as constituted by the internal market;

(6) Whereas, furthermore, the increase in scientific and technical cooperation and the coordinated introduction of new telecommunications networks in the Community necessitate and facilitate cross-border flows of personal data;

(7) Whereas the difference in levels of protection of the rights and freedoms of individuals, notably the right to privacy, with regard to the processing of personal data afforded in the Member States may prevent the transmission of such data from the territory of one Member State to that of another Member State; whereas this difference may therefore constitute an

obstacle to the pursuit of a number of economic activities at Community level, distort competition and impede authorities in the discharge of their responsibilities under Community law; whereas this difference in levels of protection is due to the existence of a wide variety of national laws, regulations and administrative provisions;

(8) Whereas, in order to remove the obstacles to flows of personal data, the level of protection of the rights and freedoms of individuals with regard to the processing of such data must be equivalent in all Member States; whereas this objective is vital to the internal market but cannot be achieved by the Member States alone, especially in view of the scale of the divergences which currently exist between the relevant laws in the Member States and the need to coordinate the laws of the Member States so as to ensure that the cross-border flow of personal data is regulated in a consistent manner that is in keeping with the objective of the internal market as provided for in Article 7a of the Treaty; whereas Community action to approximate those laws is therefore needed;

(9) Whereas, given the equivalent protection resulting from the approximation of national laws, the Member States will no longer be able to inhibit the free movement between them of personal data on grounds relating to protection of the rights and freedoms of individuals, and in particular the right to privacy; whereas Member States will be left a margin for manoeuvre, which may, in the context of implementation of the Directive, also be exercised by the business and social partners; whereas Member States will therefore be able to specify in their national law the general conditions governing the lawfulness of data processing; whereas in doing so the Member States shall strive to improve the protection currently provided by their legislation; whereas, within the limits of this margin for manoeuvre and in accordance with Community law, disparities could arise in the implementation of the Directive, and this could have an effect on the movement of data within a Member State as well as within the Community;

(10) Whereas the object of the national laws on the processing of personal data is to protect fundamental rights and freedoms, notably the right to privacy, which is recognised both in Article 8 of the European Convention for the Protection of Human Rights and Fundamental Freedoms and in the general principles of Community law; whereas, for that reason, the approximation of those laws must not result in any lessening of the protection they afford but must, on the contrary, seek to ensure a high level of protection in the Community;

(11) Whereas the principles of the protection of the rights and freedoms of individuals, notably the right to privacy, which are contained in this Directive, give substance to and amplify those contained in the Council of Europe Convention of 28 January 1981 for the Protection of Individuals with regard to Automatic Processing of Personal Data;

(12) Whereas the protection principles must apply to all processing of personal data by any person whose activities are governed by Community law; whereas there should be excluded the processing of data carried out by a natural person in the exercise of activities which are exclusively personal or domestic, such as correspondence and the holding of records of addresses;

(13) Whereas the activities referred to in Titles V and VI of the Treaty on European Union regarding public safety, defence, State security or the activities of the State in the area of criminal laws fall outside the scope of Community law, without prejudice to the obligations incumbent upon Member States under Article 56(2), Article 57 or Article 100a of the Treaty establishing the European Community; whereas the processing of personal data that is necessary to safeguard the economic well-being of the State does not fall within the scope of this Directive where such processing relates to State security matters;

(14) Whereas, given the importance of the developments under way, in the framework of the information society, of the techniques used to capture, transmit, manipulate, record, store or communicate sound and image data relating to natural persons, this Directive should be applicable to processing involving such data;

(15) Whereas the processing of such data is covered by this Directive only if it is automated or if the data processed are contained or are intended to be contained in a filing system structured according to specific criteria relating to individuals, so as to permit easy access to the personal data in question;

(16) Whereas the processing of sound and image data, such as in cases of video surveillance, does not come within the scope of this Directive if it is carried out for the purposes of public security, defence, national security or in the course of State activities relating to the area of criminal law or of other activities which do not come within the scope of Community law;

(17) Whereas, as far as the processing of sound and image data carried out for purposes of journalism or the purposes of literary or artistic expression is concerned, in particular in the audiovisual field, the principles of the Directive are to apply in a restricted manner according to the provisions laid down in Article 9;

(18) Whereas, in order to ensure that individuals are not deprived of the protection to which they are entitled under this Directive, any processing of personal data in the Community must be carried out in accordance with the law of one of the Member States; whereas, in this connection, processing carried out under the responsibility of a controller who is established in a Member State should be governed by the law of that State;

(19) Whereas establishment on the territory of a Member State implies the effective and real exercise of activity through stable arrangements; whereas the legal form of such an establishment, whether simply branch or a subsidiary with a legal personality, is not the determining factor in this respect; whereas, when a single controller is established on the territory of several Member States, particularly by means of subsidiaries, he must ensure, in order to avoid any circumvention of national rules, that each of the establishments fulfils the obligations imposed by the national law applicable to its activities;

(20) Whereas the fact that the processing of data is carried out by a person established in a third country must not stand in the way of the protection of individuals provided for in this Directive; whereas in these cases, the processing should be governed by the law of the Member State in which the means used are located, and there should be guarantees to ensure that the rights and obligations provided for in this Directive are respected in practice;

(21) Whereas this Directive is without prejudice to the rules of territoriality applicable in criminal matters;

(22) Whereas Member States shall more precisely define in the laws they enact or when bringing into force the measures taken under this Directive the general circumstances in which processing is lawful; whereas in particular Article 5, in conjunction with Articles 7 and 8, allows Member States, independently of general rules, to provide for special processing conditions for specific sectors and for the various categories of data covered by Article 8;

(23) Whereas Member States are empowered to ensure the implementation of the protection of individuals both by means of a general law on the protection of individuals as regards the processing of personal data and by sectorial laws such as those relating, for example, to statistical institutes;

(24) Whereas the legislation concerning the protection of legal persons with regard to the processing data which concerns them is not affected by this Directive;

(25) Whereas the principles of protection must be reflected, on the one hand, in the obligations imposed on persons, public authorities, enterprises, agencies or other bodies responsible for processing, in particular regarding data quality, technical security, notification to the supervisory authority, and the circumstances under which processing can be carried out, and, on the other hand, in the right conferred on individuals, the data on whom are the subject of processing, to be informed that processing is taking place, to consult the data, to request corrections and even to object to processing in certain circumstances;

(26) Whereas the principles of protection must apply to any information concerning an identified or identifiable person; whereas, to determine whether a person is identifiable, account should be taken of all the means likely reasonably to be used either by the controller or by any other person to identify the said person; whereas the principles of protection shall not apply to data rendered anonymous in such a way that the data subject is no longer identifiable; whereas codes of conduct within the meaning of Article 27 may be a useful instrument for providing guidance as to the ways in which data may be rendered anonymous and retained in a form in which identification of the data subject is no longer possible;

(27) Whereas the protection of individuals must apply as much to automatic processing of data as to manual processing; whereas the scope of this protection must not in effect depend on the techniques used, otherwise this would create a serious risk of circumvention; whereas, nonetheless, as regards manual processing, this Directive covers only filing systems, not unstructured files; whereas, in particular, the content of a filing system must be structured according to specific criteria relating to individuals allowing easy access to the personal data; whereas, in line with the definition in Article 2(c), the different criteria for determining the constituents of a structured set of personal data, and the different criteria governing access to

such a set, may be laid down by each Member State; whereas files or sets of files as well as their cover pages, which are not structured according to specific criteria, shall under no circumstances fall within the scope of this Directive;

(28) Whereas any processing of personal data must be lawful and fair to the individuals concerned; whereas, in particular, the data must be adequate, relevant and not excessive in relation to the purposes for which they are processed; whereas such purposes must be explicit and legitimate and must be determined at the time of collection of the data; whereas the purposes of processing further to collection shall not be incompatible with the purposes as they were originally specified;

(29) Whereas the further processing of personal data for historical, statistical or scientific purposes is not generally to be considered incompatible with the purposes for which the data have previously been collected provided that Member States furnish suitable safeguards; whereas these safeguards must in particular rule out the use of the data in support of measures or decisions regarding any particular individual;

(30) Whereas, in order to be lawful, the processing of personal data must in addition be carried out with the consent of the data subject or be necessary for the conclusion or performance of a contract binding on the data subject, or as a legal requirement, or for the performance of a task carried out in the public interest or in the exercise of official authority, or in the legitimate interests of a natural or legal person, provided that the interests or the rights and freedoms of the data subject are not overriding; whereas, in particular, in order to maintain a balance between the interests involved while guaranteeing effective competition, Member States may determine the circumstances in which personal data may be used or disclosed to a third party in the context of the legitimate ordinary business activities of companies and other bodies; whereas Member States may similarly specify the conditions under which personal data may be disclosed to a third party for the purposes of marketing whether carried out commercially or by a charitable organisation or by any other association or foundation, of a political nature for example, subject to the provisions allowing a data subject to object to the processing of data regarding him, at no cost and without having to state his reasons;

(31) Whereas the processing of personal data must equally be regarded as lawful where it is carried out in order to protect an interest which is essential for the data subject's life;

(32) Whereas it is for national legislation to determine whether the controller performing a task carried out in the public interest or in the exercise of official authority should be a public administration or another natural or legal person governed by public law, or by private law such as a professional association;

(33) Whereas data which are capable by their nature of infringing fundamental freedoms or privacy should not be processed unless the data subject gives his explicit consent; whereas, however, derogations from this prohibition must be explicitly provided for in respect of specific needs, in particular where the processing of these data is carried out for certain health-related purposes by persons subject to a legal obligation of professional secrecy or in the course of legitimate activities by certain associations or foundations the purpose of which is to permit the exercise of fundamental freedoms;

(34) Whereas Member States must also be authorised, when justified by grounds of important public interest, to derogate from the prohibition on processing sensitive categories of data where important reasons of public interest so justify in areas such as public health and social protection—especially in order to ensure the quality and cost-effectiveness of the procedures used for settling claims for benefits and services in the health insurance system—scientific research and government statistics; whereas it is incumbent on them, however, to provide specific and suitable safeguards so as to protect the fundamental rights and the privacy of individuals;

(35) Whereas, moreover, the processing of personal data by official authorities for achieving aims, laid down in constitutional law or international public law, of officially recognised religious associations is carried out on important grounds of public interest;

(36) Whereas where, in the course of electoral activities, the operation of the democratic system requires in certain Member States that political parties compile data on people's political opinion, the processing of such data may be permitted for reasons of important public interest, provided that appropriate safeguards are established;

(37) Whereas the processing of personal data for purposes of journalism or for purposes of literary of artistic expression, in particular in the audiovisual field, should qualify for exemption from the requirements of certain provisions of this Directive in so far as this is necessary to

reconcile the fundamental rights of individuals with freedom of information and notably the right to receive and impart information, as guaranteed in particular in Article 10 of the European Convention for the Protection of Human Rights and Fundamental Freedoms; whereas Member States should therefore lay down exemptions and derogations necessary for the purpose of balance between fundamental rights as regards general measures on the legitimacy of data processing, measures on the transfer of data to third countries and the power of the supervisory authority; whereas this should not, however, lead Member States to lay down exemptions from the measures to ensure security of processing; whereas at least the supervisory authority responsible for this sector should also be provided with certain ex-post powers, eg to publish a regular report or to refer matters to the judicial authorities;

(38) Whereas, if the processing of data is to be fair, the data subject must be in a position to learn of the existence of a processing operation and, where data are collected from him, must be given accurate and full information, bearing in mind the circumstances of the collection;

(39) Whereas certain processing operations involve data which the controller has not collected directly from the data subject; whereas, furthermore, data can be legitimately disclosed to a third party, even if the disclosure was not anticipated at the time the data were collected from the data subject; whereas, in all these cases, the data subject should be informed when the data are recorded or at the latest when the data are first disclosed to a third party;

(40) Whereas, however, it is not necessary to impose this obligation of the data subject already has the information; whereas, moreover, there will be no such obligation if the recording or disclosure are expressly provided for by law or if the provision of information to the data subject proves impossible or would involve disproportionate efforts, which could be the case where processing is for historical, statistical or scientific purposes; whereas, in this regard, the number of data subjects, the age of the data, and any compensatory measures adopted may be taken into consideration;

(41) Whereas any person must be able to exercise the right of access to data relating to him which are being processed, in order to verify in particular the accuracy of the data and the lawfulness of the processing; whereas, for the same reasons, every data subject must also have the right to know the logic involved in the automatic processing of data concerning him, at least in the case of the automated decisions referred to in Article 15(1); whereas this right must not adversely affect trade secrets or intellectual property and in particular the copyright protecting the software; whereas these considerations must not, however, result in the data subject being refused all information;

(42) Whereas Member States may, in the interest of the data subject or so as to protect the rights and freedoms of others, restrict rights of access and information; whereas they may, for example, specify that access to medical data may be obtained only through a health professional;

(43) Whereas restrictions on the rights of access and information and on certain obligations of the controller may similarly be imposed by Member States in so far as they are necessary to safeguard, for example, national security, defence, public safety, or important economic or financial interests of a Member State or the Union, as well as criminal investigations and prosecutions and action in respect of breaches of ethics in the regulated professions; whereas the list of exceptions and limitations should include the tasks of monitoring, inspection or regulation necessary in the three last-mentioned areas concerning public security, economic or financial interests and crime prevention; whereas the listing of tasks in these three areas does not affect the legitimacy of exceptions or restrictions for reasons of State security or defence;

(44) Whereas Member States may also be led, by virtue of the provisions of Community law, to derogate from the provisions of this Directive concerning the right of access, the obligation to inform individuals, and the quality of data, in order to secure certain of the purposes referred to above;

(45) Whereas, in cases where data might lawfully be processed on grounds of public interest, official authority or the legitimate interests of a natural or legal person, any data subject should nevertheless be entitled, on legitimate and compelling grounds relating to his particular situation, to object to the processing of any data relating to himself; whereas Member States may nevertheless lay down national provisions to the contrary;

(46) Whereas the protection of the rights and freedoms of data subjects with regard to the processing of personal data requires that appropriate technical and organisational measures be taken, both at the time of the design of the processing system and at the time of the processing itself, particularly in order to maintain security and thereby to prevent any unauthorised

processing; whereas it is incumbent on the Member States to ensure that controllers comply with these measures; whereas these measures must ensure an appropriate level of security, taking into account the state of the art and the costs of their implementation in relation to the risks inherent in the processing and the nature of the data to be protected;

(47) Whereas where a message containing personal data is transmitted by means of a telecommunications or electronic mail service, the sole purpose of which is the transmission of such messages, the controller in respect of the personal data contained in the message will normally be considered to be the person from whom the message originates, rather than the person offering the transmission services; whereas, nevertheless, those offering such services will normally be considered controllers in respect of the processing of the additional personal data necessary for the operation of the service;

(48) Whereas the procedures for notifying the supervisory authority are designed to ensure disclosure of the purposes and main features of any processing operation for the purpose of verification that the operation is in accordance with the national measures taken under this Directive;

(49) Whereas, in order to avoid unsuitable administrative formalities, exemptions from the obligation to notify and simplification of the notification required may be provided for by Member States in cases where processing is unlikely to affect adversely the rights and freedoms of data subjects, provided that it is in accordance with a measure taken by a Member State specifying its limits; whereas exemption or simplification may similarly be provided for by Member States where a person appointed by the controller ensures that the processing carried out is not likely adversely to affect the rights and freedoms of data subjects; whereas such a data protection official, whether or not an employee of the controller, must be in a position to exercise his functions in complete independence;

(50) Whereas exemption or simplification could be provided for in cases of processing operations whose sole purpose is the keeping of a register intended, according to national law, to provide information to the public and open to consultation by the public or by any person demonstrating a legitimate interest;

(51) Whereas, nevertheless, simplification or exemption from the obligation to notify shall not release the controller from any of the other obligations resulting from this Directive;

(52) Whereas, in this context, *ex post facto* verification by the competent authorities must in general be considered a sufficient measure;

(53) Whereas, however, certain processing operation are likely to pose specific risks to the rights and freedoms of data subjects by virtue of their nature, their scope or their purposes, such as that of excluding individuals from a right, benefit or a contract, or by virtue of the specific use of new technologies; whereas it is for Member States, if they so wish, to specify such risks in their legislation;

(54) Whereas with regard to all the processing undertaken in society, the amount posing such specific risks should be very limited; whereas Member States must provide that the supervisory authority, or the data protection official in cooperation with the authority, check such processing prior to it being carried out; whereas following this prior check, the supervisory authority may, according to its national law, give an opinion or an authorisation regarding the processing; whereas such checking may equally take place in the course of the preparation either of a measure of the national parliament or of a measure based on such a legislative measure, which defines the nature of the processing and lays down appropriate safeguards;

(55) Whereas, if the controller fails to respect the rights of data subjects, national legislation must provide for a judicial remedy; whereas any damage which a person may suffer as a result of unlawful processing must be compensated for by the controller, who may be exempted from liability if he proves that he is not responsible for the damage, in particular in cases where he establishes fault on the part of the data subject or in case of *force majeure*; whereas sanctions must be imposed on any person, whether governed by private of public law, who fails to comply with the national measures taken under this Directive;

(56) Whereas cross-border flows of personal data are necessary to the expansion of international trade; whereas the protection of individuals guaranteed in the Community by this Directive does not stand in the way of transfers of personal data to third countries which ensure an adequate level of protection; whereas the adequacy of the level of protection afforded by a third country must be assessed in the light of all the circumstances surrounding the transfer operation or set of transfer operations;

(57) Whereas, on the other hand, the transfer of personal data to a third country which does not ensure an adequate level of protection must be prohibited;

(58) Whereas provisions should be made for exemptions from this prohibition in certain circumstances where the data subject has given his consent, where the transfer is necessary in relation to a contract or a legal claim, where protection of an important public interest so requires, for example in cases of international transfers of data between tax or customs administrations or between services competent for social security matters, or where the transfer is made from a register established by law and intended for consultation by the public or persons having a legitimate interest; whereas in this case such a transfer should not involve the entirety of the data or entire categories of the data contained in the register and, when the register is intended for consultation by persons having a legitimate interest, the transfer should be made only at the request of those persons or if they are to be the recipients;

(59) Whereas particular measures may be taken to compensate for the lack of protection in a third country in cases where the controller offers appropriate safeguards; whereas, moreover, provision must be made for procedures for negotiations between the Community and such third countries;

(60) Whereas, in any event, transfers to third countries may be effected only in full compliance with the provisions adopted by the Member States pursuant to this Directive, and in particular Article 8 thereof;

(61) Whereas Member States and the Commission, in their respective spheres of competence, must encourage the trade associations and other representative organisations concerned to draw up codes of conduct so as to facilitate the application of this Directive, taking account of the specific characteristics of the processing carried out in certain sectors, and respecting the national provisions adopted for its implementation;

(62) Whereas the establishment in Member States of supervisory authorities, exercising their functions with complete independence, is an essential component of the protection of individuals with regard to the processing of personal data;

(63) Whereas such authorities must have the necessary means to perform their duties, including powers of investigation and intervention, particularly in cases of complaints from individuals, and powers to engage in legal proceedings; whereas such authorities must help to ensure transparency of processing in the Member States within whose jurisdiction they fall;

(64) Whereas the authorities in the different Member States will need to assist one another in performing their duties so as to ensure that the rules of protection are properly respected throughout the European Union;

(65) Whereas, at Community level, a Working Party on the Protection of Individuals with regard to the Processing of Personal Data must be set up and be completely independent in the performance of its functions; whereas, having regard to its specific nature, it must advise the Commission and, in particular, contribute to the uniform application of the national rules adopted pursuant to this Directive;

(66) Whereas, with regard to the transfer of data to third countries, the application of this Directive calls for the conferment of powers of implementation on the Commission and the establishment of a procedure as laid down in Council Decision 87/373/EEC;[3]

(67) Whereas an agreement on a *modus vivendi* between the European Parliament, the Council and the Commission concerning the implementing measures for acts adopted in accordance with the procedure laid down in Article 189b of the EC Treaty was reached on 20 December 1994;

(68) Whereas the principles set out in this Directive regarding the protection of the rights and freedoms of individuals, notably their right to privacy, with regard to the processing of personal data may be supplemented or clarified, in particular as far as certain sectors are concerned, by specific rules based on those principles;

(69) Whereas Member States should be allowed a period of not more than three years from the entry into force of the national measures transposing this Directive in which to apply such new national rules progressively to all processing operations already under way; whereas, in order to facilitate their cost-effective implementation, a further period expiring 12 years after the date on which this Directive is adopted will be allowed to Member States to ensure the conformity of existing manual filing systems with certain of the Directive's provisions; whereas, where data contained in such filing systems are manually processed during this extended transition period, those systems must be brought into conformity with these provisions at the time of such processing;

(70) Whereas it is not necessary for the data subject to give his consent again so as to allow the controller to continue to process, after the national provisions taken pursuant to this Directive enter into force, any sensitive data necessary for the performance of a contract concluded on the basis of free and informed consent before the entry into force of these provisions;

(71) Whereas this Directive does not stand in the way of a Member State's regulating marketing activities aimed at consumers residing in territory in so far as such regulation does not concern the protection of individuals with regard to the processing of personal data;

(72) Whereas this Directive allows the principle of public access to official documents to be taken into account when implementing the principles set out in this Directive,

NOTES
[1]  OJ C277, 5.11.90, p 3 and OJ C311, 27.11.92, p 30.
[2]  OJ C159, 17.6.91, p 38.
[3]  OJ L197, 18.7.87, p 33.

HAVE ADOPTED THIS DIRECTIVE—

## CHAPTER I
## GENERAL PROVISIONS

### Article 1

### Object of the Directive

1.  In accordance with this Directive, Member States shall protect the fundamental rights and freedoms of natural persons, and in particular their right to privacy with respect to the processing of personal data.

2.  Member States shall neither restrict nor prohibit the free flow of personal data between Member States for reasons connected with the protection afforded under paragraph 1.

### Article 2

### Definitions

For the purposes of this Directive—
- (a)  "personal data" shall mean any information relating to an identified or identifiable natural person ("data subject"); an identifiable person is one who can be identified, directly or indirectly, in particular by reference to an identification number or to one or more factors specific to his physical, physiological, mental, economic, cultural or social identity;
- (b)  "processing of personal data" ("processing") shall mean any operation or set of operations which is performed upon personal data, whether or not by automatic means, such as collection, recording, organisation, storage, adaptation or alteration, retrieval, consultation, use, disclosure by transmission, dissemination or otherwise making available, alignment or combination, blocking, erasure or destruction;
- (c)  "personal data filing system" ("filing system") shall mean any structured set of personal data which are accessible according to specific criteria, whether centralised, decentralised or dispersed on a functional or geographical basis;
- (d)  "controller" shall mean the natural or legal person, public authority, agency or any other body which alone or jointly with others determines the purposes and means of the processing of personal data; where the purposes and means of processing are determined by

national or Community laws or regulations, the controller or the specific criteria for his nomination may be designated by national or Community law;

(e) "processor" shall mean a natural or legal person, public authority, agency or any other body which processes personal data on behalf of the controller;

(f) "third party" shall mean any natural or legal person, public authority, agency or any other body other than the data subject, the controller, the processor and the persons who, under the direct authority of the controller or the processor, are authorised to process the data;

(g) "recipient" shall mean a natural or legal person, public authority, agency or any other body to whom data are disclosed, whether a third party or not; however, authorities which may receive data in the framework of a particular inquiry shall not be regarded as recipients;

(h) "the data subject's consent" shall mean any freely given specific and informed indication of his wishes by which the data subject signifies his agreement to personal data relating to him being processed.

# Article 3

## Scope

1. This Directive shall apply to the processing of personal data wholly or partly by automatic means, and to the processing otherwise than by automatic means of personal data which form part of a filing system or are intended to form part of a filing system.

2. This Directive shall not apply to the processing of personal data—

— in the course of an activity which falls outside the scope of Community law, such as those provided for by Titles V and VI of the Treaty on European Union and in any case to processing operations concerning public security, defence, State security (including the economic well-being of the State when the processing operation relates to State security matters) and the activities of the State in areas of criminal law,

— by a natural person in the course of a purely personal or household activity.

# Article 4

## National law applicable

1. Each Member State shall apply the national provisions it adopts pursuant to this Directive to the processing of personal data where—

(a) the processing is carried out in the context of the activities of an establishment of the controller on the territory of the Member State; when the same controller is established on the territory of several Member States, he must take the necessary measures to ensure that each of these establishments complies with the obligations laid down by the national law applicable;

(b) the controller is not established on the Member State's territory, but in a place where its national law applies by virtue of international public law;

(c) the controller is not established on Community territory and, for purposes of processing personal data makes use of equipment, automated or otherwise, situated on the territory of the said Member State, unless such equipment is used only for purposes of transit through the territory of the Community.

2.    In the circumstances referred to in paragraph 1(c), the controller must designate a representative established in the territory of that Member State, without prejudice to legal actions which could be initiated against the controller himself.

## CHAPTER II
## GENERAL RULES ON THE LAWFULNESS OF THE PROCESSING OF PERSONAL DATA

### Article 5

Member States shall, within the limits of the provisions of this Chapter, determine more precisely the conditions under which the processing of personal data is lawful.

## SECTION I
## PRINCIPLES RELATING TO DATA QUALITY

### Article 6

1.    Member States shall provide that personal data must be—
    (a)    processed fairly and lawfully;
    (b)    collected for specified, explicit and legitimate purposes and not further processed in a way incompatible with those purposes. Further processing of data for historical, statistical or scientific purposes shall not be considered as incompatible provided that Member States provide appropriate safeguards;
    (c)    adequate, relevant and not excessive in relation to the purposes for which they are collected and/or further processed;
    (d)    accurate and, where necessary, kept up to date; every reasonable step must be taken to ensure that data which are inaccurate or incomplete, having regard to the purposes for which they were collected or for which they are further processed, are erased or rectified;
    (e)    kept in a form which permits identification of data subjects for no longer than is necessary for the purposes for which the data were collected or for which they are further processed. Member States shall lay down appropriate safeguards for personal data stored for longer periods for historical, statistical or scientific use.

2.    It shall be for the controller to ensure that paragraph 1 is complied with.

## SECTION II
## CRITERIA FOR MAKING DATA PROCESSING LEGITIMATE

### Article 7

Member States shall provide that personal data may be processed only if—
    (a)    the data subject has unambiguously given his consent; or
    (b)    processing is necessary for the performance of a contract to which the data subject is party or in order to take steps at the request of the data subject prior to entering into a contract; or
    (c)    processing is necessary for compliance with a legal obligation to which the controller is subject; or
    (d)    processing is necessary in order to protect the vital interests of the data subject; or
    (e)    processing is necessary for the performance of a task carried out in the public interest or in the exercise of official authority vested in the controller or in a third party to whom the data are disclosed; or

(f)     processing is necessary for the purposes of the legitimate interests pursued by the controller or by the third party or parties to whom the data are disclosed, except where such interests are overridden by the interests for fundamental rights and freedoms of the data subject which require protection under Article 1(1).

## SECTION III
## SPECIAL CATEGORIES OF PROCESSING

### Article 8

### The processing of special categories of data

1.     Member States shall prohibit the processing of personal data revealing racial or ethnic origin, political opinions, religious or philosophical beliefs, trade-union membership, and the processing of data concerning health or sex life.

2.     Paragraph 1 shall not apply where—
   (a)   the data subject has given his explicit consent to the processing of those data, except where the laws of the Member State provide that the prohibition referred to in paragraph 1 may not be lifted by the data subject's giving his consent; or
   (b)   processing is necessary for the purposes of carrying out the obligations and specific rights of the controller in the field of employment law in so far as it is authorised by national law providing for adequate safeguards; or
   (c)   processing is necessary to protect the vital interests of the data subject or of another person where the data subject is physically or legally incapable of giving his consent; or
   (d)   processing is carried out in the course of its legitimate activities with appropriate guarantees by a foundation, association or any other non-profit-seeking body with a political, philosophical, religious or trade-union aim and on condition that the processing relates solely to the members of the body or to persons who have regular contact with it in connection with its purposes and that the data are not disclosed to a third party without the consent of the data subjects; or
   (e)   the processing relates to data which are manifestly made public by the data subject or is necessary for the establishment, exercise or defence of legal claims.

3.     Paragraph 1 shall not apply where processing of the data is required for the purposes of preventive medicine, medical diagnosis, the provision of care or treatment or the management of health-care services, and where those data are processed by a health professional subject under national law or rules established by national competent bodies to the obligation of professional secrecy or by another person also subject to an equivalent obligation of secrecy.

4.     Subject to the provision of suitable safeguards, Member States may, for reasons of substantial public interest, lay down exemptions in addition to those laid down in paragraph 2 either by national law or by decision of the supervisory authority.

5.     Processing of data relating to offences, criminal convictions or security measures may be carried out only under the control of official authority, or if suitable specific safeguards are provided under national law, subject to derogations which may be granted by the Member State under national provisions providing suitable specific safeguards. However, a complete register of criminal convictions may be kept only under the control of official authority.

Member States may provide that data relating to administrative sanctions or judgements in civil cases shall also be processed under the control of official authority.

6.  Derogations from paragraph 1 provided for in paragraphs 4 and 5 shall be notified to the Commission.

7.  Member States shall determine the conditions under which a national identification number or any other identifier of general application may be processed.

## Article 9

### Processing of personal data and freedom of expression

Member States shall provide for exemptions or derogations from the provisions of this Chapter, Chapter IV and Chapter VI for the processing of personal data carried out solely for journalistic purposes or the purpose of artistic or literary expression only if they are necessary to reconcile the right to privacy with the rules governing freedom of expression.

## SECTION IV
## INFORMATION TO BE GIVEN TO THE DATA SUBJECT

## Article 10

### Information in cases of collection of data from the data subject

Member States shall provide that the controller or his representative must provide a data subject from whom data relating to himself are collected with at least the following information, except where he already has it—

- (a) the identity of the controller and of his representative, if any;
- (b) the purposes of the processing for which the data are intended;
- (c) any further information such as
  - — the recipients or categories of recipients of the data,
  - — whether replies to the questions are obligatory or voluntary, as well as the possible consequences of failure to reply,
  - — the existence of the right of access to and the right to rectify the data concerning him

in so far as such further information is necessary, having regard to the specific circumstances in which the data are collected, to guarantee fair processing in respect of the data subject.

## Article 11

### Information where the data have not been obtained from the data subject

1.  Where the data have not been obtained from the data subject, Member States shall provide that the controller or his representative must at the time of undertaking the recording of personal data or if a disclosure to a third party is envisaged, no later than the time when the data are first disclosed provide the data subject with at least the following information, except where he already has it—

- (a) the identity of the controller and of his representative, if any;
- (b) the purposes of the processing;
- (c) any further information such as
  - — the categories of data concerned,
  - — the recipients or categories of recipients,
  - — the existence of the right of access to and the right to rectify the data concerning him

in so far as such further information is necessary, having regard to the specific circumstances in which the data are processed, to guarantee fair processing in respect of the data subject.

2.    Paragraph 1 shall not apply where, in particular for processing for statistical purposes or for the purposes of historical or scientific research, the provision of such information proves impossible or would involve a disproportionate effort or if recording or disclosure is expressly laid down by law. In these cases Member States shall provide appropriate safeguards.

## SECTION V
## THE DATA SUBJECT'S RIGHT OF ACCESS TO DATA

### Article 12

### Right of access

Member States shall guarantee every data subject the right to obtain from the controller—

  (a)   without constraint at reasonable intervals and without excessive delay or expense—
  
  —   confirmation as to whether or not data relating to him are being processed and information at least as to the purposes of the processing, the categories of data concerned, and the recipients or categories of recipients to whom the data are disclosed,
  
  —   communication to him in an intelligible form of the data undergoing processing and of any available information as to their source,
  
  —   knowledge of the logic involved in any automatic processing of data concerning him at least in the case of the automated decisions referred to in Article 15(1);

  (b)   as appropriate the rectification, erasure or blocking of data the processing of which does not comply with the provisions of this Directive, in particular because of the incomplete or inaccurate nature of the data;

  (c)   notification to third parties to whom the data have been disclosed of any rectification, erasure or blocking carried out in compliance with (b), unless this proves impossible or involves a disproportionate effort.

## SECTION VI
## EXEMPTIONS AND RESTRICTIONS

### Article 13

### Exemptions and restrictions

1.    Member States may adopt legislative measures to restrict the scope of the obligations and rights provided for in Articles 6(1), 10, 11(1), 12 and 21 when such a restriction constitutes a necessary measures to safeguard—

  (a)   national security;
  (b)   defence;
  (c)   public security;
  (d)   the prevention, investigation, detection and prosecution of criminal offences, or of breaches of ethics for regulated professions;
  (e)   an important economic or financial interest of a Member State or of the European Union, including monetary, budgetary and taxation matters;

(f)    a monitoring, inspection or regulatory function connected, even occasionally, with the exercise of official authority in cases referred to in (c), (d) and (e);

(g)    the protection of the data subject or of the rights and freedoms of others.

2.    Subject to adequate legal safeguards, in particular that the data are not used for taking measures or decisions regarding any particular individual, Member States may, where there is clearly no risk of breaching the privacy of the data subject, restrict by a legislative measure the rights provided for in Article 12 when data are processed solely for purposes of scientific research or are kept in personal form for a period which does not exceed the period necessary for the sole purpose of creating statistics.

## SECTION VII
## THE DATA SUBJECT'S RIGHT TO OBJECT

### Article 14

### The data subject's right to object

Member States shall grant the data subject the right—

(a)    at least in the cases referred to in Article 7(e) and (f), to object at any time on compelling legitimate grounds relating to his particular situation to the processing of data relating to him, save where otherwise provided by national legislation. Where there is a justified objection, the processing instigated by the controller may no longer involve those data;

(b)    to object, on request and free of charge, to the processing of personal data relating to him which the controller anticipates being processed for the purposes of direct marketing, or to be informed before personal data are disclosed for the first time to third parties or used on their behalf for the purposes of direct marketing, and to be expressly offered the right to object free of charge to such disclosures or uses.

Member States shall take the necessary measures to ensure that data subjects are aware of the existence of the right referred to in the first subparagraph of (b).

### Article 15

### Automated individual decisions

1.    Member States shall grant the right to every person not to be subject to a decision which produces legal effects concerning him or significantly affects him and which is based solely on automated processing of data intended to evaluate certain personal aspects relating to him, such as his performance at work, creditworthiness, reliability, conduct, etc.

2.    Subject to the other Articles of this Directive, Member States shall provide that a person may be subjected to a decision of the kind referred to in paragraph 1 if that decision—

(a)    is taken in the course of the entering into or performance of a contract, provided the request for the entering into or the performance of the contract, lodged by the data subject, has been satisfied or that there are suitable measures to safeguard his legitimate interests, such as arrangements allowing him to put his point of view; or

(b)    is authorised by a law which also lays down measures to safeguard the data subject's legitimate interests.

## SECTION VIII
## CONFIDENTIALITY AND SECURITY OF PROCESSING

### Article 16

### Confidentiality of processing

Any person acting under the authority of the controller or of the processor, including the processor himself, who has access to personal data must not process them except on instructions from the controller, unless he is required to do so by law.

### Article 17

### Security of processing

1.　Member States shall provide that the controller must implement appropriate technical and organisational measures to protect personal data against accidental or unlawful destruction or accidental loss, alteration, unauthorised disclosure or access, in particular where the processing involves the transmission of data over a network, and against all other unlawful forms of processing.

Having regard to the state of the art and the cost of their implementation, such measures shall ensure a level of security appropriate to the risks represented by the processing and the nature of the data to be protected.

2.　The Member States shall provide that the controller must, where processing is carried out on his behalf, choose a processor providing sufficient guarantees in respect of the technical security measures and organisational measures governing the processing to be carried out, and must ensure compliance with those measures.

3.　The carrying out of processing by way of a processor must be governed by a contract or legal act binding the processor to the controller and stipulating in particular that—
- the processor shall act only on instructions from the controller,
- the obligations set out in paragraph 1, as defined by the law of the Member State in which the processor is established, shall also be incumbent on the processor.

4.　For the purposes of keeping proof, the parts of the contract or the legal act relating to data protection and the requirements relating to the measures referred to in paragraph 1 shall be in writing or in another equivalent form.

## SECTION IX
## NOTIFICATION

### Article 18

### Obligation to notify the supervisory authority

1.　Member States shall provide that the controller or his representative, if any, must notify the supervisory authority referred to in Article 28 before carrying out any wholly or partly automatic processing operation or set of such operations intended to serve a single purpose or several related purposes.

2.　Member States may provide for the simplification of or exemption from notification only in the following cases and under the following conditions—
- where, for categories of processing operations which are unlikely, taking account of the data to be processed, to affect adversely the rights and freedoms of data subjects, they specify the purposes of the processing, the data or categories of data undergoing processing, the

category or categories of data subject, the recipients or categories of recipient to whom the data are to be disclosed and the length of time the data are to be stored, and/or
— where the controller, in compliance with the national law which governs him, appoints a personal data protection official, responsible in particular—
  — for ensuring in an independent manner the internal application of the national provisions taken pursuant to this Directive
  — for keeping the register of processing operations carried out by the controller, containing the items of information referred to in Article 21(2),
thereby ensuring that the rights and freedoms of the data subjects are unlikely to be adversely affected by the processing operations.

3. Member States may provide that paragraph 1 does not apply to processing whose sole purpose is the keeping of a register which according to laws or regulations is intended to provide information to the public and which is open to consultation either by the public in general or by any person demonstrating a legitimate interest.

4. Member States may provide for an exemption from the obligation to notify or a simplification of the notification in the case of processing operations referred to in Article 8(2)(d).

5. Member States may stipulate that certain or all non-automatic processing operations involving personal data shall be notified, or provide for these processing operations to be subject to simplified notification.

## Article 19

### Contents of notification

1. Member States shall specify the information to be given in the notification. It shall include at least—
   (a) the name and address of the controller and of his representative, if any;
   (b) the purpose or purposes of the processing;
   (c) a description of the category or categories of data subject and of the data or categories of data relating to them;
   (d) the recipients or categories of recipient to whom the data might be disclosed;
   (e) proposed transfers of data to third countries;
   (f) a general description allowing a preliminary assessment to be made of the appropriateness of the measures taken pursuant to Article 17 to ensure security of processing.

2. Member States shall specify the procedures under which any change affecting the information referred to in paragraph 1 must be notified to the supervisory authority.

## Article 20

### Prior checking

1. Member States shall determine the processing operations likely to present specific risks to the rights and freedoms of data subjects and shall check that these processing operations are examined prior to the start thereof.

2. Such prior checks shall be carried out by the supervisory authority following receipt of a notification from the controller or by the data protection official, who, in cases of doubt, must consult the supervisory authority.

3. Member States may also carry out such checks in the context of preparation either of a measure of the national parliament or of a measure based on such a legislative measure, which define the nature of the processing and lay down appropriate safeguards.

## Article 21

### Publicising of processing operations

1. Member States shall take measures to ensure that processing operations are publicised.

2. Member States shall provide that a register of processing operations notified in accordance with Article 18 shall be kept by the supervisory authority.

The register shall contain at least the information listed in Article 19(1)(a) to (e).

The register may be inspected by any person.

3. Member States shall provide, in relation to processing operations not subject to notification, that controllers or another body appointed by the Member States make available at least the information referred to in Article 19(1)(a) to (e) in an appropriate form to any person on request.

Member States may provide that this provision does not apply to processing whose sole purpose is the keeping of a register which according to laws or regulations is intended to provide information to the public and which is open to consultation either by the public in general or by any person who can provide proof of a legitimate interest.

## CHAPTER III
## JUDICIAL REMEDIES, LIABILITY AND SANCTIONS

## Article 22

### Remedies

Without prejudice to any administrative remedy for which provision may be made, *inter alia* before the supervisory authority referred to in Article 28, prior to referral to the judicial authority, Member States shall provide for the right of every person to a judicial remedy for any breach of the rights guaranteed him by the national law applicable to the processing in question.

## Article 23

### Liability

1. Member States shall provide that any person who has suffered damage as a result of an unlawful processing operation or of any act incompatible with the national provisions adopted pursuant to this Directive is entitled to receive compensation from the controller for the damage suffered.

2. The controller may be exempted from this liability, in whole or in part, if he proves that he is not responsible for the event giving rise to the damage.

## Article 24

### Sanctions

The Member States shall adopt suitable measures to ensure the full implementation of the provisions of this Directive and shall in particular lay down the sanctions to be imposed in case of infringement of the provisions adopted pursuant to this Directive.

# CHAPTER IV
## TRANSFER OF PERSONAL DATA TO THIRD COUNTRIES

### Article 25

### Principles

1.    The Member States shall provide that the transfer to a third country of personal data which are undergoing processing or are intended for processing after transfer may take place only if, without prejudice to compliance with the national provisions adopted pursuant to the other provisions of this Directive, the third country in question ensures an adequate level of protection.

2.    The adequacy of the level of protection afforded by a third country shall be assessed in the light of all the circumstances surrounding a data transfer operation or set of data transfer operations; particular consideration shall be given to the nature of the data, the purpose and duration of the proposed processing operation or operations, the country of origin and country of final destination, the rules of law, both general and sectoral, in force in the third country in question and the professional rules and security measures which are complied with in that country.

3.    The Member States and the Commission shall inform each other of cases where they consider that a third country does not ensure an adequate level of protection within the meaning of paragraph 2.

4.    Where the Commission finds, under the procedure provided for in Article 31(2), that a third country does not ensure an adequate level of protection within the meaning of paragraph 2 of this Article, Member States shall take the measures necessary to prevent any transfer of data of the same type to the third country in question.

5.    At the appropriate time, the Commission shall enter into negotiations with a view to remedying the situation resulting from the finding made pursuant to paragraph 4.

6.    The Commission may find, in accordance with the procedure referred to in Article 31(2), that a third country ensures an adequate level of protection within the meaning of paragraph 2 of this Article, by reason of its domestic law or of the international commitments it has entered into, particularly upon conclusion of the negotiations referred to in paragraph 5, for the protection of the private lives and basic freedoms and rights of individuals.

Member States shall take the measures necessary to comply with the Commission's decision.

### Article 26

### Derogations

1.    By way of derogation from Article 25 and save where otherwise provided by domestic law governing particular cases, Member States shall provide that a transfer or a set of transfers of personal data to a third country which does not ensure an adequate level of protection within the meaning of Article 25(2) may take place on condition that—
      (a)   the data subject has given his consent unambiguously to the proposed transfer; or
      (b)   the transfer is necessary for the performance of a contract between the data subject and the controller or the implementation of precontractual measures taken in response to the data subject's request; or

    (c)    the transfer is necessary for the conclusion or performance of a contract concluded in the interest of the data subject between the controller and a third party; or

    (d)    the transfer is necessary or legally required on important public interest grounds, or for the establishment, exercise or defence of legal claims; or

    (e)    the transfer is necessary in order to protect the vital interests of the data subject; or

    (f)    the transfer is made from a register which according to laws or regulations is intended to provide information to the public and which is open to consultation either by the public in general or by any person who can demonstrate legitimate interest, to the extent that the conditions laid down in law for consultation are fulfilled in the particular case.

2.    Without prejudice to paragraph 1, a Member State may authorise a transfer or a set of transfers of personal data to a third country which does not ensure an adequate level of protection within the meaning of Article 25(2), where the controller adduces adequate safeguards with respect to the protection of the privacy and fundamental rights and freedoms of individuals and as regards the exercise of the corresponding rights; such safeguards may in particular result from appropriate contractual clauses.

3.    The Member State shall inform the Commission and the other Member States of the authorisations it grants pursuant to paragraph 2.

If a Member State or the Commission objects on justified grounds involving the protection of the privacy and fundamental rights and freedoms of individuals, the Commission shall take appropriate measures in accordance with the procedure laid down in Article 31(2).

Member States shall take the necessary measures to comply with the Commission's decision.

4.    Where the Commission decides, in accordance with the procedure referred to in Article 31(2), that certain standard contractual clauses offer sufficient safeguards as required by paragraph 2, Member States shall take the necessary measures to comply with the Commission's decision.

## CHAPTER V
## CODES OF CONDUCT

### Article 27

1.    The Member States and the Commission shall encourage the drawing up of codes of conduct intended to contribute to the proper implementation of the national provisions adopted by the Member States pursuant to this Directive, taking account of the specific features of the various sectors.

2.    Member States shall make provision for trade associations and other bodies representing other categories of controllers which have drawn up draft national codes or which have the intention of amending or extending existing national codes to be able to submit them to the opinion of the national authority.

Member States shall make provision for this authority to ascertain, among other things, whether the drafts submitted to it are in accordance with the national provisions adopted pursuant to this Directive. If it sees fit, the authority shall seek the views of data subjects or their representatives.

3.    Draft Community codes, and amendments or extensions to existing Community codes, may be submitted to the Working Party referred to in Article 29. This Working Party shall determine, among other things, whether the drafts

submitted to it are in accordance with the national provisions adopted pursuant to this Directive. If it sees fit, the authority shall seek the views of data subjects or their representatives. The Commission may ensure appropriate publicity for the codes which have been approved by the Working Party.

## CHAPTER VI
## SUPERVISORY AUTHORITY AND WORKING PARTY ON THE PROTECTION OF INDIVIDUALS WITH REGARD TO THE PROCESSING OF PERSONAL DATA

### Article 28

### Supervisory authority

1. Each Member State shall provide that one or more public authorities are responsible for monitoring the application within its territory of the provisions adopted by the Member States pursuant to this Directive.

These authorities shall act with complete independence in exercising the functions entrusted to them.

2. Each Member State shall provide that the supervisory authorities are consulted when drawing up administrative measures or regulations relating to the protection of individuals' rights and freedoms with regard to the processing of personal data.

3. Each authority shall in particular be endowed with—
  — investigative powers, such as powers of access to data forming the subject-matter of processing operations and powers to collect all the information necessary for the performance of its supervisory duties,
  — effective powers of intervention, such as, for example, that of delivering opinions before processing operations are carried out, in accordance with Article 20, and ensuring appropriate publication of such opinions, of ordering the blocking, erasure or destruction of data, of imposing a temporary or definitive ban on processing, of warning or admonishing the controller, or that of referring the matter to national parliaments or other political institutions,
  — the power to engage in legal proceedings where the national provisions adopted pursuant to this Directive have been violated or to bring these violations to the attention of the judicial authorities.

Decisions by the supervisory authority which give rise to complaints may be appealed against through the courts.

4. Each supervisory authority shall hear claims lodged by any person, or by an association representing that person, concerning the protection of his rights and freedoms in regard to the processing of personal data. The person concerned shall be informed of the outcome of the claim.

Each supervisory authority shall, in particular, hear claims for checks on the lawfulness of data processing lodged by any person when the national provisions adopted pursuant to Article 13 of this Directive apply. The person shall at any rate be informed that a check has taken place.

5. Each supervisory authority shall draw up a report on its activities at regular intervals. The report shall be made public.

6. Each supervisory authority is competent, whatever the national law applicable to the processing in question, to exercise, on the territory of its own Member State, the powers conferred on it in accordance with paragraph 3. Each authority may be requested to exercise its powers by an authority of another Member State.

The supervisory authorities shall cooperate with one another to the extent necessary for the performance of their duties, in particular by exchanging all useful information.

7.     Member States shall provide that the members and staff of the supervisory authority, even after their employment has ended, are to be subject to a duty of professional secrecy with regard to confidential information to which they have access.

## Article 29

### Working Party on the Protection of Individuals with regard to the Processing of Personal Data

1.     A Working Party on the Protection of Individuals with regard to the Processing of Personal Data, hereinafter referred to as "the Working Party", is hereby set up.

It shall have advisory status and act independently.

2.     The Working Party shall be composed of a representative of the supervisory authority or authorities designated by each Member State and of a representative of the authority or authorities established for the Community institutions and bodies, and of a representative of the Commission.

Each member of the Working Party shall be designated by the institution, authority or authorities which he represents. Where a Member State has designated more than one supervisory authority, they shall nominate a joint representative. The same shall apply to the authorities established for Community institutions and bodies.

3.     The Working Party shall take decisions by a simple majority of the representatives of the supervisory authorities.

4.     The Working Party shall elect its chairman. The chairman's term of office shall be two years. His appointment shall be renewable.

5.     The Working Party's secretariat shall be provided by the Commission.

6.     The Working Party shall adopt its own rules of procedure.

7.     The Working Party shall consider items placed on its agenda by its chairman, either on his own initiative or at the request of a representative of the supervisory authorities or at the Commission's request.

## Article 30

1.     The Working Party shall—
    (a)    examine any question covering the application of the national measures adopted under this Directive in order to contribute to the uniform application of such measures;
    (b)    give the Commission an opinion on the level of protection in the Community and in third countries;
    (c)    advise the Commission on any proposed amendment of this Directive, on any additional or specific measures to safeguard the rights and freedoms of natural persons with regard to the processing of personal data and on any other proposed Community measures affecting such rights and freedoms;
    (d)    give an opinion on codes of conduct drawn up at Community level.

2.     If the Working Party finds that divergences likely to affect the equivalence of protection for persons with regard to the processing of personal data in the Community are arising between the laws or practices of Member States, it shall inform the Commission accordingly.

3.     The Working Party may, on its own initiative, make recommendations on all matters relating to the protection of persons with regard to the processing of personal data in the Community.

4.     The Working Party's opinions and recommendations shall be forwarded to the Commission and to the committee referred to in Article 31.

5.     The Commission shall inform the Working Party of the action it has taken in response to its opinions and recommendations. It shall do so in a report which shall also be forwarded to the European Parliament and the Council. The report shall be made public.

6.     The Working Party shall draw up an annual report on the situation regarding the protection of natural persons with regard to the processing of personal data in the Community and in third countries, which it shall transmit to the Commission, the European Parliament and the Council. The report shall be made public.

## CHAPTER VII
## COMMUNITY IMPLEMENTING MEASURES

### Article 31

### The Committee

1.     The Commission shall be assisted by a committee composed of the representatives of the Member States and chaired by the representative of the Commission.

2.     The representative of the Commission shall submit to the committee a draft of the measures to be taken. The committee shall deliver its opinion on the draft within a time limit which the chairman may lay down according to the urgency of the matter.

The opinion shall be delivered by the majority laid down in Article 148(2) of the Treaty. The votes of the representatives of the Member States within the committee shall be weighted in the manner set out in that Article. The chairman shall not vote.

The Commission shall adopt measures which shall apply immediately. However, if these measures are not in accordance with the opinion of the committee, they shall be communicated by the Commission to the Council forthwith. It that event—

—     the Commission shall defer application of the measures which it has decided for a period of three months from the date of communication,

—     the Council, acting by a qualified majority, may take a different decision within the time limit referred to in the first indent.

## FINAL PROVISIONS

### Article 32

1.     Member States shall bring into force the laws, regulations and administrative provisions necessary to comply with this Directive at the latest at the end of a period of three years from the date of its adoption.

When Member States adopt these measures, they shall contain a reference to this Directive or be accompanied by such reference on the occasion of their official publication. The methods of making such reference shall be laid down by the Member States.

2.     Member States shall ensure that processing already under way on the date the national provisions adopted pursuant to this Directive enter into force, is brought into conformity with these provisions within three years of this date.

By way of derogation from the preceding subparagraph, Member States may provide that the processing of data already held in manual filing systems on the date of entry into force of the national provisions adopted in implementation of this Directive shall be brought into conformity with Articles 6, 7 and 8 of this Directive within 12 years of the date on which it is adopted. Member States shall, however, grant the data subject the right to obtain, at his request and in particular at the time of exercising his right of access, the rectification, erasure or blocking of data which are incomplete, inaccurate or stored in a way incompatible with the legitimate purposes pursued by the controller.

3.    By way of derogation from paragraph 2, Member States may provide, subject to suitable safeguards, that data kept for the sole purpose of historical research need not be brought into conformity with Articles 6, 7 and 8 of this Directive.

4.    Member States shall communicate to the Commission the text of the provisions of domestic law which they adopt in the field covered by this Directive.

### Article 33

The Commission shall report to the Council and the European Parliament at regular intervals, starting not later than three years after the date referred to in Article 32(1), on the implementation of this Directive, attaching to its report, if necessary, suitable proposals for amendments. The report shall be made public.

The Commission shall examine, in particular, the application of this Directive to the data processing of sound and image data relating to natural persons and shall submit any appropriate proposals which prove to be necessary, taking account of developments in information technology and in the light of the state of progress in the information society.

### Article 34

This Directive is addressed to the Member States.

Done at Luxembourg, 24 October 1995.

# DIRECTIVE OF THE EUROPEAN PARLIAMENT AND OF THE COUNCIL

## of 15 December 1997

### concerning the processing of personal data and the protection of privacy in the telecommunications sector

(97/66/EC)

NOTES
    Date of Publication in OJ: OJ L24, 30.1.98, p 1.

## THE EUROPEAN PARLIAMENT AND THE COUNCIL OF THE EUROPEAN UNION,

Having regard to the Treaty establishing the European Community, and in particular Article 100a thereof,

Having regard to the proposal from the Commission,[1]

Having regard to the opinion of the Economic and Social Committee,[2]

Acting in accordance with the procedure laid down in Article 189b of the Treaty,[3] in the light of the joint text approved by the Conciliation Committee on 6 November 1997,

(1) Whereas Directive 95/46/EC of the European Parliament and of the Council of 24 October 1995 on the protection of individuals with regard to the processing of personal data and on the free movement of such data[4] requires Member States to ensure the rights and freedoms of natural persons with regard to the processing of personal data, and in particular their right to privacy, in order to ensure the free flow of personal data in the Community;

(2) Whereas confidentiality of communications is guaranteed in accordance with the international instruments relating to human rights (in particular the European Convention for the Protection of Human Rights and Fundamental Freedoms) and the constitutions of the Member States;

(3) Whereas currently in the Community new advanced digital technologies are introduced in public telecommunications networks, which give rise to specific requirements concerning the protection of personal data and privacy of the user; whereas the development of the information society is characterised by the introduction of new telecommunications services; whereas the successful cross-border development of these services, such as video-on-demand, interactive television, is partly dependent on the confidence of the users that their privacy will not be at risk;

(4) Whereas this is the case, in particular, with the introduction of the Integrated Services Digital Network (ISDN) and digital mobile networks;

(5) Whereas the Council, in its Resolution of 30 June 1988 on the development of the common market for telecommunications services and equipment up to 1992,[5] called for steps to be taken to protect personal data, in order to create an appropriate environment for the future development of telecommunications in the Community; whereas the Council re-emphasised the importance of the protection of personal data and privacy in its Resolution of 18 July 1989 on the strengthening of the coordination for the introduction of the Integrated Services Digital Network (ISDN) in the European Community up to 1992;[6]

(6) Whereas the European Parliament has underlined the importance of the protection of personal data and privacy in the telecommunications networks, in particular with regard to the introduction of the Integrated Services Digital Network (ISDN);

(7) Whereas, in the case of public telecommunications networks, specific legal, regulatory, and technical provisions must be made in order to protect fundamental rights and freedoms of natural persons and legitimate interests of legal persons, in particular with regard to the increasing risk connected with automated storage and processing of data relating to subscribers and users;

(8) Whereas legal, regulatory, and technical provisions adopted by the Member States concerning the protection of personal data, privacy and the legitimate interest of legal persons, in the telecommunications sector, must be harmonised in order to avoid obstacles to the internal market for telecommunications in conformity with the objective set out in Article 7a of the Treaty; whereas the harmonisation is limited to requirements that are necessary to guarantee that the promotion and development of new telecommunications services and networks between Member States will not be hindered;

(9) Whereas the Member States, providers and users concerned, together with the competent Community bodies, should cooperate in introducing and developing the relevant technologies where this is necessary to apply the guarantees provided for by the provisions of this Directive.

(10) Whereas these new services include interactive television and video on demand;

(11) Whereas, in the telecommunications sector, in particular for all matters concerning protection of fundamental rights and freedoms, which are not specifically covered by the provisions of this Directive, including the obligations on the controller and the rights of individuals, Directive 95/46/EC applies; whereas Directive 95/46/EC applies to non-publicly available telecommunications services;

(12) Whereas this Directive, similarly to what is provided for by Article 3 of Directive 95/46/EC, does not address issues of protection of fundamental rights and freedoms related to activities which are not governed by Community law; whereas it is for Member States to take such measures as they consider necessary for the protection of public security, defence, State security (including the economic well-being of the State when the activities relate to State security matters) and the enforcement of criminal law; whereas this Directive shall not affect the ability of Member States to carry out lawful interception of telecommunications, for any of these purposes;

(13) Whereas subscribers of a publicly available telecommunications service may be natural or legal persons; whereas the provisions of this Directive are aimed to protect, by supplementing Directive 95/46/EC, the fundamental rights of natural persons and particularly their right to privacy, as well as the legitimate interests of legal persons; whereas these provisions may in no case entail an obligation for Member States to extend the application of Directive 95/46/EC to the protection of the legitimate interests of legal persons; whereas this protection is ensured within the framework of the applicable Community and national legislation;

(14) Whereas the application of certain requirements relating to presentation and restriction of calling and connected line identification and to automatic call forwarding to subscriber lines connected to analogue exchanges must not be made mandatory in specific cases where such application would prove to be technically impossible or would require a disproportionate economic effort; whereas it is important for interested parties to be informed of such cases and the Member States should therefore notify them to the Commission;

(15) Whereas service providers must take appropriate measures to safeguard the security of their services, if necessary in conjunction with the provider of the network, and inform subscribers of any special risks of a breach of the security of the network; whereas security is appraised in the light of the provision of Article 17 of Directive 95/46/EC;

(16) Whereas measures must be taken to prevent the unauthorised access to communications in order to protect the confidentiality of communications by means of public telecommunications networks and publicly available telecommunications services; whereas national legislation in some Member States only prohibits intentional unauthorised access to communications;

(17) Whereas the data relating to subscribers processed to establish calls contain information on the private life of natural persons and concern the right to respect for their correspondence or concern the legitimate interests of legal persons; whereas such data may only be stored to the extent that is necessary for the provision of the service for the purpose of billing and for interconnection payments, and for a limited time; whereas any further processing which the provider of the publicly available telecommunications services may want to perform for the marketing of its own telecommunications services may only be allowed if the subscriber has agreed to this on the basis of accurate and full information given by the provider of the publicly available telecommunications services about the types of further processing he intends to perform;

(18) Whereas the introduction of itemised bills has improved the possibilities for the subscriber to verify the correctness of the fees charged by the service provider; whereas, at the same time, it may jeopardise the privacy of the users of publicly available telecommunications services; whereas therefore, in order to preserve the privacy of the user, Member States must encourage the development of telecommunications service options such as alternative payment facilities which allow anonymous or strictly private access to publicly available telecommunications services, for example calling cards and facilities for payment by credit card; whereas, alternatively, Member States may, for the same purpose, require the deletion of a certain number of digits from the called numbers mentioned in itemised bills;

(19) Whereas it is necessary, as regards calling line identification, to protect the right of the calling party to withhold the presentation of the identification of the line from which the call is being made and the right of the called party to reject calls from unidentified lines; whereas it is justified to override the elimination of calling line identification presentation in specific cases; whereas certain subscribers, in particular helplines and similar organisations, have an interest in guaranteeing the anonymity of their callers; whereas it is necessary, as regards connected line identification, to protect the right and the legitimate interest of the called party to withhold the presentation of the identification of the line to which the calling party is actually connected, in particular in the case of forwarded calls; whereas the providers of publicly available telecommunications services must inform their subscribers of the existence of calling and connected line identification in the network and of all services which are offered on the basis of calling and connected line identification and about the privacy options which are available; whereas this will allow the subscribers to make an informed choice about the privacy facilities they may want to use; whereas the privacy options which are offered on a per-line basis do not necessarily have to be available as an automatic network service but may

be obtainable through a simple request to the provider of the publicly available telecommunications service;

(20) Whereas safeguards must be provided for subscribers against the nuisance which may be caused by automatic call forwarding by others; whereas, in such cases, it must be possible for subscribers to stop the forwarded calls being passed on to their terminals by simple request to the provider of the publicly available telecommunications service;

(21) Whereas directories are widely distributed and publicly available; whereas the right to privacy of natural persons and the legitimate interest of legal persons require that subscribers are able to determine the extent to which their personal data are published in a directory; whereas Member States may limit this possibility to subscribers who are natural persons;

(22) Whereas safeguards must be provided for subscribers against intrusion into their privacy by means of unsolicited calls and telefaxes; whereas Member States may limit such safeguards to subscribers who are natural persons;

(23) Whereas it is necessary to ensure that the introduction of technical features of telecommunications equipment for data protection purposes is harmonised in order to be compatible with the implementation of the internal market;

(24) Whereas in particular, similarly to what is provided for by Article 13 of Directive 95/46/EC, Member States can restrict the scope of subscribers' obligations and rights in certain circumstances, for example by ensuring that the provider of a publicly available telecommunications service may override the elimination of the presentation of calling line identification in conformity with national legislation for the purpose of prevention or detection of criminal offences or State security;

(25) Whereas where the rights of the users and subscribers are not respected, national legislation must provide for judicial remedy; whereas sanctions must be imposed on any person, whether governed by private or public law, who fails to comply with the national measures taken under this Directive;

(26) Whereas it is useful in the field of application of this Directive to draw on the experience of the Working Party on the protection of individuals with regard to the processing of personal data composed of representatives of the supervisory authorities of the Member States, set up by Article 29 of Directive 95/46/EC;

(27) Whereas, given the technological developments and the attendant evolution of the services on offer, it will be necessary technically to specify the categories of data listed in the Annex to this Directive for the application of Article 6 of this Directive with the assistance of the Committee composed of representatives of the Member States set up in Article 31 of Directive 95/46/EC in order to ensure a coherent application of the requirements set out in this Directive regardless of changes in technology; whereas this procedure applies solely to specifications necessary to adapt the Annex to new technological developments, taking into consideration changes in market and consumer demand; whereas the Commission must duly inform the European Parliament of its intention to apply this procedure and whereas, otherwise, the procedure laid down in Article 100a of the Treaty shall apply;

(28) Whereas, to facilitate compliance with the provisions of this Directive, certain specific arrangements are needed for processing of data already under way on the date that national implementing legislation pursuant to this Directive enters into force,

NOTES
1    OJ C200, 22.7.94, p 4.
2    OJ C159, 17.6.91, p 38.
3    Opinion of the European Parliament of 11 March 1992 (OJ C94, 13.4.92, p 198). Council Common Position of 12 September 1996 (OJ C315, 24.10.96, p 30) and Decision of the European Parliament of 16 January 1997 (OJ C33, 3.2.97, p 78). Decision of the European Parliament of 20 November 1997 (OJ C371, 8.12.97). Council Decision of 1 December 1997.
4    OJ L281, 23.11.95, p 31.
5    OJ C257, 4.10.88, p 1.
6    OJ C196, 1.8.89, p 4.

# HAVE ADOPTED THIS DIRECTIVE—

## Article 1

### Object and scope

1.    This Directive provides for the harmonisation of the provisions of the Member States required to ensure an equivalent level of protection of fundamental rights and freedoms, and in particular the right to privacy, with respect to the processing of personal data in the telecommunications sector and to ensure the free movement of such data and of telecommunications equipment and services in the Community.

2.    The provisions of this Directive particularise and complement Directive 95/46/EC for the purposes mentioned in paragraph 1. Moreover, they provide for protection of legitimate interests of subscribers who are legal persons.

3.    This Directive shall not apply to the activities which fall outside the scope of Community law, such as those provided for by Titles V and VI of the Treaty on European Union, and in any case to activities concerning public security, defence, State security (including the economic well-being of the State when the activities relate to State security matters) and the activities of the State in areas of criminal law.

## Article 2

### Definitions

In addition to the definitions given in Directive 95/46/EC, for the purposes of this Directive—

(a)    "subscriber" shall mean any natural or legal person who or which is party to a contract with the provider of publicly available telecommunications services for the supply of such services;

(b)    "user" shall mean any natural person using a publicly available telecommunications service, for private or business purposes, without necessarily having subscribed to this service;

(c)    "public telecommunications network" shall mean transmission systems and, where applicable, switching equipment and other resources which permit the conveyance of signals between defined termination points by wire, by radio, by optical or by other electromagnetic means, which are used, in whole or in part, for the provision of publicly available telecommunications services;

(d)    "telecommunications service" shall mean services whose provision consists wholly or partly in the transmission and routing of signals on telecommunications networks, with the exception of radio- and television broadcasting.

## Article 3

### Services concerned

1.    This Directive shall apply to the processing of personal data in connection with the provision of publicly available telecommunications services in public telecommunications networks in the Community, in particular via the Integrated Services Digital Network (ISDN) and public digital mobile networks.

2.    Articles 8, 9 and 10 shall apply to subscriber lines connected to digital exchanges and, where technically possible and if it does not require a disproportionate economic effort, to subscriber lines connected to analogue exchanges.

3.    Cases where it would be technically impossible or require a disproportionate investment to fulfil the requirements of Articles 8, 9 and 10 shall be notified to the Commission by the Member States.

## Article 4

### Security

1.    The provider of a publicly available telecommunications service must take appropriate technical and organisational measures to safeguard security of its services, if necessary in conjunction with the provider of the public telecommunications network with respect to network security. Having regard to the state of the art and the cost of their implementation, these measures shall ensure a level of security appropriate to the risk presented.

2.    In case of a particular risk of a breach of the security of the network, the provider of a publicly available telecommunications service must inform the subscribers concerning such risk and any possible remedies, including the costs involved.

## Article 5

### Confidentiality of the communications

1.    Member States shall ensure via national regulations the confidentiality of communications by means of a public telecommunications network and publicly available telecommunications services. In particular, they shall prohibit listening, tapping, storage or other kinds of interception or surveillance of communications, by others than users, without the consent of the users concerned, except when legally authorised, in accordance with Article 14(1).

2.    Paragraph 1 shall not affect any legally authorised recording of communications in the course of lawful business practice for the purpose of providing evidence of a commercial transaction or of any other business communication.

## Article 6

### Traffic and billing data

1.    Traffic data relating to subscribers and users processed to establish calls and stored by the provider of a public telecommunications network and/or publicly available telecommunications service must be erased or made anonymous upon termination of the call without prejudice to the provisions of paragraphs 2, 3 and 4.

2.    For the purpose of subscriber billing and interconnection payments, data indicated in the Annex may be processed. Such processing is permissible only up to the end of the period during which the bill may lawfully be challenged or payment may be pursued.

3.    For the purpose of marketing its own telecommunications services, the provider of a publicly available telecommunications service may process the data referred to in paragraph 2, if the subscriber has given his consent.

4.    Processing of traffic and billing data must be restricted to persons acting under the authority of providers of the public telecommunications networks and/or publicly available telecommunications services handling billing or traffic management, customer enquiries, fraud detection and marketing the provider's own telecommunications services and it must be restricted to what is necessary for the purposes of such activities.

5.    Paragraphs 1, 2, 3 and 4 shall apply without prejudice to the possibility for competent authorities to be informed of billing or traffic data in conformity with applicable legislation in view of settling disputes, in particular interconnection or billing disputes.

## Article 7

### Itemised billing

1.    Subscribers shall have the right to receive non-itemised bills.

2.    Member States shall apply national provisions in order to reconcile the rights of subscribers receiving itemised bills with the right to privacy of calling users and called subscribers, for example by ensuring that sufficient alternative modalities for communications or payments are available to such users and subscribers.

## Article 8

### Presentation and restriction of calling and connected line identification

1.    Where presentation of calling-line identification is offered, the calling user must have the possibility via a simple means, free of charge, to eliminate the presentation of the calling-line identification on a per-call basis. The calling subscriber must have this possibility on a per-line basis.

2.    Where presentation of calling-line identification is offered, the called subscriber must have the possibility via a simple means, free of charge for reasonable use of this function, to prevent the presentation of the calling line identification of incoming calls.

3.    Where presentation of calling line identification is offered and where the calling line identification is presented prior to the call being established, the called subscriber must have the possibility via a simple means to reject incoming calls where the presentation of the calling line identification has been eliminated by the calling user or subscriber.

4.    Where presentation of connected line identification is offered, the called subscriber must have the possibility via a simple means, free of charge, to eliminate the presentation of the connected line identification to the calling user.

5.    The provisions set out in paragraph 1 shall also apply with regard to calls to third countries originating in the Community; the provisions set out in paragraphs 2, 3 and 4 shall also apply to incoming calls originating in third countries.

6.    Member States shall ensure that where presentation of calling and/or connected line identification is offered, the providers of publicly available telecommunications services inform the public thereof and of the possibilities set out in paragraphs 1, 2, 3 and 4.

## Article 9

### Exceptions

Member States shall ensure that there are transparent procedures governing the way in which a provider of a public telecommunications network and/or a publicly available telecommunications service may override the elimination of the presentation of calling line identification—

   (a)    on a temporary basis, upon application of a subscriber requesting the tracing of malicious or nuisance calls; in this case, in accordance with national law, the data containing the identification of the calling subscriber will be stored and be made available by the provider of a public telecommunications network and/or publicly available telecommunications service;

   (b)    on a per-line basis for organisations dealing with emergency calls and recognised as such by a Member State, including law enforcement agencies, ambulance services and fire brigades, for the purpose of answering such calls.

## Article 10

### Automatic call forwarding

Member States shall ensure that any subscriber is provided, free of charge and via a simple means, with the possibility to stop automatic call forwarding by a third party to the subscriber's terminal.

## Article 11

### Directories of subscribers

1. Personal data contained in printed or electronic directories of subscribers available to the public or obtainable through directory enquiry services should be limited to what is necessary to identify a particular subscriber, unless the subscriber has given his unambiguous consent to the publication of additional personal data. The subscriber shall be entitled, free of charge, to be omitted from a printed or electronic directory at his or her request, to indicate that his or her personal data may not be used for the purpose of direct marketing, to have his or her address omitted in part and not to have a reference revealing his or her sex, where this is applicable linguistically.

2. Notwithstanding paragraph 1, Member States may allow operators to require a payment from subscribers wishing to ensure that their particulars are not entered in a directory, provided that the sum involved does not act as a disincentive to the exercise of this right, and that, taking account of the quality requirements of the public directory in the light of the universal service, it is limited to the actual costs incurred by the operator for the adaptation and updating of the list of subscribers not to be included in the public directory.

3. The rights conferred by paragraph 1 shall apply to subscribers who are natural persons. Member States shall also guarantee, in the framework of Community law and applicable national legislation, that the legitimate interests of subscribers other than natural persons with regard to their entry in public directories are sufficiently protected.

## Article 12

### Unsolicited calls

1. The use of automated calling systems without human intervention (automatic calling machine) or facsimile machines (fax) for the purposes of direct marketing may only be allowed in respect of subscribers who have given their prior consent.

2. Member States shall take appropriate measures to ensure that, free of charge, unsolicited calls for purposes of direct marketing, by means other than those referred to in paragraph 1, are not allowed either without the consent of the subscribers concerned or in respect of subscribers who do not wish to receive these calls, the choice between these options to be determined by national legislation.

3. The rights conferred by paragraphs 1 and 2 shall apply to subscribers who are natural persons. Member States shall also guarantee, in the framework of Community law and applicable national legislation, that the legitimate interests of subscribers other than natural persons with regard to unsolicited calls are sufficiently protected.

## Article 13

### Technical features and standardisation

1. In implementing the provisions of this Directive, Member States shall ensure, subject to paragraphs 2 and 3, that no mandatory requirements for specific technical

features are imposed on terminal or other telecommunications equipment which could impede the placing of equipment on the market and the free circulation of such equipment in and between Member States.

2.     Where provisions of this Directive can be implemented only by requiring specific technical features, Member States shall inform the Commission according to the procedures provided for by Directive 83/189/EEC[1] which lays down a procedure for the provision of information in the field of technical standards and regulations.

3.     Where required, the Commission will ensure the drawing up of common European standards for the implementation of specific technical features, in accordance with Community legislation on the approximation of the laws of the Member States concerning telecommunications terminal equipment, including the mutual recognition of their conformity, and Council Decision 87/95/EEC of 22 December 1986 on standardisation in the field of information technology and telecommunications.[2]

NOTES

[1]     OJ L109, 26.4.83, p 8. Directive as last amended by Directive 94/10/EC (OJ L100, 19.4.94, p 30).

[2]     OJ L36, 7.2.87, p 31. Decision as last amended by the 1994 Act of Accession.

## Article 14

### Extension of the scope of application of certain provisions of Directive 95/46/EC

1.     Member States may adopt legislative measures to restrict the scope of the obligations and rights provided for in Articles 5, 6 and Article 8(1), (2), (3) and (4), when such restriction constitutes a necessary measure to safeguard national security, defence, public security, the prevention, investigation, detection and prosecution of criminal offences or of unauthorised use of the telecommunications system, as referred to in Article 13(1) of Directive 95/46/EC.

2.     The provisions of Chapter III on judicial remedies, liability and sanctions of Directive 95/46/EC shall apply with regard to national provisions adopted pursuant to this Directive and with regard to the individual rights derived from this Directive.

3.     The Working Party on the Protection of Individuals with regard to the Processing of Personal Data established according to Article 29 of Directive 95/46/EC shall carry out the tasks laid down in Article 30 of the abovementioned Directive also with regard to the protection of fundamental rights and freedoms and of legitimate interests in the telecommunications sector, which is the subject of this Directive.

4.     The Commission, assisted by the Committee established by Article 31 of Directive 95/46/EC, shall technically specify the Annex according to the procedure mentioned in this Article. The aforesaid Committee shall be convened specifically for the subjects covered by this Directive.

## Article 15

### Implementation of the Directive

1.     Member States shall bring into force the laws, regulations and administrative provisions necessary for them to comply with this Directive not later than 24 October 1998.

By way of derogation from the first subparagraph, Member States shall bring into force the laws, regulations and administrative provisions necessary for them to comply with Article 5 of this Directive not later than 24 October 2000.

When Member States adopt these measures, they shall contain a reference to this Directive or shall be accompanied by such a reference at the time of their official publication. The procedure for such reference shall be adopted by Member States.

2.     By way of derogation from Article 6(3), consent is not required with respect to processing already under way on the date the national provisions adopted pursuant to this Directive enter into force. In those cases the subscribers shall be informed of this processing and if they do not express their dissent within a period to be determined by the Member State, they shall be deemed to have given their consent.

3.     Article 11 shall not apply to editions of directories which have been published before the national provisions adopted pursuant to this Directive enter into force.

4.     Member States shall communicate to the Commission the text of the provisions of national law which they adopt in the field governed by this Directive.

## Article 16

### Addressees

This Directive is addressed to the Member States.

Done at Brussels, 15 December 1997.

## ANNEX
## LIST OF DATA

For the purpose referred to in Article 6(2) the following data may be processed—

Data containing the—
- number or identification of the subscriber station,
- address of the subscriber and the type of station,
- total number of units to be charged for the accounting period,
- called subscriber number,
- type, starting time and duration of the calls made and/or the data volume transmitted,
- date of the call/service,
- other information concerning payments such as advance payment, payments by instalments, disconnection and reminders.

# Index